# THE BURNING FOUNTAIN

*A Study in the Language
of Symbolism*

## The Burning Fountain

*Dust to the dust: but the pure spirit shall flow*
*Back to the burning fountain whence it came,*
*A portion of the Eternal, which must glow*
*Through time and change, unquenchably the same . . .*

SHELLEY, Adonais

# THE BURNING FOUNTAIN

*A Study in the Language*
*of Symbolism*

By PHILIP WHEELWRIGHT

NEW AND REVISED EDITION

GLOUCESTER, MASS.
PETER SMITH
1982

To
MAUDE
*(without whom, not)*

# Contents

## Preface to the Revised Edition

"A book should be a ball of light in one's hands," Ezra Pound has said. In the original edition of *The Burning Fountain,* published some fourteen years ago, there were, as I gradually came to realize, some blurring smudges on the crystal. When Indiana University Press invited me to revise the book for the purposes of a paperback edition I gladly seized the opportunity to improve it. I hope I have done so. Certain parts of the older version, including two entire chapters, have been discarded as being inferior and outside the stream of argument. Partly by rearrangement, occasionally by rephrasing, I have sought to produce a firmer logic without loss of tone.

In essence the book is unchanged. Its pervading outlook continues to rest upon two basic principles: that of the intrinsically threshold character of experience and that of the ontological status of linguistic ordering. Both principles are of deep importance, I believe, for a mature confrontation of the problematic What which we call reality. The latter of them is more immediately germane to the theme of *The Burning Fountain,* and whether explicitly or not it affirms itself in every chapter. The former, the paradox of the irreducibly liminal character of human experience, receives a provisional statement in Chapter

Two, but must await a later occasion for the fuller examination which it demands.

Special thanks go to Professors Leonard H. Frey of San Diego State College and Peter Fuss of the University of California, Riverside. Both of these scholars gave their critical attention to my typescript during the last stages of its preparation, the one from the vantage-point of literature and philology, the other from that of existential philosophy. Miss Jeane Wheelwright has helped me immeasurably with stylistic criticisms and suggestions. At longer range there are the many reviewers and correspondents whose criticisms of the original book, even when I could not accept them wholly, have been of vast help in letting me see my exposition through other eyes than my own. On this basis I am particularly grateful for the published reviews and discussions by Meyer Abrams in *The Kenyon Review,* Edward A. Bloom in *The Saturday Review,* Robert F. Creegan in *Philosophy and Phenomenological Research,* F. Cudworth Flint in *The Dartmouth Alumni Magazine,* Charles I. Glicksberg in *The Arizona Quarterly* ("a telling shot fired in the war raging at present against the monopolistic truth-claims made for the scientific method"), Alfred M. Hayes in *The Chicago Review,* Albert William Levi in *Ethics,* J. J. A. Mooij in *Foundations of Language* (Netherlands), Sherman Paul in *Accent,* Julia A. Randall in *The Baltimore Daily Sun,* Sister Ritamary, C. H. M., in *The Catholic Messenger* (Davenport, Iowa), Catherine Rau in *The Journal of Aesthetics and Art Criticism* (in the course of a review of *Metaphor and Reality*), Nathan A. Scott, Jr., in *The Christian Scholar,* George N. Shuster in *The Phi Beta Kappa Key* ("an exploration of what happens when one turns the tables. . . . a critical, or dialectical, consideration of what can be realized with the whole depth of our experience through analogue and symbol"), Kersten Svendsen in *The Daily Oklahoman* ("its central argument can be grasped in a moment:

literature is a way of knowing, not merely a way of saying"),
Eliseo Vivas in *Perspectives USA,* and W. K. Wimsatt in his
book *Hateful Contraries.* My remaining acknowledgment is reserved for the Dedication.

P. W.

*Santa Barbara, California*
*January, 1968*

# ACKNOWLEDGMENTS

Acknowledgment is made to the following publishers who have granted permission to quote from the books indicated: Case Western Reserve University Press, *The Collected Poems of Dilys Laing;* John Day Company, Alan Porter *Signature of Pain;* E. P. Dutton Company, Helen Gardner *The Art of T. S. Eliot;* Harcourt, Brace and World, T. S. Eliot *The Complete Poems and Plays* and I. A. Richards *The Principles of Literary Criticism;* Harvard University Press, Susanne K. Langer *Philosophy in a New Key;* W. W. Norton and Company, Bertrand Russell *An Inquiry into Meaning and Truth;* Princeton University Press, Allen Tate (editor) *The Language of Poetry;* Rockcliff Publishing Corporation, Jean Louis Barrault *Reflections on the Theatre;* University of Oklahoma Press, Silvanus J. Morley and Delia Goetz (translators) *Popol Vuh.*

Chapters Three and Ten have been developed out of lectures given at Indiana University on the Mahlon Powell Foundation, and acknowledgment is made to the University and the Foundation for permission to use this material.

# THE BURNING
# FOUNTAIN

*A Study in the Language
of Symbolism*

# I

## Symbol, Language, Meaning

There is a legend in Estonia that the god of song Wanne-munne once descended onto the Domberg, and there, in a sacred wood, played and sang music of divine beauty. All creatures were invited to listen, and they each learned some fragment of the celestial sound: the forest learned its rustling, the stream its roar; the wind caught and learned to re-echo the shrillest tones, and the birds the prelude of the song. The fishes stuck their heads as far as the eyes out of the water, but left their ears below the surface; they saw the movements of the god's mouth and imitated them, but remained dumb. Man alone grasped it all, and therefore his song pierces into the depths of the heart, and mounts upward to the dwellings of the gods.[1]

The present book is concerned with ways in which men have aspired to imitate the god worthily and sing the full song. The majority of human utterances are thin pipings, as though (Nietzsche remarked) the Eroica Symphony were to be scored for two flutes. The language of the full song may be called *expressive language* or *depth language,* and one of my aims in the early chapters will be to distinguish its nature and potentialities from those of literal language, or, as I shall sometimes call it for brevity's sake, *steno-language*—a distinction to be analyzed in some detail in Chapter Five. Man's everyday intercourse employs both kinds of language to some degree, often in uncritical conjunction, besides mixing them up with phatic modes of utterance, which is to say emotional or merely perfunctory vaporizings. The greater uses of depth language, as exemplified by the best utterances in poetry, in religion, and in myth, represent approximately the scope and focus of this book; whose central thesis, which I shall clarify and defend in the early chapters, is that religious, poetic, and mythic utterances at their best really mean something, make a kind of transsubjective reference, although their methods of referring and the nature of what is referred to need to be understood and judged on their own merits, not by standards of meaning imported from outside.

Our contemporary vision tends to be limited and prejudiced by certain prevalent habits of interpretation and expectancy. I don't say there haven't been other limitations and prejudices at other times; that, however, is not especially our business. The task of a rational being is to see beyond his own prejudices, not to deride the prejudices of another. An age of technosophy— an age, that is to say, in which our ways of interpreting and appraising experience tend to be influenced more and more by the streamlined methods and glittering results of technology— encourages us to think in certain ways and inhibits or dissuades us from thinking in other ways. Our current intellectual mores permit us to envision a world of invisible electronic patterns on the one hand, and hidden subconscious motivations on the other; they do not permit us to envision—at least not with an equal degree of seriousness and public accountability—gods and daemons, fairies and elves, or (in anything like a firm sense) inspiration by the Muses. They restrict us, by and large, to the naturalistic point of view, allowing few or no beliefs save such as can be validated by scientific method.

The inquiry upon which I am embarking is partly ontological, partly semantic. Let ontology be understood to mean the study of the major ways in which anything can be said to really *be*. When Jesus speaks of our Father in Heaven, or when Prometheus in Aeschylus' *Prometheus Bound* denounces the tyranny of Zeus, in each case something is being spoken about. Neither Jesus nor Aeschylus is merely vaporizing; each of them has a certain beliefful attitude toward that which he is characterizing. On the other hand, neither of them is speaking about that Something Other in literal everyday terms. Jesus does not mean that God is a father in quite the same sense as an earthly father; Aeschylus does not mean that God is a tyrant in quite the same sense as an earthly monarch might be. Both are employing the language of analogy—or, in the most adequate sense of the phrase, the language of poetic vision. Each is speaking about something which he regards as very real, but of a different order of being from that of common familiarity. And we, as readers and hearers, if we want to understand such teachers instead of imposing our own conceptualizations upon them, must try to find our way back into their ontological perspective—into that way of confronting the world and asking questions about it which is the realizing medium of their mode of thought and utterance—i.e., the medium through which and in terms of which the object spoken about is real. The discipline of grasping such a viewpoint, of effecting such a translation of basic intellectual reliance, is an ontological discipline—a discipline with respect to the way in which Being is grasped and interpreted.

Now ontology is closely involved with semantics—which is to say, with the study of meanings and of how they can be expressed and communicated. Being, in its various modes, has to be articulated in language, and the habits and customs and styles and limitations of language set barriers to the ways in which Being can be understood. Thus, substitute the word "psyche" for "soul," and see how differently the entourage of problems tends to shape itself! Or again, consider with how much more innocence it was possible to use the word "God" a few centuries ago, when Christian assumptions permeated every stratum of daily life, than in these days of the locust and the dry wind. The two factors—our intimations of what *is* and our limited ways of saying it—affect each other mutually. A critical method must examine them as complementaries: it must try to report the radical character of things so far as a disciplined exercise of philosophical intuition can discover it, and at the same time, with a touch of irony, acknowledge that this discovery, too, is conditioned and limited (we never know just how far) by the linguistic resources which are at once the instruments of expression and largely also the conditioning media of thought itself.

## Definition of Symbol

A symbol cannot be understood in itself, it must be taken correlatively with what it means. A symbol owes its symbolic character to the fact that it stands for something other than, or at least more than, what it immediately is. As Mary Anita Ewer has written:

> A word is a symbol because it stands for its meaning. The sign + is a symbol, because it stands for the operation of addition. A lily, in religious art, is a symbol, because it stands for purity. The creature which, in a terrifying dream, threatens to devour the dreamer, is a symbol, because it stands for some situation in the environment or some conflict in the inner life which threatens to engulf the personality. The flag in battle is a symbol, because it

stands for the ideals and the honor of the mother country. In theology, the Cross is a symbol, because it stands for a truth which words cannot completely express.[2]

What all these many kinds of symbol have in common is the property of *being more in intention than they are in existence.* In the words of an older vocabulary the symbol is ideally self-transcendent. Which is to say, it *means* something.

Now *meaning* is a very broad term indeed. Like *being* and *relation* it is too fundamental to allow of definition: to ask what meaning means is obviously question-begging. Nevertheless, while it is impossible to define meaning from the outside by reference to a larger category, we can clarify the concept internally by distinguishing its main forms and expressions. To keep our bearings in such an examination we must acknowledge from first to last that every human experience has meaning in some way or other, whether clear or vague, articulate or dumb, intellectually respectable or offbeat. By such non-partisan procedure we can avoid the danger of systematically omitting (as a seeming exercise of methodological virtue) unorthodox kinds of significant question.

The most general truth that can be affirmed about meaning, or a meaningful situation, is that it always involves two aspects: what means and what is meant, a semantic carrier and a semantic content, or (in I. A. Richards' suggested terminology) *vehicle* and *tenor*, $V$ and $T$. Now $V$ may be anything without exception; for we can inquire of anything to which our attention is turned, and implicitly we do inquire, what it means. In asking what $V$ means we seek to give shape to its $T$ and to that specific $V$-$T$ relation. $T$ may also be spoken of as the *referend* (from the Latin gerund, "to be referred to") or *meaning* of $V$.

The forms of the $V$-$T$ relation are manifold. The relation may be distinct (e.g., the word "dog" vis-à-vis the animal itself), or on the other hand $V$ may coalesce with $T$ and participate in it (as a friend's face will signify, and indicate the presence of, the friend himself, of whom the face is a part, and as a sacred dance may pay symbolic homage to a divine presence of which the dance is regarded as a manifestation). Or taking a different approach we may distinguish between those *V-T* relations that grow up naturally in a given cultural nexus (e.g., the bull as a symbol-manifestation of divine potency) as against those established stipulatively by deliberate choice (e.g., the Greek letter $\pi$ to stand for the ratio of a circle's circumference to its diameter). Each of these two ways of distinguishing between different kinds of *V-T* relation develops its own set of problems for poetic interpretation and theory. The former distinction suggests questions of clarity vs. vagueness and their pattern of interrelations in a poem, and more generally the relation between overt statement and the overtones of innuendo suggested by imagery, tone, and cadence. The latter distinction, on the other hand, suggests questions about the poet's acceptance of established meanings in contrast with his creative renewal of meanings through linguistic remolding.

Behind every semantic situation there lies the question of "for whom." The word "dog" carries a definite meaning for those who know the English language, and quite possibly no meaning at all for others. Here the requirements of being a fit interpreter of the word are fairly obvious: viz., to have had some acquaintance with the kind of animal in question or with pictures of it, and to have learnt that the English word "dog" is commonly employed to stand for any member of that species. In many other cases the question of the fit interpreter is much more problematic. Particularly as we move toward the larger and more variable meanings in poeto-cultural and religio-cultural fields we find ourselves less and less able to say with assurance just who the fit interpreters are. Nevertheless the concept of the fit interpreter is indispensable in principle. For if we are to think, judge, and communicate, we cannot avoid supposing, however tentatively, that some ways of understanding a given matter are more adequate and nearer to the truth than other ways.

We are now in a better position to say what a symbol is— i.e., to say how the word "symbol" should be used. Here as in all definitions there has to be some compromise between actual usage and conceptual identification (prescribed usage)—with an eye to practicality on the one hand, to order and clarity on the other. Accordingly we can specify three main characteristics as distinguishing the symbol from other kinds of semantic vehicle.

First, the attitude which a symbol represents and to which it appeals is contemplative rather than directive or pragmatic. A symbol refers to what supposedly *is*, not (or at least not directly) to what one is to do. It is the *logos theorêtikos*, not the *logos praktikos*, that the symbol in its symbolic role expresses. Thus a red traffic light, although it indubitably "means something," is not a symbol, it is a signal. But if, on the other hand, some sermonizer were to devise a remark like "The atomic bomb is God's red traffic light," then in that metaphorical usage the familiar signal would have been turned into a symbol.

It seems probable that man alone among the animals can think contemplatively in this precise sense of giving and receiving signs not only as stimuli to behavioral and emotive responses but also as symbols—that is, as representing something for its own sake. The psychophysical difference between the two attitudes has been stated by Susanne K. Langer as follows:

> To a clever dog, the name of a person is a signal that the person is present; you say the name, he pricks up his ears and looks for its object. If you say "dinner," he becomes restive, expecting food. You cannot make any communication to him that is not taken as a signal of something immediately forthcoming. His mind is a simple and direct

*transmitter* of messages from the world to his motor centers.
With men it is different. We use certain "signs" among ourselves that do not point to anything in our actual surroundings. Most of our words are not signs in the sense of signals.
They are used to talk *about* things, not to direct our eyes
and ears and noses toward them.[3]

Accordingly Professor Langer offers the highly suggestive hypothesis that man's basic need, the one function that most truly
distinguishes him from beasts, is the need for *symbolization*, the
need to form conceptions of things.

Secondly, a symbol is to be distinguished from a natural sign.
Where the vehicle of a meaningful relation is a symbol, the
relation between $V$ and $T$ is not determined by natural causation, but involves a contributing factor of human choice—
whether individual or collective, and whether conscious or unconscious. A rapidly clouding sky points to the prospect of a
storm; we can even say that the clouded sky "means" that a
storm is brewing. Nevertheless, although the sky is a sign of the
coming storm, it is not a symbol. It signifies or indicates the
likelihood of a storm purely by virtue of its causal connection
with stormy weather, to a mind which has learned of that
connection through previous experience. A natural sign is not
used with any purpose or intention of communicating; it works
by causal efficacy alone.

A given thing, event, or situation may occasionally function
in all three of the aforementioned ways. Thunder, for example,
is a natural sign insofar as it indicates the probability that rain
will follow; it is a signal insofar as it warns us to seek shelter.
But also, in the *Brihad-Aranyaka Upanishad*, it functions symbolically when it represents the voice of Prajapati issuing divine
commands to gods, to asuras, and to men.[4] In the context of
Vedanta philosophy, as in many another religio-cosmological
context, the sound of thunder not only indicates but means.

Thirdly, a symbol has a certain stability: it endures beyond one or a few occasions. For instance, a man might make a spontaneous gesture of contempt and the onlookers might understand well enough what he meant by it: his gesture would then be meaningful, but it would not be a symbol. On the other hand the gesture of thumbing the nose, the accepted meaning of which has been commonly understood for several generations, has become a symbol of contempt. Again, a landscape seen from a train window may stir one's mind to childhood recollections—perhaps because of some resemblance, or some emotional affinity, to a place which one had known as a child. The landscape is then an associative stimulus, evoking memories either by reason of certain observed similarities or because of some more hidden and personal psychic connection—some emotive congruity that mysteriously produces a particular response. But since the stimulus merely acts upon the observer by certain psycho-physical propulsions and is not taken by him to stand for anything, it does not have the status of a symbol.

Now there are three main ways in which the $V$-$T$ relation can get stabilized so that the $V$ functions as a symbol of one sort or another: by passive habituation, by stipulation, and by creative development.

Habituation, the way of the marketplace, of journalese, and of personal default, produces the *common symbol*. Its examples are numerous and various: anything that we habitually accept as a carrier of certain shared complexes of feeling and perhaps thought, which doubtless includes most of the words and phrases of our everyday speech, respectable and slang expressions alike. Popular language may, to be sure, degenerate into clichés, phatic utterances, perfunctory commonplaces that have lost any truly symbolic function. Such conventional remarks as "Nice day!" or "I swear to God," or "Oh, damn!" are evidently off-shoots of what were formerly common symbols but have now become little more than linguistic reflexes called forth by certain types of situation. However, not all common speech becomes thus semantically deflated. People do communicate with one another, and they can do so only if they share some knowledge of what their linguistic expressions indicate. When one person says to another, "I felt awfully bad about what happened," he is surely communicating something, however vaguely and incompletely. Where this occurs without enforced exactitude on the one hand and without imaginative renewal on the other, it is a case of common symbolism.

Stipulation involves the strict employment of language as an instrument of wide communication and maximum stabilization of meaning. Its utility up to a point is obvious, particularly in a contractual and technological society. Collective living requires agreements and contracts, and these can operate only if the terms of them are identically understood and are kept unchanged. Equitable social arrangements and valid scientific investigation are alike in this, that both of them require a clarity of language that is understandable and accepted by all workers in the field. Imagine the plight of a geographer who, after comparing certain distances in miles, were to find himself wondering whether all the miles were of equal length! The principles of logical clarity and consistency must be enforced rigidly on such symbols as arithmetical numbers, the square root sign and other such mathematical indicators, the terms and relations of logic, the terms of legal documents and binding agreements, and (hopefully if not always quite successfully) the language of any body of knowledge that presumes or aspires to be scientific. In all such cases we can speak of the *stipulative symbol,* or more briefly of the *steno-symbol.*

Of central interest to the inquiry that motivates the present volume, however, is the *organic symbol,* which from another point of view may be called the *expressive symbol,* and from still another the *depth symbol*. Where this kind of living symbol is concerned, the stability of the *V-T* relation is not just an accidental happening, nor again is it achieved and kept unvarying by fiat; it is developed and modulated by the creative and discriminating activity of man, in his human capacity as the being who can apprehend and express meanings through language. His materials are drawn from his experiences, from his imaginative expansions of experience, and from various kinds of psychic association, some of which may have erupted unaccountably from the depths of his unconscious. An important part of the artist's role is to develop such associative stimuli, through the medium of his craft, into freshly expressive and (if he is lucky) sharable symbols. Thus the madeleine dipped in a cup of tea was originally an associative stimulus in Proust's experience, whether actual or imagined, but through his memorable account of its effects, and his contextualization of the incident as a theme in the orchestration of his novel, the taste of madeleine in tea was made into a symbolic vehicle whereby Proust could communicate expressively and concretely something of his personal discoveries about memory and time. Similarly, Mallarmé's *faune,* Rilke's angels, Eliot's waste land, Flannery O'Connor's genteel deteriorated southern folk, and so on, are expressive symbols that have been developed, by selection and guided association, out of commonly shared or imagined experiences.

## The Two Strategies of Language

How are the terms *language* and *symbolism* interrelated? Both terms are indispensable to the course of our argument; the shifting relation between them is illustrated by the slight inconsistency between the book's subtitle, where symbolism is treated as a species of language, and the first chapter title, where the two terms appear to be somehow distinct. Such ambiguity cannot be totally removed without artificial restrictions, for the terms as generally understood are neither entirely separate nor entirely identical. While we can speak on the one hand of non-linguistic symbols (e.g., Indian smoke puffs, recognized gestures, the Cross, the Wheel) and of non-symbolic language on the other (e.g., nonsense talk, phatic phrases of greeting, pure lyric, pure exclamation), the most fully interesting specimens for study are linguistic and symbolic at once—both adjectives being taken in breadth. The principal meanings of symbol have been discussed; those of language must be analyzed a little differently.

Language, with its subtle variations of syntax, verbal shading, innuendo and other devices, offers far greater possibilities of richness and energy combined with clarity and precision than any other form of semantic activity. Music can sometimes express more energetically, and to the intuition of a musical creator it may even seem a more accurate way of representing subtleties and shifts of mood and of suggested meaning. The technical symbolism of mathematical logic, on the other hand, is an instrument of unsurpassed precision within its specialized field of relevance. But what music "says"—what it expresses and communicates—is for non-musical people slight and perhaps non-existent; while by contrast the nearly perfect clarity of mathematics and mathematical logic is of so technical a kind that it has little if any bearing upon poetry, politics, religion, love, moral choice, or the alluring irrelevancies of playful nonsense. In fields of real human concern it is the language of word and syntax that offers generally the least inadequate kind of semantic vehicle by which mature meanings can be discovered, created, and communicated.

Semantically considered—i.e., with respect to what it *means*—language can be conceived as having two main complementary uses: to designate clearly for the sake of efficient and widespread communication, and to express with humanly significant fullness. Although reconcilable and combinable in some instances, these different aims pose a problem in others. When they conflict, which of them shall be given preference? Granted that the linguistic ideal should be to combine logical precision and richly vigorous expressiveness both to the highest degree, yet the achievement is a hard one, for which even the most accomplished writers strive with but fluctuating success. The question of precedence will be answered differently, no doubt, according to the nature and dominant purpose of the occasion. And so far as we set primary importance upon wide-scale communicability or upon associative depth and fullness, we tend to engage in one or other of two basic types of semantic strategy: to employ steno-language (the language of plain sense as it becomes logical) or to employ depth language, which is to say expressive language (the language of poetic imagination). Correspondingly we may distinguish symbols as either steno-symbols or depth-symbols (expressive symbols), regardless of whether they have a linguistic form or not.

The distinction-but-relation between the two modes of language, and between their affiliated modes of symbolism, is so central to the purport of this book that I need to warn against two threatening kinds of misunderstanding, each of which did in fact mislead certain reviewers of the original edition. Some of the early critics took the central distinction as necessarily involving the traditional philosophical dualism between object and subject, between what *is* and what *seems,* between the objectively real and the subjectively apparent. Others, even when they did not fall into that post-Cartesian trap, conceived the distinction in terms of a sharply separated dualism, a semantic dichotomy between opposed types of meaning. Both misinterpretations must be avoided if the argument of the book is to be understood.

Today's version of post-Cartesian dualism, by which virtually all of us to greater or less degree have been brainwashed, consists in defining "the real world" in terms of propositions that in the long run can be publicly verified and in relegating all else to the dubious status of someone's private subjectivity. Such is the positivist stance, an ampler look at which must await Chapter Four. Meanwhile a provisional warning should be sounded against falling into a stereotyped notion of what objective and subjective mean. When employed sparingly the two adjectives can usefully indicate contrasting emphases and directions of attention, particularly the contrast between what is grasped and felt by oneself and what is known alike to oneself and others. Yet while the distinction may be of great practical utility and even on certain occasions necessary, the line of demarcation between objective and subjective is not perfectly fixed but tends to waver and shift according to the circumstances, mood, and interpretative aim. The words "object" and "subject" can become dangerously prejudicial when applied wholesale and without suitable qualifications.

My other caveat is against rigorization of the difference between expressive language and steno-language by treating it as an out-and-out dualism. It is one thing to recognize that the language of *Hamlet* or *Le cimetière marin* or *The Man with the Blue Guitar* is significantly and wonderfully different from the language of a telephone directory; it is quite another to treat this difference as a conceptual chasm. Shakespeare, Valéry, and Stevens employ many words and idioms in almost their ordinary sense; where they transcend semantic usualness it is not so much by simple opposition as by an imaginative enlargement which presupposes a common language as its initiating base of operations. Expressive language offers subtle possibilities of discourse which steno-language does not, but its possibilities are various both in kind and in degree, as Chapter Five will show by analysis and illustration. Steno-language at its best, which is to say strictly logical language, has the cold purity that comes from adherence to rules; and ultimately there is but a single kind of logical purity, the set ideal of all logical thinking. By contrast, expressive language at its best, which is to say poetic language, has no single standard of purity; its semantic achievements are various and unexpected, involving perpetually new discoveries, creating unique triumphs of momentary unity over mixture. In critical terms, the relation between the two modes of language is not one of balanced antithesis; rather, steno-language is the purely negative limit, the condition to which expressive language may approximate whenever and insofar as its free imaginative life is inoperative. Steno-language is a *must*, expressive language is a *can* and *may*.

This book is about expressive language, particularly about that guilefully responsible kind of expressive language which is to be described as poetic. Before turning pointed attention to its characteristic possibilities, however, I want to explore certain ontological and psychological assumptions on which the inquiry rests and then to examine dialectically the logical status of the problem. These three preliminary exercises will occupy Chapters Two, Three, and Four respectively. Thereafter I shall be in a better position to discuss, with such partial accuracy as the elusive nature of the subject matter allows, the nature of poetic meaning and of poetic affirmation.

# 2

## Man's Threshold Existence

Man lives always on the verge, always on the borderland of a something more. He is the only animal, apparently, who has built restlessness into a metaphysical principle. Even in the practical sphere he is restless in ways that mark him off, for good *and* for ill, from his fellow animals. Human desires, winged by imagination, fly beyond the scope of natural instinct and mock at our efforts to satisfy them. Such is a favorite theme of moralists. But even when—perhaps especially when—we succeed in allaying the grosser forms of uneasiness, the sense of a beyond and the urge to wonder about it remain.

Indeed, the intimation of a something more, a beyond the horizon, belongs to the very nature of consciousness. To be conscious is not simply a fact or event like those determinate facts and events which make up our physical world. If we call it a fact, or event, or process, or function, we do so by analogy, and in any analogy the differences can be as important as the resemblances. To be conscious is not just to be; it is to mean, to intend, to point beyond oneself, to testify that some kind of beyond exists, and to be ever on the verge of entering into it although never in the state of having fully entered. The existen-

18

tial structure of human life is radically, irreducibly *liminal*.[1]

That is why there can be no science of man. You can study a man scientifically to just the extent that you can grasp and systematize his thinglike characteristics, which form the physical substructure of every one of us; but the man in his wholeness, which is to say in his distinctively human character, eludes every network of rational concepts that may be thrown out to cover him. In our technosophic age it is especially important to remember and reaffirm this inalienable first principle of the human condition. For when we sink back into the passivity and complacency of the Nothing Else But, and ignore the radically threshold situation that is our birthright—at once the glory and the tragic finitude of being human—we throw away the one chance, however small and precarious, of fulfilling our destiny as rational and (in the sense which I hope will gradually become clear in these chapters) spiritual creatures.

## The Threshold of Time

A continual reminder of our liminal condition, our radical incompleteness, is furnished by the passage of time. All existence, as we can humanly know it, is in the process of change: an unremitting passage out of *what just was* into *what is just about to be*. This familiar truism has more significance than appears at first glance. Our minds tend to minimize time's radically destructive power by forming a concept of time: of ourselves existing "in" the present, with the past behind us and the future ahead. The conceptualization has its uses; we employ it whenever we write a history or prognosticate tomorrow's events. But it distorts the reality of the one kind of time we can ever directly know—the present.

What is this present in which I seem to find myself? What does it mean to be between past and future? Both "in" and "between"

connote spatial relations, and our readiness to rely on these prepositions confirms Bergson's theory that the concept of time, as distinguished from pure experience of it, is always built on a space model. Present does not stand between future and past in the way that Indiana lies between Ohio and Illinois. To think in such terms is to substitute a spacelike concept for the experiential fact of time as directly known. Time future and time past interpenetrate to form the present moment; for man's first recognition of his situational existence involves as its essential elements the having-been in a somewhat different situation, remembered or half-remembered, and the about-to-be in another and not yet realized situation, vaguely and tentatively expected. It is for this reason that Julián Marías defines the human situation as "intrinsically historical," in the sense that it consists simultaneously of what it is emerging out of and what it is moving into[2]—of the Just Was and the Just About To Be.

But if that were all—the continual dying to the past and being reborn to the future—we could not know ourselves; the "I" of one moment would have no discernible identity with the "I" of the next. It is man's eminently human prerogative to be conscious of time's passage. To be conscious that the present moment is but a moment, that passage into the future is a death and a birth, is to transcend the bondage of the moment in the only way that is humanly possible to us. Memory and imagination give the past and future a shape; contemplative awareness of them reduces their power over us—or at any rate over that part of us which matters most. Thus metaphorically we can say that human existence, so far as we live it on the human level, is an interweaving not only of moment with moment, but of the transiency of moments with the permanency of that which sustains us in their passage, and which we can gradually realize by learning to identify with what the ancients described as the still point at the center of the revolving wheel.

But the existential awareness of time's passage, and of one's own relatively enduring poise with regard to it, is not to be confused with the conceptualization of time. Conceptualization is not so much a transcendence as an intellectual sidestepping. To conceptualize time, as already remarked, is to spatialize it; for it is only thus that time can be divided into units—whether these units correspond to the markings on the face of a clock, or the notches on a sundial, or the amounts of sand or water passing through an aperture, or the diminished length of burning candles. All such devices have their utility, to be sure; the measured burning of candles in medieval monasteries seems to have originated from the need of assembling the monks for prayers on time. Utility, however, is not to the point. Our present inquiry concerns being, not doing; it is ontological and semantic, not pragmatic. Ontologically there is the double existential aspect of temporal and super-temporal transcendency ("Today will be yesterday tomorrow," on the one hand; "Future and past I survey with equal mind," on the other); semantically this situation provides a clue, though but a partial one, to the meaning of paradox.

## The Threshold of Otherness

For there is another dimension of the liminal and paradoxical in human existence—quite as fundamental as the temporal dimension, logically independent of it, and perhaps even more manifoldly significant. In any of my conscious moments I seem to be aware, vaguely or clearly, of otherness—i.e., of much that I consider as existing somehow in its own right, as other than myself. Nothing seems more basic and obvious than this, although when it gets articulated verbally it tends to assume an air of paradox. Classical empiricists, notably Berkeley and Hume, have accentuated the paradox by launching their inquiries from conceptually refined products rather than from original awarenesses. It is true that if I formulate the epistemological question in Berkeleyan or Humean terms, presupposing all sure knowledge to consist of "my" images and ideas, there is no possible way of proving that anything more than these mental possessions of mine really exists. Solipsism is the only honest outcome of such procedure. But the procedure itself is an unnatural one. Otherness cannot be either proved or disproved; for the assured acceptance of it, in some terms or other, precedes all queries and all proofs.

The important thing is not proof but perspective. Why are we normally so convinced that Berkeley was wrong, despite the bright cogency of his arguments? Because it is unnatural, and unreasonable, for the mind to maintain its rationality in so isolationist a way. One's mind becomes partially identified with an object at the moment of knowing it; never wholly, however, for one feels instinctively sure that there is more to the object than immediately shows itself. Dr. Johnson in kicking the stone did not refute Berkeley, who had foreseen that kind of objection and had answered it in advance.[3] But although his logic was inferior to the Bishop's, his perspective was more reasonable.

For we stand, as it were, on the verge of the circumambient world—a fluctuating stance, with phases of incomplete participation and incomplete withdrawal. The dual tendency, the in-and-out movement of the mind seeking to know an object in its otherness, frames every experience with the irony of its own finitude. In the distractions of practical life and in the resolute secularity of theorizing we may lose sight of that irony; and not the least of the poet's tasks is to bring us back, by evocative cadence or the jolt of a fresh metaphor, to the bright ambiguity of our primal situation.

The epistemological question remains, accordingly, obdurately problematical, not yielding to a single answer. For all answers to it are contingent upon the mode of interpretation chosen. Let it be granted that you can, if you force the issue hard enough, render any component of experience—whether the greenness of a grassplot, or its oblong shape, or the invisible molecules of which it is composed, or the gay and friendly aspect it wears after a spring rain—as either subjective or objective, either a possession of your mind or an aspect of the world confronting you. Some of the grassplot's characteristics—its measurable length and width, the mass of its particles, etc.—are extremely stubborn and, like a man with only one idea who declaims it again and again, they give constant evidence of ontological rigidity: they are just what they are, and while we can exploit their characteristics and turn them to our uses, they maintain their own kind of existence in apparently total disregard of how we choose to think about them. Other characteristics are ontologically more flexible, more adaptable to varying moods, to differences of perceptual and emotive response. What presents itself to one man as a gloomy and hostile landscape may seem mysteriously alluring to another, perhaps even friendly and promising to a third; and a painter can train his eyes to see shades and colors differently from the way they immediately impressed him. Doubtless it is reasonable, then, to say that the grimness of a gray weatherbeaten cliff is a *more* subjective characteristic than its measurable height or the percentage of silicon in its chemical make-up. But to call it "merely subjective" is to ride a partial insight too hard. In the moment of living experience the grimness and grayness appear as real qualities out there, in the rock itself and not in the perceiver of it. It is only when we fear the testimony of the burning moment and take refuge in a currently fashionable thought-pattern, that we can deny such qualities as grayness and grimness their discovered place in the world that confronts us.

Something is always presented—a certain *such*ness, never

adequately captured and expressed by ordinary word usage. The reason for linguistic inadequacy is plain enough. Several individuals look simultaneously at the grim gray cliffs, and each receives his own perceptual and emotive impression. Their shared assent to the description "grim and gray" represents a common denominator of experience, hence is in that sense an abstraction. What then? Is everything other than the shared abstraction to be dismissed as merely a subjective residue on the part of one or another of the observers? But suppose one of them is a poet—not as a publisher of verses but as an explorer of language as a means of fuller communication with his fellows? Can he succeed in extending, through sly linguistic maneuvers, the ordinarily narrow areas of shared mentality? He can but try. If he manages to do so, then what might have been doomed to subjectivity has become, in part, by the creative magic of the word, trans-subjective. The bard and his hearers may perhaps move a little forward (who can ever say how far?) along the unsure threshold. The radically presential, the pristine *such*ness of it, is not hopelessly and totally incommunicable; it offers an ever shifting challenge to communicative ingenuity and taste.

### *"Aha!" and "Hello!"*

The presential, which is to say sheer experienced otherness, comes to us in two main ways—that which we merely observe and that which we can both observe and greet—roughly, what we conceptualize as the distinction between things and persons. Every person is a thing also, and can be treated as such; in fact we do treat other persons as things much of the time in subtly disguised ways. Whether or not this is always regrettable is a question for moralists, and outside the present scope. Moreover, there are various kinds of borderland cases, such as pet animals, babies, maniacs, and lobotomy patients; these complicate the general problem, but need not detain us. The essential distinction is easy enough to draw, however hard the problems of application may be. It is a question of significant reciprocity. Can that of which I am aware be aware of me? Does the transliminal $x$, to which my liminal sensitivity responds, have a reciprocal liminal sensitivity toward myself? Whatever may be the grounds on which we believe in such ontological reciprocity,[4] we do in fact believe in it. We may doubt that the reciprocity is being actively exercised on a given occasion or on the part of a given person, but everyone inherently believes in its general possibility. Loneliness, alienation, and even solipsism draw their meaning from an underlying expectation of reciprocity, which in the first two cases is felt to be unfulfilled and which in the case of solipsism is declared on rational grounds to be unfulfillable. It is on the basis of this radical belief (i.e., this root-belief) that we can say "Hello!" to some beings and not, or at least not seriously, to others. We *address* the former group, inviting a reply, and not the latter. The difference is of major importance, not only ontologically and ethically but also for a semantics of expressive discourse, for at bottom it is such ontological reciprocity that justifies our employment of the *you*-vocabulary—i.e., of what grammarians call the second person singular.

To address is to invite dialogue. That is the difference between addressing someone and haranguing him. (To "give an address" is not to address, but is merely to harangue from the respectable elevation of a platform.) The dialogical "you" of "What do you think?" is not the peremptive "you" of "Hey, you, get off the grass!" Nor is it the sentimental "you" of "Aren't you a good doggie!" Neither of these latter instances employs the word "you" with full intent. To address someone as "you" not only in words but in full actuality, is to let the *I-you* relation become, in the same dialogical act, a *you-I* relation. I not only utter the word, I also listen for the word in reply.

All this is so evident perhaps as to seem hardly worth setting down. What has been said here is little more than what had been variously advanced by Ebner, Buber, Marcel, Calogero, and other proponents of the *I-you* method of analysis.[5] Nevertheless the topic is indispensable to our inquiry. For if we are to study the characteristics and powers of expressive language, which steno-language deprecates or excludes, we must not overlook variables of ontological mutuality—variable degrees to which a discourse not merely tells but addresses, not merely declares but also invokes—degrees to which the speaker both speaks and listens as twin aspects of a single dialogical act, where ideally the speaking and the listening are like convex and concave sides of the same arc.

## The Upward Threshold

Just as we may describe man's threshold situation, metaphorically, as having a "forward" dimension in time and an "outward" dimension in its sense of otherness and in the development of that sense into a conception of "the world," so with like metaphorical indirection we may speak of an "upward" dimension—intending to mean, as a first step, man's sense of a reality "higher"—i.e., intrinsically worthier and more real—than himself and his temporal and worldly preoccupations. Here, however, we must exercise a far greater linguistic caution than in the two preceding cases. For while it is possible enough to be mistaken about the future and about the environing world, the possibilities not only of error but of all kinds of fanciful nonsense are much greater when we try to articulate in speech the nature of existential upwardness.

If at this point I introduce the word "religious," it must be understood in a minimal sense, without any of the mythological and theological associations that usually accompany it. We need to extricate ourselves from the bondage of the spatial metaphor of upwardness; for of course there is no virtue in physical upwardness itself, which is the semantic vehicle here; and moreover the metaphor is a survival from pre-relativistic and even pre-Copernican ages, when men presumed they knew what absolute up and down rightly meant. Furthermore, apart from any doubts about the fixity of spatial directions, it is notable that the major religious metaphors have as their imagistic vehicles not only the Upward, with its numerous mythologies of a sky god or gods in an upstairs world, but also the Downward, with its mythically powerful underworld sources of life and death, and the Inward, as the ideal center of the moving wheel of life.[6] Can we say anything meaningful—i.e., not-nonsensical—about the religious dimension of human existence without falling into the trap of taking some of these metaphors literally? By putting the question in this form we establish its clear relevance to our general investigation of poetic, metapoetic, and mythopoeic symbolism. It is largely, even primarily, with reference to his religious concerns that man is most dependent upon symbolic indirection in attempting to say, and even to ask, what he means.

Whether it be called the "upward" or the "religious" dimension, the point is that men tend to discover, however dimly and variously, a Something affecting their experience and intelligence, not as an ingredient of these but as a challenge to them—a challenge which somehow gives a basic significance and direction to one's living and thinking, which would seem more empty and pointless without having such a challenge and making a serious attempt to respond to it. Let us view this general existential situation in its full cultural breadth. Vergil described Aeneas awakening in Carthage with the clear and undoubting conviction that the god Mercury had come to him in a dream commanding him to put to sea with his fleet. Numerous Christians and ex-Christians, who can take seriously, even if they do not wholly believe, the account of Jahveh's command to the boy Samuel in the night and the reproach of the risen Christ to Saul (later St. Paul) on the road to Damascus, would not for a moment regard the apparition of Mercury as anything more than a subconsciously invented fancy. Genuine ontological inquiry, on the other hand, will look without preestablished favor on all such reported situations alike. Each makes an ontological claim—not in abstract philosophical terms, but embodied in the symbolic language and mytho-theological context of its own culture and interpretative habits. But since the literal truth of such narratives seems so empirically improbable, there arise in the later stages of every advanced culture sophisticates who, deriding the naiveté of the literal narrative, think they thereby justify a dismissal of the religious tenor along with it. Meaning, however, is by no means as clear-cut as that. The upward adumbration remains. And it is the task of mythopoeic language to find ways of symbolically indicating the chronic ambivalence of the proto-religious affirmation, and of keeping the possibility of it alive despite opposition from literal believers on the one side and sceptical iconoclasts on the other.

But even when all the sensible qualifications have been lodged there still remains one final question, the most persistently problematic of all. It is this: Can the *I-you* relation, the relation of ontological mutuality, apply to the upward dimension of experience with fully as much validity as we all believe it applies in our normal outward intercourse with other human beings? That I can speak to a fellow-human and reasonably hope to be spoken to in return is implicitly accepted by everyone, whatever his theories and speculations. But turn the same questional structure into the upward dimension, and it is well known that men's opinions sharply differ. Is it possible and meaningful (not-non-sensical) to address Divinity in prayer and reasonably hope to be addressed, however deviously and mysteriously, by Divinity in return? There is a real issue at stake here. For if one's answer is "No," that is tantamount to denying that Divinity in any significant sense exists. It may be that religious language and some of its attendant attitudes are retained, but how can they be then anything more than a semantic proxy for whatever is of highest excellence in the world, in oneself, and in other human beings? How, in short, after such denial can religion be anything more than pantheism? The pros and cons of pantheism are not here in question, but it is essential to discover just what we are talking about, and what the possibilities of meaning are in any question under discussion. The meaning of the question, "Does God exist?" can be translated, as William James has argued, into the question, "Can we legitimately say *thou* to the universe?" (Or, I would append, to a significant non-human aspect of the universe?) On this interpretation the current "God is dead" slogan turns out to be saying something both real and important —namely that for many, perhaps most people today, the possibility of dialogue with God is no longer real or even meaningful.

This question, of whether the *I-you* relation can legitimately apply to the universe as a whole, or to some significant area of it other than the person-to-person intercourse among human individuals, is in itself an ontological rather than a semantical question. But the two kinds of question are inextricable, and it is important to construe semantics openly enough to avoid prejudging what the ontological answer must be. In terms of steno-semantics there can be but two possible replies to the primary question of religious ontology: the reply of positivism and that of supernaturalism. Whatever their disguises, qualifications, and confusions these represent the only logical possibilities; there can be no third. For when the question of religious transcendence is put in steno-linguistic terms, so that reality is conceived on the model of physical-like entities, it follows (by the law of excluded middle) that one of two things must be the case—that either there exist superhuman physical-like entities or else there do not. On that basis religious supernaturalism must have as its only alternative religious nihilism. These are the two logical alternatives whenever the semantics of steno-language is maintained. What the steno-semanticists rarely see is that if they were fully consistent they would have to face the same pair of alternatives with respect to human aliosubjectivity. For although everyone does in fact believe in the existence of other persons as independent centers of subjectivity, yet this utterly basic human fact (without the acceptance of which there could be no significant social life) cannot be directly described by the techniques of steno-language. Ultimately our steno-alternatives have to be these: on the one side, behaviorism; on the other, belief in a soul-substance residing in the body—what Gilbert Ryle has called "the ghost in the machine."

It will be replied by some that so precise an analysis of the religious relationship is misleading, and that any explicit formulation of divine response to prayer is forever inadequate and misleading. But I agree! That, in fact, is precisely the point of the foregoing argument. If we wish to avoid the horns of the dilemma, positivism vs. supernaturalism, we need to develop more expressive linguistic means of approaching the problem of transcendence. Every good writer, to be sure, finds and develops his own means of linguistic expressiveness in practice; his writing would be ineffective if he did not. But serious argument is still likely to be impeded and confused by a half-acknowledged over-restrictive theory. What the revised linguistic assumptions are—nothing new, indeed, for in their perhaps unacknowledged operation they are as old as language itself—will be set forth in Chapter Five; and certain of the metapoetic categories discussed in that chapter will have special bearing on the question of how the mystery and paradox of upward liminal experience are to be expressed and presented—most notably the categories of concrete universality, indirection, soft focus, and assertorial lightness. Meanwhile, in the chapter just ahead, in the context of a general phenomenological inquiry into the nature of poetic imagination, the same question of liminal upwardness will be centrally involved in the section entitled "Archetypal Imagining."

# 3

## Four Ways of Imagination

*A revolution in the imagery of poetry is in reality a revolution in metaphysics.*
EDMUND WILSON, *Axel's Castle*

What mainly produces depth-meanings, distinguishing them from steno-meanings, is the greater vivacity of imagination that goes into their making. Authentic imagining is far more than the play of fancy. Particularly since Kant's doctrine of "imagination" (*Einbildungskraft*) began to affect informed critical opinion it has become more and more generally accepted that the human imagination is neither that mere decay of sensation which Hobbes had supposed it to be nor an irresponsible commentator upon a world already given, but an original contributor to the very nature of the world. Coleridge, employing an independent vocabulary and drawing upon his own ample reserves of poetic insight, renewed and confirmed Kant's doctrine that the mind is more than an onlooker, that it is largely producer and constituent of the very world which it knows.[1]

To look at a tree and recognize it as the thing we humans mean by the word "tree" is possible only because one's mind is actively fusing the fleeting impingements of sensation into a meaningful, recognizable whole. A woodpecker, a dog, and a man has each his separate business with the tree; and as each responds differently to it, so each perceives and recognizes it in a manner largely impervious to the others. The outreaching of the mind, in that primordial, preconscious enterprise of comparison and selective recognition, is what Kant calls the Transcendental Unity of Apperception, and Coleridge the Primary Imagination. What Coleridge calls the Secondary Imagination—the more concrete activity of imagining that is employed in the poetic art—is a continuation and reflection of that "living power and prime agent of all human perception" which is the Primary Imagination. This conceptual layout gives Coleridge a theoretical criterion for distinguishing genuine poetry from artificial. The imagination that generates and guides an authentic poem, although Secondary by definition, maintains a living unity with the Primary; it is "a repetition in the finite mind of the eternal act of creation in the infinite I AM."[2]

Keeping in mind this Coleridgean doctrine of continuity between man's primary (or constitutive) imagination and his secondary (or poetic) imagination—for where the continuity gets broken the constitutive imagination hardens into steno-thinking and the poetic imagination deteriorates into fancy and whim—let us examine the principal ways in which poetic imagination appears to operate. That is to say, instead of appealing to usual psychological treatments of the subject let us distinguish among the aspects of imagination as they appear from the standpoint and through the perspective of poetic expression. Four main emphases may be regarded as primary, and their subtle interrelations supply much of the creative force that goes into the making of poetic utterance. There is the Confrontative Imagination, which acts upon its object by particularizing and intensifying it. There is the Stylistic Imagination, which acts upon its object by distancing and stylizing it. There is the Compositive Imagination, which fuses heterogeneous elements into some kind of unity. And there is the Archetypal Imagination, which sees the particular object in the light of a larger conception or of a higher concern.

Although our attention here is directed mainly to problems of poetic meaning, I want to suggest, as a theme for possible further study, that the fourfold scheme applies not only to poetic ("secondary") but also to constitutive ("primary") imagination. The suggestion if pursued, would lead us into the outreaching areas of epistemology and metaphysics, and indeed might lay the conceptual grounds for a discussion of metapoetical ontology.[3] No doubt occasional adumbrations of such inquiry, or at least of ontological uneasiness, will show themselves during the course of the present volume. Such overtones are inevitable if, as Coleridge taught and as is postulated throughout these investigations, there is essential continuity between the constitutive imagination (the *Einbildungskraft* which, according to Kant's theory, actively molds the world and gives it form in our every attempt to understand it) and the poetic imagination, which cannot entirely break off from the constitutive without forfeiting its genuineness, but which extends, enriches, qualifies, playfully laughs at, and throws into dialogical doubt the caked familiarities that get taken for "reality" when poetic sensitivity is at a minimum.

## Confrontative Imagining

What is directly confronted in experience is always, in its first phase, something individual. When you pass from generalizations about mankind to direct acquaintance with Bill Smith, and with some particular grief or enthusiasm that Bill Smith is undergoing, you pass from concepts to real existence. The great evil encouraged by a technological and bureaucratic way of life is to forget that the individual exists and to treat him as a mere instance of a generality. Granted that generalizations are sometimes a practical necessity; yet when we make them so much a habit that they become substitutes for the bright world itself the result is a travesty of human reason, whether done in the name of business efficiency or political necessity or alleged science. Cassiodorus, the sixth century statesman and monk, declared: "God is really wonderful and extremely wise in having distinguished each one of his creatures by a unique dispensation lest unseemly confusion overwhelm them." The depth words here are "unique" and "confusion." Each of us is unique; each is a *Gestalt*, an *ousia*, an essence, not quite identical with any other. And every experience, every moment of beauty or of pain, of rapture or disgust or despair, is likewise unique. But the Devil seeks ever to confuse, or (in the potent old word of the English prayer book) to confound us, into forgetting that precise and ultimate fact. Commonplace language plays into the Devil's hands by dulling the edges between one experience and another; poetic language undertakes to speak of the concrete particulars with directness and experiential precision. "To particularize is the alone distinction of merit," said Blake.[4]

Accordingly, the first and most indispensable attribute of poetic language is its radical particularity of reference, its presentative immediacy. Poetry's first urgency is, in Richard Hovey's words, to "have business with the grass"; it presents as well as represents, it evokes something of the very quality, tone, and flavor of the concrete *quâ* concrete with a directness and a full experiential relevance that steno-symbols cannot do. Authentic poetry will always have this attribute to some degree, for—to paraphrase Yeats—poetry is love, and only the concrete is loved.

Now the point I especially want to make in this connection is that a lively recognition of the particular and unique in experience is an imaginative achievement, and that when keyed to the highest pitch it may become an imaginative achievement of a very high order.

> Down dropt the breeze, the sails dropt down.

John Livingston Lowes speaks of this powerfully laconic line from *The Ancient Mariner* as descending "with an abruptness like that of the fall of the shot bird off the Cape."[5] But the simile, though rationally justified, is explicit only in the critic's account; in the poet's it is left implied, an unspoken overtone at most. The main thrust of imagination here is not exercised to blend and fuse diverse particulars so much as to intensify the immediate experience itself, the horror of tropical seas to men becalmed.

Experiential immediacy of a contrasting tone and mood is expressed in the quatrain:

> The fair breeze blew, the white foam flew,
> The furrow followed free;
> We were the first that ever burst
> Into that silent sea.

It may be true, as Lowes plausibly argues, that Coleridge has here drawn upon two or more accounts of seamen's voyages—notably Marborough's account of Magellan's first passage through the Straits of Cape Horn into the Pacific Ocean and George Forster's *A Voyage round the World, in his British Majesty's Sloop, Resolution.* If such be the case I would think that the synthesis and fusion of these accounts took place prior to the decisive imaginative act that informs and moves the poetry. The poetic imagination in the quatrain is wholly taken up with the perceptual qualities of the breeze and foam and furrow and with the unique awe of aloneness, of being the first men ever to have penetrated that watery region.

Coleridge himself recognizes the intensifying function of imagination. Although the compositive receives greatest emphasis in his major declarations of theory, he shows often enough a recognition of the first factor, too: "For from my very childhood I have been accustomed to abstract, and as it were, to unrealize whatever of more than common interest my eyes dwelt on."[6] Note that in the context of Coleridge's discussion the verbs "abstract" and "unrealize" are virtually synonymous. As such they throw further light upon the process of imaginative intensifying. The individual—whether it has the guise of thing or person, event or situation or quality—is "abs-tracted," which is to say "drawn away from," the reputedly "real" world with its demanding network of causal and definitional associations, so that it is then possible, Coleridge continues, "by a sort of transfusion of my consciousness to identify myself with the object." That is to say, after the initial "bracketing off" from the normally so-called "real" world the poet is then in a position to contemplate with fullest relevant attention the phenomenological object which he wants to describe.

The ability to extract such intensified transfused insights out of a mass of heterogeneous material is what principally defines *poetic sensitivity*. In the poet such sensitivity goes into the original creation, in the fit reader it makes possible an imaginative re-creation of what, with luck, may hover not too far from the poet's original. For brevity, then, we can resort to metonymy and speak of the poem itself as characterized by sensitivity—implying (a) that the poem appears to have been created out of such a sensitivity, and (b) that it has the *dynamis*, the potentiality of producing some not altogether alien sensitivity in an equipped and responsive reader.

Although poetic sensitivity has a way of finding nourishment in the most unpromising materials, it still seems to be true that some materials are more promising than others. Some situations invite poetic response more intensely or more dramatically or perhaps more subtly and caressingly than others. Reviving a phrase that was dropped in the preceding chapter I suggest that some situations—i.e., some moments, phases, elements, areas, qualities, or aspects of existence—have more ontological tenderness than others—i.e., greater potentialities of fuller poetic response and development. Such a judgment of course must be variable and tentative at best; for poetic receptivity and response will differ not only from person to person but also, in any single person, from one realizing glimpse to the next. Thus the attribution of whatever degree of ontological austerity or ontological tenderness will apply not to what we call "the objective world"—that public common denominator of already conceptualized schemes of relations and possibilities—but to the phenomenological object, which is to say the object as apprehended by poetically responsive consciousness. There is unavoidable circularity here, and unavoidable paradox. For on the one hand the poetic consciousness largely makes and articulates its own phenomenological object—and makes it, too, through the articulating of it—while on the other hand the phenomenological object confronts the poetic consciousness with relevant properties of tenderness and austerity, offering certain possibilities, indefinitely limited, of one sort or another for poetic response. Such quandaries are inevitably the by-products of intellectual analysis. Consider two passages from Wordsworth's "Evening on Calais Beach":

> The holy time is quiet as a Nun
> Breathless with adoration

and shortly thereafter:

> Listen! the mighty Being is awake,
> And doth with his eternal motion make
> A sound like thunder . . .

That there is a striking poetic sensitivity in both passages will perhaps be generally agreed. And this, as I have suggested, implies the double affirmation that such sensitivity characterizes Wordsworth in his specific role as the maker of this poem, and that a not altogether dissimilar sensitivity is demanded of a reader. But there is still something more. For the total poetic situation includes not only the poet, his hearer, and the language that passes from the one to the other; it includes also, and indispensably, the tenor of the poem—the meaning that is communicated by the language. This $x$ that is communicated by the poem is the poetic tenor, the poetic and phenomenological object.

The phenomenological object must not be viewed as having the sharply defined characteristics that a conceptual object normally has. The kinds of variability, vagueness, and problematicity of which the phenomenological object is susceptible are roughly correlative with those that characterize expressive language—a matter to be examined more fully in Chapter Five. For the guiding structure obtains: as steno-language serves the conceptual object, so expressive language, with its indefinitely greater potentialities of significant suggestiveness, serves the phenomenological object—with the added qualification that in the latter case the semantic service in question is also to some extent semantic creation as well. The question, if pursued, would carry us into ontological questions beyond the scope of the present volume.

The foregoing passages from Wordsworth are especially instructive in that both of them lead to the verge, although not into the domain, of personification, and because in both cases the unfulfilled suggestion of that step proceeds so clearly out of the phenomenological object itself and the confrontative immediacy which it has for poet and reader. Comparing the quietude of the holy time to a nun breathless with adoration is no adventitious simile, but grows out of the living quality of the confrontative description; the same is true in the uncompleted personification of "Listen! the mighty Being is awake . . ." An object as directly confronted tends to be not merely described but also addressed. Confrontative immediacy contains the seed of the *I-you* relationship, even though the grammatical form of expression may remain in the third person. Wordsworth's occasional departures into rhetorical apostrophe as explicit conveyor of direct address—

> And O ye Fountains, Meadows, Hills, and Groves
> Forbode not any severing of our loves
> (from *Intimations of Immortality*)

do not seem to evoke the sense of *thou*hood in nature quite as effectively as those third-person examples previously quoted. The grammar is not the main determinant. Imaginative awareness of an individual presence in its radical individuality tends often to pass into that mood of heightened confrontation that is the essence of *I-you* relationship. This, surely, is a main motive in the natural and imaginative, as opposed to fanciful, process of personalization.

## Imaginative Distancing

But we do not wish to carry our hearts too much on display. An *I-you* relation is possible without grimaces, sighs, or backslappings; indeed it can often achieve a sounder depth when its expressions are decently restrained. Alan Porter has sung:

> Let him that beds a princess fear
> To show himself too free,
> And ceremoniously draw near:
> There should between two lovers be
> An excellent immodesty.[7]

A sense of right distance is an imaginative achievement and one of the conducements to civilized living. It is the primary factor of style, both in life and in art.

Edward Bullough in his familiar essay "Psychical Distance" says some enlightening things about the aesthetic importance of this element. Not merely distance in space, so important to painters in the guise of visual perspective; not merely distance in time, which Aristotle saw as an ingredient of tragic *mimêsis*, considering tragedy most effective when built around events of long ago. There is also a kind of distancing in relation to the whole object of experience, which consists, as Bullough says, of "putting the phenomenon, so to speak, out of gear with our practical, actual self" and thereby looking at it with a fresh objectivity. Thus there is at once a negative and a positive side to the experience of Distance: a refusal to be concerned with the practical commonplace aspect of things, and an elaboration of the experience exhibited within the framework which this closeted standpoint establishes. In normal workaday situations our attention is given to those sides of experience which by habit and accident float up to the surface of our consciousness. So much, so very much that we could attend to is ignored. What art contrives to do is give us a "sudden view of things from the reverse unnoticed side." Thus aesthetic distancing has an element of the impersonal, although of a quite different sort from the impersonality of science. Unlike science, art does not rule out or regard as of lesser importance the subjective and personal factors in a situation. "It describes a personal relation, often emotionally colored, but of a peculiar character. Its peculiarity lies in that the personal character of the relation has been, so to speak, filtered. It has been cleared of the practical, concrete nature of its appeal, without, however, thereby losing its original constitution."[8]

How much distancing is desirable for effective art? No easy

answer is possible. Over-distancing breaks the circuit between the work of art and one's own prepared field of receptivity; under-distancing destroys the aesthetic character of the experience. The ideal spectator at a performance of *Othello* is neither he who lacks the emotional potentiality of being jealous nor yet he who is actively harassed by pangs of jealousy at the very time.

The one kind of over-distancing which Bullough analyzes is that of idealistic art, which he explains as "the subordination of Art to some extraneous purpose of an impressive, exceptional character." When art is put to subserve commemorative or hieratic functions, in either a religious or a patriotic context, the object to be honored has to be distinguished as markedly as possible from profaner objects in the environment and has to be invested with an air of sanctity by a symbolic removal from its ordinary context of occurrence. Certain objects of nature, especially (in a mythopoeic society) the curious and unusual and the apparently potent, would meet this tendency halfway by assuming divine rank; the process then gets completed by the distancing power of art—through selective exaggeration and accentuation of special features, or contrariwise by the removal of all features that were noticeably individualistic and concrete: a process which achieves loftiest development in Greek sculpture of the classical period.

The kind of over-distancing which confronts us typically in contemporary art, on the other hand, is not idealistic but dissociationistic. Much of modern art involves, as Ortega has remarked, a process of dehumanization. There have been those who fell in love with La Gioconda; but it would be impossible for anyone, and indeed meaningless, to fall in love with a Picasso female whose eyes, mouth and breasts have been transposed to suit the painter's ruthlessly neo-geometrising spirit. Whatever aesthetic pleasure we take from such an un-portrait arises not from anything human but from the triumph over what is human. Why is this? What is the motive for such over-distancing? The new sensibility, Ortega believes, is dominated by an uneasiness toward the human in art very similar to the uneasiness which a sensitive person has always felt before waxworks:

> In the presence of wax figures we have all felt a peculiar uneasiness. This springs from the ambiguous impression they make on us, which prevents our adopting a definite attitude toward them. When we feel them as human beings they mock us, and if we see them as fictions they seem to quiver in irritation. There is no way of reducing them to mere objects. Looking at them we are confused with the suspicion that it is they who are looking at us, and we end by feeling a loathing toward this kind of superior corpse. The wax figure is pure melodrama.[9]

The theater is an art-form which offers interesting analogies in the matter of distancing. Jean-Louis Barrault observes out of his distinguished experience as actor and director that in a classic drama such as the tragedies of Racine, where the essential virtues are measure and design, the actor must make both his utterance and his gesticulation calculated, chosen, and rhythmic. If he fails to do so, "any transition from gesture to speech becomes impossible, for a synthesis of what is seen and what is heard cannot take place. The 'chemical precipitate' of this delicate operation cannot come about, the theatrical phenomenon ceases to exist," and the characters seem to be ordinary men and women speaking in an affected and unnatural way. Consequently, Barrault declares:

> When we play the classics we have to abandon naturalism and yet remain *true* when operating within a particular *tone*. The problem is to find the tone and at the same time to remain true. The other day I observed a newspaper

seller. He didn't have to be as it were *present* in his cries, because he had found the correct tone. If you want to teach someone how to sell papers it is no good telling him to "think carefully about what you're saying." No, he must find the right tone and it follows that his cry will produce the right sound. The right tone is the key to style.[10]

Style in poetry, as in the other arts, is partly "a playful demonstration of the properties of the medium itself"—an independent dance of the mind along its imagistic and musical patterns. But a dance to have pattern must be disciplined; and the stylization of poetic language is an imaginative emphasizing of certain features and toning down of others in accordance with the rhythmic life of the language itself. "Even in the most imaginative flights," T. E. Hulme has written, "there is always a holding back, a reservation. The classical poet never forgets this finiteness, this limit of man. He remembers always that he is mixed up with earth."[11]

If that were all, however, poetry would finally be reduced to the condition of music; and by the logic of the diagram in the next chapter its language would thus be but a mingling of the phatic and the ejaculative. Poetry is typically more than that. Its language is expressive, which implies that there is something to express. Stylization is the medium through which the expression is realized; and most of all this is seen in rhythm, the purpose of which, Yeats has said, is "to prolong the moment of contemplation, the moment when we are both asleep and awake, which is the one moment of creation, by hushing us with an alluring monotony, while it holds us waking by its variety, to keep us in that state of perhaps real trance, in which the mind, liberated from the pressure of the will, is unfolded in symbols."[12] Style involves a hushing of ordinary compulsions, a veiling of ordinary associations, and therein makes its unique semantic contribution, as even somehow a creator and revealer of meanings which only in that style could be uttered at all. The Imagist Manifesto of four decades ago declared: "In poetry a new cadence means a new idea."[13] Imagination, even in its stylizing and distancing aspect, is more than play of fancy; it is subtly but effectively a real contributor to the very nature and significance of "our world."

## Compositive Imagining

Having thus recognized in the foregoing sections the importance of both the intensifying and the distancing functions of poetic imagination, we are now ready to consider the kind of imaginative activity that consists in the blending of disparate elements. Coleridge describes such activity as "esemplastic," and it is what he has in mind when he makes his familiar statement of how the poet, "described in ideal perfection," operates:

> He diffuses a tone and spirit of unity, that blends, and (as it were) *fuses*, each into each, by that synthetic and magical power, to which I would exclusively appropriate the name of Imagination.[14]

Such activity characteristically reveals itself, Colerdige continues, in "the balance or reconcilement of opposite or discordant qualities." The imagination, to his view (in Walter Jackson Bate's paraphrase) is "a process of realization by which the products and insights of two [or more] distinct aspects of mind become transmuted and funneled into a single stream of awareness." It is in his occasional role as philosopher of literature, rather than as practicing poet, that Coleridge thinks thus; for in his verses, as the excerpts in an earlier section have exemplified, a spontaneously wider range of imaginative activity is to be found.

The compositive factor in poetry, and in art generally, has

been put in a philosophical context in the writings of the late José Vasconcelos, Mexican philosopher, ex-revolutionary and short story writer. Vasconcelos proceeds from the principle stressed by Kant in the *Critique of Pure Reason*, that all knowledge takes place through a unifying act of the mind as it receives the manifold of sense-impressions and pre-consciously arranges them into intelligible patterns. "Knowledge," he writes in his *Aesthetics*, "consists essentially in a unifying act which integrates instantaneously any given multiplicity into an organic whole that has meaning": so far Vasconcelos is a good Kantian. But the unifying process does not normally occur in the formal manner postulated by Kant's doctrine of the categories. If the unification really went on in that way, he argues, the world would be as clear and distinct as a geometrical figure. The world by which we actually find ourselves surrounded is by no means completely or even predominantly rational—unless we insist on judging it so by ignoring or discounting every evidence to the contrary. It is a world full of surprises, confusions, subtly blended qualities, dramatic oppositions—generally speaking, "a world of maximum concretion."

Now if we accept this observed fact on the one hand, and on the other Vasconcelos' Kantian principle that all knowing takes place through a unifying act of the mind, what must we conclude? The next step of his argument lays an epistemological basis for the distinction between what I am here calling steno-awareness and the wider ranges of human awareness. In unifying the heterogeneous elements presented to it as raw materials for cognition, he argues, the mind *may* act in the manner described by Kant: viz., it may unify in such a way that the radical heterogeneity of the raw materials is virtually nullified in the process. The result in that case is a conceptual one: we see the world as rationally ordered, in terms of cause and effect, substances and attributes, measurable space and time or space-time, necessities and probabilities, and so on. But the synthesis which expresses our actual living encounter with the world—the "vitalistic" synthesis—"tends to preserve the heterogeneous in its natural character (i.e., in its heterogeneity), thereby giving it a place in a meaningful world that is not mechanical but vital." Our world thus contains an irrepressible element of paradox, of dramatic tension, and of unresolved ambiguity. In his later writings Vasconcelos erected this principle of "the unification of the heterogeneous" (*la unificación de los heterogéneos*) into a proposition of full metaphysical import, declaring: "The very concept of truth in our time has become something different from formerly. It becomes a function of the unification of disparate elements which are combined without being subjected to logical identification"—i. e., without being subsumed under logical class-concepts.[15]

"As a poet," Hart Crane writes, "I may very possibly be more interested in the so-called illogical impingements of words on the consciousness (and their combinations and interplay in metaphor on this basis) than I am interested in the preservation of their logically rigid significations at the cost of limiting my subject matter and perceptions involved in the poem."[16] Crane's point can be put more academically by saying that poetic meanings can, and deeply need to, overreach the raw datum of sensation in quite different ways, along quite different lines, and by quite different techniques from those which characterize logical literal meanings. An adequate semantics, therefore, must recognize and make room for whatever fresh, unexpected, and unpredictably diverse modes of synthesis may find expression when the mind operates at levels and at moments of highest poetic intensity.

Two complementary metaphysical principles can be seen, on analysis, in the insistence upon the basic validity of this aspect of poetic imagination: on the one hand the principle of radical interpenetration, on the other the principle of radical novelty, or, from another point of view, what has been described by some philosophers as "creative synthesis." The former principle is indicated by Julián Marías' remark that as in the world of Anaxagoras, so in life, *there is a bit of everything in everything else.*[17] Sheer confusion would result if that were the last word, but Marías constructively adds that "The decisive factor, for us as for him, is the perspective taken, the functional articulation of the elements."

The other metaphysical principle, not contradicting but supplementing the first, is that of the possibility of *radical novelty through synthesis of heterogeneous elements.* The principle is essential, at different levels, both to cosmology and to poetry. As Boutroux and Bergson have shown, even so scientific a concept as evolution would be meaningless without it; for if something has evolved it must be something that had not existed before. Analogously, since a genuine poem is one that says something which is not a mere repetition of what has been said before, it must involve some juxtaposition and arrangement of elements that produces novelty—not necessarily a striking novelty, perhaps not an easily identifiable one, but a something distinctive, or else the poem is counterfeit. Every artist assumes the principle whenever he experiments; every poet makes discoveries of novel effects through new collections of materials. In a poem that has become familiar the impact of the original novelty may be somewhat diminished, but it is always there for the seeking. When Hamlet in the Queen's closet scene declares:

> Nay, but to live
> In the rank sweat of an enseamed bed
> Stew'd in corruption, honeying and making love
> Over the nasty sty . . .
> 
> > (*Hamlet,* Act III, Scene iv)

he creates out of such disparate components as stew, honey, and rank sweat a unique meaningful description of the situation which none of the components by itself could begin to express.

But of course not every synthesis of disparate materials will produce something of significance and value. The helterskelter quality of much contemporary writing often results from combining very disparate elements without adequately harmonizing them. Of course critical judgment should not be hasty; for many a marriage that in its early years seemed headed for the divorce courts may settle down at last into a strange viable harmony of its own. In literature, what at first looks to the established critics like "the most heterogeneous ideas yoked by violence together," as Dr. Johnson put it, may by the very abruptness of its challenge develop new habits of response in explorative readers and in uncloseted critics.

Nevertheless, audience adaptability is not the entire problem. One poetic synthesis may still be better and more promising than another. It comes down to this, I think: that while there is always an indeterminable measure of chance, of fortuitous free play in all poetic creation and in all critical response, there must also be, in any authentic artist however wayward and unpredictable, a degree of unified sensibility as well. The double requirement of a large heterogeneity of elements and an artistically effective fusion of them finds recognition in what Murray Krieger calls the "organic theory of poetic creation," particularly reflected in his remark that "Eliot sees the poet of unified sensibility as impressing the stamp of his unique psychological integration on everything around him, thereby giving it newness of life."[18] The statement distills into contemporary critical language what Coleridge had found most important in the concept of imagination as distinguished from fancy.

The semantic principle involved in the compositive aspect of imagination can now be summed up as follows. All meaning

has as its subjective condition a certain mental responsiveness—
a readiness to make connections and to associate this with that,
a readiness to see this and that in a single perspective, as forming a single individuality, a single semantic object, an *ousia*, a
Something Meant. Steno-meanings, whether scientifically stip-
ulated or more roughly stereotyped by custom, represent fixed
sets of associations, necessary no doubt for carrying on much
of the world's work but meager in experiential reference.
Fresh associations can generate fresh meanings, and the semantic function of poetry consists largely in this: that poetry quickens and guides the associative faculty, keeps it in athletic trim,
and thus actually generates new meanings—meanings that would
lose their identity outside the individual poetic context, but
which are authentically real within it.

## Archetypal Imagining

The fourth kind of poetic imagination, never found without
some admixture of the other three, consists in seeing the particular as somehow embodying and expressing a more universal
significance—that is, a "higher" or "deeper" meaning than itself.
My juxtaposition of these two opposite metaphysical vehicles is
deliberate—the Platonic figure of height and the Freudian figure
of depth—inasmuch as each of them represents an expressive
aspect of what is meant: depth connotes the complex psychical
basis, while height connotes valuational'superiority. The word
"archetype" introduces yet a third metaphor, since etymologically it connotes primacy, with overtones of temporal historical
primacy, and hence suggests what Shakespeare's Prospero calls
"the dark backward and abysm of time." Complete avoidance of
metaphorical language is impossible; the best we can do is se-
lect two or more different metaphors, each appropriate from

some point of view to what is intended, and balance these judiciously.

The role of universals in a poem, which Aristotle affirms in his famous distinction between poetry and history, and the way in which poetic imagination takes account of or has implicit reference to such universals is often obscured by wrong emphasis. Few poets, I dare say, would subscribe fully to Brunetière's remark: "What, after all, is poetry but metaphysics made manifest through sensible images?" Dante, Spenser and Traherne, let's say, might have found each some carefully guarded sense in which they could accept it, but one can scarcely think of Homer or Chaucer or almost any twentieth century poet as doing so. Naturally it is important to recognize and respond to the universal hints and implications of a poem so far as they are really present. When a poet exploits the depth dimension (which is also, from another critical standpoint, the height dimension) by stirring archetypal associations, we cannot ignore that dimension if we are to understand and adequately respond to the poem. Still, the depth dimension is more insistent and relevant in some poems than in others: more so in *Faust* than in *Egmont*, and in *Faust Part II* than in *Faust Part I;* more so in *Measure for Measure* than in *Othello;* more so in *Adonais* than in *Ode to the West Wind.* In offering such comparisons I do not mean to suggest that archetypal hints are ever entirely lacking, nor again am I proposing that either term of a comparison is poetically superior to the other. The question at present is not of evaluation but of interpretation; the inquiry is a semantic one—i.e., whether in a given poem the dimension of depth-meaning is or is not prominent, and how it is related to the organic totality of response-inviting elements which is the poem.

Moreover, there is the question of the manner in which a universal enters into a poem. Preferably not as an abstract universal, the same in all its appearances, unchanged by its temporary commerce with poetic discourse. A poem that emphasizes abstract universals in their abstract character is didactic, and if it employs sustained symbolism it is allegorical; its particulars tend to become little more than illustrations of a generality that can be formulated independently of the poem. When a poem succeeds in being didactic and poetic at once—Lucretius' *De Rerum Natura* and Pope's *Essay on Criticism* come to mind—it is by virtue of fresh insights and occasional twists of metaphorical imagery in Lucretius' case; chiefly by irony, nuance, and subtlety of framing in Pope's. Such cases are rather special. More characteristically the universals that enter into poetry are concrete and radically implicit universals; which is to say, the universal idea cannot be separated from the given context, cannot be logically explicated, without suffering distortion. For its universality exists by analogy only, not by definition, not by independent conceptualization. There are significant analogies between *Oedipus at Colonus* and *King Lear*, but any attempts to formulate them in critical language are feeble and abstract, compared with the insights we can draw from either of them in the reading, when our memories and potential response to the other are subdued and unconscious, not explicit. Coleridge is acknowledging the importance of concrete universality when he praises Shakespeare for effecting a "union and interpenetration of the universal and the particular," and again when he remarks that Shakespeare "had the universal which is potentially within each particular opened out to him."[19] Hegel says much the same thing in characterizing a work of art as something which though *sensuous* is at the same time essentially addressed to the *mind*. And W. K. Wimsatt has observed that "in one terminology or another this idea of a concrete universal is found in most metaphysical aesthetics of the eighteenth and nineteenth centuries." And throughout literary criticism, too, there has been a recurrent concern with what Professor Wimsatt calls "an object which in a mysterious and special way is both highly general and highly particular."[20]

Perhaps the most interesting case of a great poet who consciously made concrete universality the governing condition of his poetry is Goethe. "Every character," he declared to Eckermann, "however peculiar it may be, and every representation, from stone all the way up the scale to man, has a certain universality; for everything repeats itself, and there is nothing in the world that has happened only once."[21] All nature, in Goethe's view, is variously and changingly interrelated, but the phenomena which manifest themselves on the surface not only interpenetrate one another but variously reveal the perduring archetypes which they express and symbolize. For Goethe holds that the world is intrinsically symbolic: by which he means that every quality, character, happening, is at once concrete event (*Phänomenon*) and archetype (*Urphänomen*). The Goethean archetype, however, is not like the Platonic *eidos* something separate in existence or even in thought from the particular; it exists only in and through the particular, and hence can be known only by opening our eyes and ears and hearts to the sensuous living world. There is an undercurrent of Goethean seriousness in Mephistopheles' chaffing of the pedantic scholar:

> Grau, theurer Freund, ist alle Theorie,
> Und grün des Lebens goldner Baum.

The green and golden archetype, as distinguished from the gray abstract idea, is at once genuinely universal and undivorcibly concrete.

Certain particulars have more of an archetypal content than others: that is to say, they are *"eminent instances"* which stand forth in a characteristic amplitude as representatives of many others; they enclose in themselves a certain totality, arranged in a certain way, stirring in the soul something at once familiar and strange, and thus outwardly as well as inwardly they lay claim to a certain unity and generality. Such eminent instances are the keystone of Goethe's conception of art; for he defines beauty, or the beautiful, as "a disclosure of secret natural laws, which would have remained forever hidden if it had not been for just this manifestation." The beautiful, to Goethe, carries a connotation of the symbolic, to greater or lesser degree. But symbolism ("a living-moment disclosure of the inscrutable") must not be confused with allegory ("a dream or a shadow"):

> It makes a great difference whether the poet starts with a universal idea and then looks for suitable particulars, or beholds the universal *in* the particular. The former method produces allegory, where the particular has status merely as an instance, an example of the universal. The latter, by contrast, is what reveals poetry in its true nature: it speaks forth a particular without independently thinking of or referring to a universal, but in grasping the particular in its living character it implicitly apprehends the universal along with it.[22]

The notion of archetype has come into greater public prominence within the last few decades because of the prestige of the late Dr. Carl G. Jung and the controversies aroused by his psychological theory of archetypes. My own discussions of archetypes are unaffected by the truth or falsity of Jung's special theories of the collective unconscious and of whether its "primordial images" are transmitted by inheritance. Jung is quite palpably right to this extent, that the primordial images are "as much feelings as thoughts" but that their strong feeling-tone does not by any means reduce them to the status of merely subjective occurrences. Their subjectivity has its origin somehow (unlike Jung I can't suggest how) beyond the confines of the individual. A genuine archetype shows itself to have a life of its own, far older and more comprehensive than ideas belonging to the individual consciousness or to the shared consciousness of particular communities. The Divine Father, the Earth Mother, the World Tree, the satyr or centaur or other man-animal amalgam, the descent into Hell, the Purgatorial stair or other pathway of trials, the washing away of sin, the castle of attainment, the culture-hero such as Prometheus bringing fire or other basic gift to mankind, the treacherous betrayal of the hero, the sacrificial death of the god, the god in disguise or the prince under an enchantment—these and many other mythologems (as Jung calls them, following Herder) are persistent patterns of human thought and expression, and have become story-elements repeatedly in the literature of many different and often unrelated races. They are closer to man's natural human vision than are the products of brain-ingenuity; and I agree with Jung that the genuine philosopher conceptualizes his ideas not by arbitrary stipulation and not merely as intellectual exercises, but as transmutations and developments of the "primitive and purely natural vision" which the archetypes originally express. When it comes to inquiring just how a given archetype is to be interpreted, however, in relation to the rooted meanings and values of human life, I fear that either Freud's or Jung's insistence upon the priority of a single method and a single theory and upon judging the archetypes on the basis of discoveries made or claimed to be made in modern clinics, tends to increase the obscurities of the problem instead of lessening them. No method is foolproof, but the most promising methods are likely to be, other things equal, the least prejudiced; and this involves the gathering of archetypal evidences on a broad base from literature, myth, religion, and art, and seeking to understand such evidences on their own terms as far as possible instead of imposing extrinsically oriented interpretations upon them.

# 4

## The Limits of Plain Sense

*When people stammer together that is thinking.*
GERTRUDE STEIN

There is no more ironic illusion than to suppose that one has escaped from illusions. So subtly do the real and the illusory interpenetrate that their difference is never finally clear. Mind is by nature a meddler, and there are no self-evident criteria by which to discriminate its insights from its commentaries. Still, the quest for certainty persists. The history of philosophy, save for sceptical interludes, is a record of men's shifting intellectual stratagems by which to secure some firm line of demarcation between truth and error.

In the everyday business of living we do indeed establish convenient rules of thumb to indicate, for practical convenience, what can be handled and by what laws it may be expected to operate. Such public operables, actual and potential, constitute our physical world; the study of their regularities of operation is empirical science, and the practical exploitation of those regularities is technology. From time to time, but especially in our day, certain theorists, impressed by the science and technology and wishing a short-cut to first principles, advance this study of public operables as the one valid form of cognition, the sole way of escape from illusionistic muddle, and the system of public operables themselves as the only genuine kind of reality. Such postulation generates the philosophy known variously as materialism, naturalism, and positivism. The last name, positivism, being freest of adventitious connotations, is the one I shall mainly employ: it can be defined precisely as the philosophy which identifies "reality" with the public operables that can be scientifically determined (space-time events and their correlations), and "truth" with the system of empirically verified propositions about such operables and their interrelations, together perhaps with propositions established by deduction from mathematical and logical axioms.

Positivism in the twentieth century goes beyond older forms of materialism: not only because of its recognition of revolutionary new scientific developments, but also—what pertains to the theme of this book—by virtue of having worked out a semantic, which is to say a theory of meaning, of its own. Positivism in this guise may be called *semantic positivism*. Whereas a positivist in general is anyone who identifies reality with the system of public operables that constitutes the physical world, and truth with the system of verifiable propositions describing that reality, a semantic positivist takes the yet more drastic step of identifying *meaning* with such terms and propositions as denote such operables. In other words, the semantic positivist starts off with a judgment about *language*. The only language that really means anything, he declares, is language which refers to things, events, and relations in the physical world. If it does not refer to the physical world, it does not refer to anything (for nothing else exists), and is therefore, strictly speaking, meaningless. By this bold stratagem the positivist gains an enviable advantage: instead of having to argue with dissenters he need only declare that the terms in which they formulate their opposition do not conform to the conditions of meaningfulness which he has set up; in short, he dismisses them as talking nonsense.

Semantic positivism represents, on its affirmative side, the excellent intention of promoting intelligibility and avoiding confusion. It proceeds from the principle that we ought to be as clear as possible about the meaning of our utterances, and be able to know when we are speaking sense and when we are just vaporizing. With this general aim every candid thinker will agree. The question is, where the line between sense and vaporizing is to be drawn. Semantic positivists have no difficulty in drawing it. Language, they declare, may on the one hand assert something in the form of a proposition about what is "actually the case"; on the other it may, in the words of Rudolf Carnap, "express the emotions, fancies, images, or wishes of the speaker, and under proper conditions evoke emotions, wishes, or resolutions in the hearer."[1]

The same semantic dichotomy is proclaimed in the earlier writings of I. A. Richards. Since Professor Richards is a sensitive literary critic and a generally alert thinker, it may not seem fair to saddle his present reputation with a view which he expressed over four decades ago. His more recent writings, although never repudiating, have shown a tendency to liberalize and soften the hard semantic postulates which he advocated during the 'twenties. Nevertheless the influence of those early books has persisted in certain critical circles, and the point of view which they represent is still very much alive. Inasmuch as that point of view, consistently developed, destroys the very basis of that mythopoeic vision of the world which alone can give human life its transcendental significance, there is as much pertinence now as there ever was in subjecting it to critical scrutiny. A succinct statement of the view in question is offered in this passage from Richards' *Principles of Literary Criticism* (1924):

> A statement may be used for the sake of *reference*, true or false, which it causes. This is the *scientific* use of language. But it may also be used for the sake of the effects in emotion and attitude produced by the reference it occasions. This is the *emotive* use. The distinction once clearly grasped is simple. We may either use words for the sake of the reference they promote, or we may use them for the sake of the attitudes and emotions which ensue.[2]

The distinction is simple enough, to be sure; indeed, far too over-simple. What follows from so uncompromising an "either-or"? The consequences for poetry and religion had been indicated a few years earlier in *The Meaning of Meaning* (written in collaboration with C. K. Ogden), where it is asserted that as poetry and religion do not employ words scientifically, so neither of them employs words referentially—which is to say, neither of them is capable of speaking *about* anything. For the one plain test of whether a given use of words is essentially symbolic and referential or essentially emotive is declared to be the question, "Is it true or false in the ordinary strict scientific sense?"

The ontological basis of Richards' semantic position became clarified in his article, "Between Truth and Truth," published in 1931. Two years earlier, in *Practical Criticism*, he had pursued more fully the question of communication in literature. From that standpoint he now reformulated his position. A poem, he now declared, describes and communicates something, but what? "Two alternatives, and not more I think, are before us, two main senses of 'describe' and 'communicate.' . . . The first sense is that in which a form of words describes or communicates the state of mind or experience of the speaker; the second is that in which it describes or communicates some state of affairs or fact which the speaker is thinking of or knowing (something in all but one case, that of introspection, *other than* the experience which is his thinking of it or knowing it)."[3] Richards then turns to John Clare's description of the primrose—

> With its crimp and curdled leaf
> And its little brimming eye,

about which, in an earlier article, John Middleton Murry had remarked that it "is surely an accurate description, but accurate with an accuracy unknown to and unachievable by science." Richards complains: Mr. Murry "does not say explicitly whether he takes it as a description of an object (the primrose) or of the experience of seeing one." And he adds: "It seems to me not likely that there will be widespread disagreement with the view that the description applies to the experience of sensing or imagining a primrose rather than to actual primroses."

But the "rather than" naively over-simplifies the matter. For what is an "actual" primrose? Surely any observant flower lover, unless constrained by loyalty to a preconceived theory, will find actuality in the qualitative kind of thing that John Clare describes. Neither the lexicographer's definition of the primrose as a "plant or flower of the genus Primula" nor a botanist's or biochemist's analysis of it into scientifically discoverable elements and processes can describe the perceived primrose in its full living actuality as adequately as Clare's lines have done. If we are willing to consider such words as "crimp" and "curdled" in their descriptive function (as Richards has done in formulating his complaint against Murry above), then clearly it is not the *experience of* a primrose that is being described (for it is not my experience that is crimp and curdled) but *the primrose as experienced.*

The trouble is that Professor Richards has fallen here without realizing it into the trap of metaphysics. The defection is especially noticeable in a footnote to the article just mentioned, where he distinguishes the "sensed or imagined primrose" from the "inferred or constructed common or gardener's primrose" on the ground that the former lacks such scientifically determinable characteristics as weight. His distinction does not stand up under examination. The very same primrose which I see as crimp and curdled I can also pick up and feel as having a bit of weight. Such visual and such kinaesthetic experiences refer to what I naturally and reasonably regard as constituting a single object. So too, but less directly, do the experiences of looking at the notches on a scale on which the primrose is being weighed. On the basis of this latter type of experience (mine or another's) the primrose is assigned a numerical figure which we call its "objective weight"—bearing some relation no doubt, but not a strictly determinable one, to the kinaesthetic experience of lightness which I feel when I take the flower in my hand. Now the fallacy of the semantic positivist is to reject the "crimp and curdled" kind of experience and the kinaesthetic kind of experience ("Why, this flower weighs practically nothing!") and to accept as "real" only the kind of experience which consists in looking at notches on a scale. For the notch on the scale to which the pointer turns can be securely agreed on by everyone who is capable of seeing or touching; whereas no such agreement can normally be reached in the case of the other qualities mentioned.

When I say that the logical positivist "rejects," of course I do not mean that he wants nothing to do with the more colorful and feelingful qualities of things. He may indeed, as Mr. Richards explicitly does, consider them "more valuable" for the larger human purposes than a knowledge of such abstract properties as length and weight. His rejection is not practical but ontological. He asserts that only *abstract objects*, like the scientist's primrose with its numerical length and weight and its chemical properties, have real existence, whereas concrete objects, like

Clare's primrose with its plenitude of warmly experienced qualities, are not really objects at all. He asserts, therefore, that when a poet or anyone else appears to be speaking about such qualities he is not really speaking *about* anything, but is merely ejaculating the history of his mind, "his feelings and attitudes in the moment of speaking, and conditions of their governance in the future." Thus the positivist when he turns literary critic has no recourse but to fall into what Wimsatt and Beardsley have called the Affective Fallacy; for how can he logically say anything about the poetry of a poem except to tell how it affects him subjectively?

Naturally I do not deny that poetry does and should express in some degree the poet's feelings, nor that it may and should have for a reader the beneficial and equilibrating effects which Richards has well described in *The Principles of Literary Criticism.* These things have their own kind of importance, but from the standpoint of interpreting *what a poem says* they are strictly secondary and sometimes quite irrelevant. Every science has its proper object; and the object of poetic interpretation, rightly conceived, is the poem under consideration, and not either the poet's supposed feelings or the reader's expected benefits. An adequate study of the meaning of poetry, then—what I am calling *the semantics of poetry*—must first establish unhampering postulates and find a suitable language whereby the nature and meaning of poetic utterance can be indicated without stepping into fields of discourse peripheral and sometimes alien to poetry.

Positivists who lack Mr. Richards' sound taste have produced some quaint monsters when occasionally they have ventured to raise questions of literary theory. Consider, for example, Bertrand Russell's analysis of the experience of reading a drama:

> We experience "Hamlet," not Hamlet; but our emotions in reading the play have to do with Hamlet, not with "Hamlet." "Hamlet" is a word of six letters; whether it

should be or not be is a question of little interest, and it
certainly could not make its quietus with a bare bodkin.
Thus the play "Hamlet" consists entirely of false propositions, which transcend experience, but which are certainly
significant, since they can arouse emotions. When I say
that our emotions are about Hamlet, not "Hamlet," I must
qualify this statement: they are really not about anything,
but we think they are about a man named "Hamlet." The
propositions in the play are false because there was no
such man; they are significant because we know from experience the noise "Hamlet," the meaning of "name" and the
meaning of "man." .The fundamental falsehood in the play
is the proposition: the noise "Hamlet" is a name.[4]

There are only two ways of taking Lord Russell's odd pronouncement, so far as I can see. Either he is saying something
intended to be practical, about how to respond to the play in
question, or else he is merely telling how he chooses to delimit
the word "experience." On the former interpretation I believe
he is plainly wrong; for it is neither necessary nor desirable to
focus our experience upon a noise and a six-letter word while
allowing our emotions to expend themselves upon we know not
what. Serious emotional experience is better integrated than
that. The feelings we entertain toward Hamlet grow out of the
experience we have of him in reading the play or seeing it
performed; take away the experience of Hamlet and his sea of
troubles and my emotions about him will either vanish or fall
into confusion and bathos. A fit response to the play and to the
predicament of its main character involves experience and feeling as inseparable aspects of the same response.

If, on the other hand, Lord Russell is only intending to prescribe how the word "experience" should be employed—i.e., that
it should be limited to sensory data such as visible letters and
audible noises together with the act of apprehending them, then
I would reply that such linguistic procedure has no backing in

the common idiom, nor can it be justified as clarifying the situation. It is both arbitrary and needlessly confusing. When someone speaks of a play as "a moving experience" no one takes him to refer primarily to the quality of noises that proceed from the actors' larynxes, but to the dramatic action which those noises (aided by gesture, staging, etc.) reveal. Moreover, there is a worse evil than the negative ones of violating common practice and failing to clarify. For to insist that the word "experience" should denote only the mechanics of seeing and hearing is to prejudice the issue in advance. Other readers think that in some important sense they experience Hamlet's character and predicament; the semantic positivist rules out this possibility by arbitrary definition. Thus upon either interpretation of Lord Russell's remarks there is the radical vice of critical irrelevance— a kind of self-imposed obtuseness to the poetic and dramatic meaning of the play and the characters in it. The positivistic assumptions and vocabulary are as inapplicable to poetry as an axe would be to wood-carving. The result in either case is splinters, not significant shape.

That positivism naturally leads to a stress upon the emotive effects of a poem, rather than to an examination on its own terms of what it means, is shown from a somewhat different angle, and with a more explicitly behavioristic emphasis, in the writings of the American philosopher Charles W. Morris.[5] Adopting Charles Peirce's word "semiotics" for the general theory of signs —"whether the signs be those of animals or of men, . . . whether they are signs in science or signs in art, technology, religion, or philosophy,"—Morris subdivides this general science into three sub-sciences: *pragmatics* (study of the origin, use, and effects of signs), *semantics* (study of significations), and *syntactics* (study of the mutual relations of signs). Now if we were to apply this scheme tentatively and experimentally to the critical study of literature (and to *no* conceptual scheme should a literary critic ever become permanently wedded), the critical task would then be conceived in terms of a combined semantic and syntactical approach. The meaning of poetic discourse is inseparable from the interplay and intervitalization of words, and whether or not these two complementary aspects are to be described as semantical and syntactical, at any rate it is within the area of their double focus that the critic's task is to be found.

Professor Morris, however, believes that what art "designates" is values, and since he further believes that the meaning of a value must be interpreted behaviorally—that it should be put "in terms descriptive of behavioral processes,"—a curious result follows. Poetry, he declares, is "an example of discourse which is appraisive-valuative" and "its primary aim is to cause the interpreter to accord to what is signified the preferential place in his behavior signified by the appraisors." What can this pair of statements mean except that the function of poetry (and of literature generally) is essentially akin to that of propaganda? It may use subtler and more varied techniques than the kind of thing we normally call propaganda, and presumably its aims are less clearly defined; but if its primary aim is to cause in the reader a change of the valuations that determine his behavior, surely that is just what propaganda commonly means. It is revealing, I think, that in the whole of Mr. Morris' book, *Signs, Language and Behavior,* there is only one poetic quotation, which consists of five lines from Walt Whitman's *A Song of Myself:* "I believe in the flesh and the appetites . . . The scent of these arm-pits finer than prayer . . ." Such lines as these do, no doubt, encourage a behavioristic-valuative interpretation and little else, but is the signification of all poetry equally limited? Even *A Song of Myself* turns out to mean a great deal more when the imagistic patterns and referential thrust of the entire poem are taken into account; and it is only in this larger context that we are dealing with questions of poetic meaning, which are scarcely pertinent to the above quoted lines taken by themselves.

My objection to the theory which I have been examining under the general name of "semantic positivism" may now be summed up. It requires, in effect, that the truth of a poem, or of a religious belief, or of a philosophical insight—of anything, in short, which is not a scientific statement either of verifiable fact or of logically analytical ("tautologous") relations—must be judged ultimately by its emotive and conative affects. Hence it can aptly be spoken of as the Affective Theory of poetic, religious, and philosophical truth.[6] From its standpoint the existence of poetry can be justified only on one or other of two grounds: either on the hedonistic ground that it gives pleasure to those who happen to like it, or on the clinical ground defended by the earlier Richards and implicit in Morris, that it tends to promote a healthier equilibrium of attitudes in the reader and therefore possibly in the society wherein he moves. Even religion can be given no firmer justification than one or the other of these, if the Affective Theory is true. There are, however, two grave flaws in that theory, one in the flower and one in the root. Experientially, the theory does not do justice to the full nature of either poetic or religious experience; and logically, it rests upon an arbitrary (and I believe false) presupposition.

On the first count let it be considered that neither the pleasurable nor the therapeutic effects of poetry or religion are fortuitous. While those of poetry may partly proceed from the direct propulsions of rhythm and imagery upon the physio-psychic organism, they most characteristically involve something more. A poem affects a mature reader as it does partly because it seems to him, notwithstanding its fantasies and pseudo-statements, to be offering a kind of genuine insight and thereby to be revealing, however obscurely and elusively, a kind of truth. In *King Lear*, for example, the language and imagery and character developments and story are inseparable aspects of the total poem and legitimate factors in its appeal. But *King Lear's* principal claim to greatness transcends these components: it is great because in and through such poetic devices it reveals depth-meaning—it adumbrates truths and quasi-truths of high importance about such matters as human nature, old age, false seeming, and self-confrontation through suffering. The depth-meaning of *Lear*— the "poetic truth" to be discovered in the play—is what mainly accounts for and justifies the Fit Reader's full response, an inseparable blending of emotive and intellectual factors. In the absence of such a depth-meaning the reader's response won't be the same. Impoverishment or distortion of the intellectual response will involve alteration of the emotive. To regard the specifically poetic response as exclusively emotive, then, is a naive way of psychologizing.

With regard to religion the shallowness of the positivistic interpretation is even more evident. For in religion the depth-meaning is *all* that matters. If you ignore the depth-meanings of Sophocles or Dante or Shakespeare, something of the nature of poetry still remains in them; and those whose response is limited to story, imagery, and versification may still be responding in a way proper to poetry, although inadequately so. But if you ignore the depth-meanings of religion, what you have remaining is not religion at all, but sabbatical play-acting. Prayer and worship can be justified as psychic therapy only if the postulant and worshiper believes that his utterance is somehow heard and somehow responded to. Now it is possible of course—I mean it is *logically* possible—that the religious believer is deceived, and that his conviction of entering into a responsive relationship with a Power or Powers transcending the human condition is illusory. Whether transcendental existence and men's intercommunication with it are real or illusory is, as Pascal insisted, the most important question of all, and it cannot be settled by ruling out all answers but one as "meaningless." An adequate semantic organon should make it possible to formulate theories about religious reality intelligibly. A semantic theory which denies meaning to any and all specifically religious affirmations of reality cuts off open discussion at the source. Its denial of meaning to any religious ontology is a disguised way of rejecting a whole set of truth-claims apriori, and thus of prejudging questions of a certain type wholesale.

The other and more analytic objection to the Affective Theory concerns the presumed dichotomy on which it rests. Two types or modes or uses of discourse are sharply distinguished; most contemporary positivists designate them the referential and the emotive. Referential statements are postulated or defined to be true insofar as they truly describe what is actually the case, false insofar as they do the contrary; and it is further postulated that in all instances of a referential statement it is possible to specify the empirical conditions under which it could be verified or disproved. Emotive discourse, on the other hand, is taken as expressing some emotive-conative state of the writer (or speaker) or as aiming to arouse such a state in the reader (or hearer), and therefore as not being intrinsically referential. The unguarded inference from "intrinsically emotive" to "not intrinsically referential" reveals the main fallacy of the Affective Theory: i.e., the unexamined assumption that language which is intrinsically the one cannot be intrinsically the other—the assumption that the terms "referential" and "emotive" constitute a natural dichotomy. This is a proposition which must now be challenged.

The following diagram shows schematically how such a challenge is logically possible. The diagram is based on the plainly evident fact that "referential" and "emotive" are not contradictory in their meaning (unless we beg the question by arbitrarily interpreting them in that manner); to conceive them without presupposition is to conceive them as independent variables. An utterance can be more or less of either of them without thereby having to be less or more of the other. For the negative of *referential* is not emotive but *non-referential,* and the negative of *emotive* is not referential but *non-emotive.* This logical truism enables us to construct a two-dimensional graph in which the vertical axis has "referential" (R) and "non-referential" (non-R) as its poles, the horizontal axis "emotive" (E) and "non-emotive" (non-E). Four areas are thus established, representing four interactive modes of discourse:

MODES OF DISCOURSE

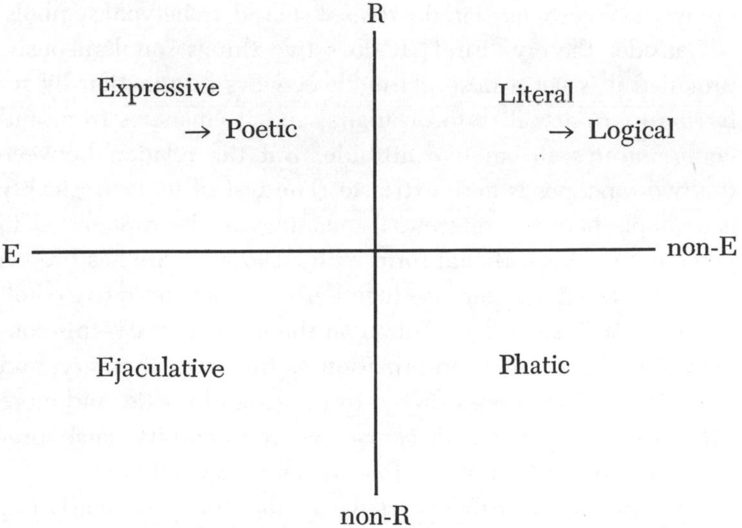

R

Expressive            Literal

→ Poetic            → Logical

E ————————————————————— non-E

Ejaculative           Phatic

non-R

R, non-E: *Literal discourse:* ordinary everyday language .in its referential mode. *Logical discourse* is its ideally perfected form.

Non-R, non-E: *Phatic discourse:* "Good morning," etc.

Non-R, E: *Ejaculative discourse:* "Oh, damn!" etc.—where, as distinguished from phatic discourse, something is really felt. For clarity's sake let us avoid the practice of certain semanticists, of applying the word "expressive" in this connection.

R, E: *Expressive discourse:* language which is referential and emotive at once—not by incidental conjunction as in a cry of "Fire!" but in the more organic sense that the referential function, the full proper meaning, takes at least some of its essential character from the precise emotivity of the language, and changes therefore as the emotivity changes. *Poetic discourse* is a species of expressive discourse, in which the main part of the meaning is controlled by the poet's art rather than by developing social customs as in the case of shared archetypal symbols.

Consider the cry "Fire!" It does two things simultaneously, provided it is not a false alarm: it conveys information by referring to an actual state of affairs, and it emanates from and communicates an emotive attitude. But the relation between the two functions is here extrinsic. The test of its extrinsicality is a simple one: the referential meaning can be expounded in non-emotive propositional form without loss. "A fire has broken out in this building," perhaps together with some hortative corollary such as "Escape!" or "Summon the fire engines!"—this conveys virtually the same information as the original outcry, and indeed conveys it more exactly. In the case of poetic, and more generally of expressive discourse, on the contrary, such prosaical restatement is not possible without essential loss.

My thesis is that truly expressive symbolism—particularly but not exclusively in a poem—means, refers, awakens insight, *in and through* the emotions it engenders, and that where an appropriate emotion is not aroused the full insight is not awakened. Granted that irrelevant emotions may be aroused, still the problem of learning to know and understand a poem is largely also the problem of distinguishing the relevant from the irrelevant—of distinguishing, that is to say, the responses aroused by the whole poem's intrinsic emotivity from the incidental responses aroused by isolated parts and fortuitous associations. In religious insight, too, (as distinguished from blind acceptance on the one hand and theological ratiocination on the other) emotion, if properly focussed, plays a legitimate role. But it is of utmost importance to distinguish the quality of emotion which reveals some aspect of the Divine from the quality of emotion which obscures and confuses—to distinguish the clarifying act of self-transcending reverence from the muck and muddle of self-deluding religiosity. In short, I am asserting that poetic and religious emotions, when they are depth-oriented and are purified as much as possible from emotions produced by superficial reactions and associations, may have or may come to have distinctively ontological bearings of their own. Whether one agrees or disagrees with this central thesis, it is by no means a new or a trifling one, and it ought not to be ruled out by the apriori maneuver of setting up a dichotomy that leaves no room for it.

What I am proposing, then, and what the diagram represents, is a sort of Copernican Revolution in semantics. Or perhaps non-Euclidean, or trans-Euclidean, would offer an apter analogy. For whereas Euclidean geometry was once regarded as the be-all and end-all of geometrical truth, modern mathematicians are able to regard a form of space in which the postulate of parallels holds true, as merely a *limiting case* (perhaps also an actual one) in the universe of possibilities. Analogously we may construe the semantic positivist as residing too doggedly in a Euclidean-like world. The aim, the instrument, and the presuppositions of logical discourse, as developed by the formal sciences, they accept without serious question. And my belief is that they are wrong, dead wrong—not of course in the contributions they have made to logical clarity in fields where it suitably belongs, but in their refusal to admit the possibility of other kinds of semantic objectivity—the possibility of real meanings other than those which logical language can formulate. Such paralogical meanings are of dominant importance in religion, in poetry and expressive prose literature, in all the arts that "say" anything, and in moral wisdom as distinguished from moral rules; they are present helter-skelter in the vagaries of daily experience; and they even, I suspect, play a bigger role than is usually admitted in science, particularly when it comes to the discovery of fresh hypotheses. Accordingly, what any adequate theory of semantics should include, and what has not yet been systematically attempted so far as I am aware, is an exposition of the basic principles of metalogical signification as embodied in expressive language. One proposed such exposition, so far as the nebulous nature of the material allows, is the purport of the next chapter.

# 5

## Traits of Expressive Language

What are the main characteristics of expressive language
(i.e., of poeto-language in the broadest sense of the term) which
differentiate it from steno-language? In attempting to answer
this question I must insist for clarity's sake upon three general
qualifications: first, that the differentiation is by no means absolute but admits of the most varied and subtle degrees, disguises, and overlappings; secondly that steno-language is not to
be confused with any actual body of linguistic usage, notably the
scientific (cf. the unnatural dichotomy "science vs. poetry,"
promoted by Coleridge and Richards); while thirdly there is the
need of keeping the semantic distinction, between expressive
and steno-language, quite clear of a pair of philosophical dual-
isms with which certain writers have confused it.

As to the first point, the distinction between the two modes
of linguistic procedure should be conceived not as a dichotomy,
not as a frontier between two equal armies, but rather on the
model of variables approaching a limit. By analogy, consider the
relation between audible tones and silence. Sounds can differ
from one another with enormous variety in both quality and
intensity, some of them being so faint as to approximate silence

without reaching it; silence, on the other hand, is always and only silence, the uttermost negative limit. A somewhat more adequate illustration, because it offers plurality on the negative side, may be found in the relation between technicolor and black-and-white movies. The former can differ among themselves by having various degrees of brightness and dimness, sometimes doing little more than enliven the sensory surface of the film by adding a greenish or sepia tint to what would otherwise be a variety of sheer grays. While the lower degrees of technicoloring bring a film indefinitely closer to the condition of the black-and-white film, the latter type, on the contrary, cannot vary in this respect— it provides a limit which technicolor films approach but do not reach as their coloring diminishes. In much the same way expressive language has rich possibilities of variation, in at least the seven respects that are about to be listed; these represent seven possibilities of enriching or softening the meaning or making it more pliant. Steno-language *by definition* represents the negative limit of expressive language, its absolute minimum in all seven respects; thus abstractly the role of steno-language is analogous to that of silence and of the black-and-white film vis-à-vis unlimited varieties of sound and of technicolor respectively. Consequently these seven traits of expressive language are not to be regarded as equally necessary requirements if expressive language is to exist, but rather as seven dimensions of possibility which expressive language offers but does not impose. Some of them are better realized in one specimen of expressive language, others in another. And yet, when this important qualification has duly been emphasized, it still remains true that there is a significant difference between sound and silence, between cinematic technicolor and cinematic black-and-white, and so also between expressive language and steno-language.

The second general remark is also in the nature of a disclaimer. I am not asserting that any specific type of language in actual use—and this applies especially to all forms of language employed by any of the sciences—must necessarily be pure steno-language bereft of any expressive characteristics. Cases have to be judged individually. If a scientist, in whatever special field and for whatever purpose, chooses to employ language that is expressive in one or more of the seven mentioned ways, the critic's role will be not to dispute property rights but only to describe and evaluate the expressive elements that he finds employed. Our business as critics is not to prescribe what semantic devices are to be employed in this or that field of discourse, but to possess an intelligible criterion whereby we can judge what is being done. There is no contradiction in saying of a certain scientist that he states his theories expressively; the important thing is to know precisely what we mean when we say it.

The third and last of the general warnings to be made is that the distinction between expressive language and steno-language is semantic only; it entails no metaphysical or epistemological judgment about any supposed distinction between reality and appearance or between objective and subjective. The conceptual blunder that weakens Dr. Richards' theory seems to involve one or both of these confusions, as was suggested in the preceding chapter. His theory is clouded, as I see it, by a blurring of the semantic concept of expressive fullness (which is the central concern of this chapter and of this book) with the metaphysical concept of reality vs. mere appearance and with the epistemological concept of objective vs. merely subjective. Let us try to unconfuse and specify. We can do this best by "bracketing off" and gracefully ignoring, at least in the earlier stages of our investtigation, both the metaphysical question of what is "real" and the epistemological question of what is "objective." Both questions are heavily theoretical and they can offer no help, but only distraction, to one who seeks to discover the nature of poetic meaning. Let us keep our critical attention focussed on the poeto-semantic question of how far and in what respects a given specimen of language is poetically expressive, and how far and in what respects it is prosaic, stenolinguistic and inert. The seven potential characteristics that are now to be discussed (no exhaustive list presumably, but highly important so far as they go) indicate seven major aspects of such semantic expressibility.

1. *Referential congruity.* Steno-language is ultimately stipulative; for basically it is a matter of free choice what word or other symbol is to be used to designate a given meaning. Red and green traffic lights mean *Stop* and *Go*, not by virtue of any intrinsic connection, but stipulatively first, and afterwards by public habituation. Or turning from directive signs to symbols, consider the Arabic digits employed in arithmetic. The familiar shapes—1, 2, 3, 4, etc.—bear no essential relation to their tenor, which is to say, to the structural relations of numbers. Mathematical relations are completely unaffected by whatever signs are chosen to designate them: two sets of six units and three sets of four units will always be exactly equal, regardless of what symbols are used. If someone were to choose to write $a$, $b$, $c$, $d$ for 2, 3, 4, 6 respectively, it would still be true, exactly and invariably so, that $a$ sets of $d$ units form a totality equal to $b$ sets of $c$ units. When, on the other hand, the semantic situation is expressive and organic the problem of switching vehicles is vastly more complex. In *Metaphor and Reality* I have remarked:

> If some Greek letter, not $\pi$, had originally been chosen to represent the ratio of circumference to diameter of a circle, the mathematical relations and laws would not have been altered a whit thereby; but if Shakespeare had decided to let the Weird Sisters inhabit water, like the Rhine Maidens, instead of "fog and filthie air," the whole play of *Macbeth* would have been profoundly different.[1]

Semantic congruity is likely to be of importance wherever

the relation between vehicle and tenor is organic and interactive, not mechanical and external. It may be that as the steno-linguistic core dwindles to zero the surface-phenomenon tends to lose its vehicular character and to approach the condition of music, which from a semantic standpoint is self-intentive rather than alio-intentive. I shall not pursue the paradox, however; for such cases are wholly aesthetic, not poeto-semantic, and accordingly they escape our area of inquiry. The more interesting kinds of situation, and those that concern our present study, are aesthetic and semantic at once; the vehicle is both self-intentive and alio-intentive, it presents as well as represents, even as a verse may be both pleasing as a song and haunting in its suggestiveness. Here there is a kind of semantic *methexis*,[2] a mutual participation between vehicle and tenor; for the quality of the song helps to open up and perhaps to limit the suggestions of meaning, while on the other hand one's sense of the meaning modifies the discoverable quality of the song.

The most natural way in which to express and convey a concrete situation (as distinguished from a *class* of situations or any other abstract relation, which can usually be represented by a steno-symbol) is by employing a linguistic vehicle that is somehow imitative; for a concrete situation in being imitated is more nearly presented, although by proxy, than when it is represented by conventional symbols. Imitation consists, as we know, in stressing certain similarities chosen for accentuation, and these can be of three types according to which of our avenues of sense is chiefly employed. Where the similarity and the imitation are visual in type, there is *iconic* representation (e.g., a map); where they are auditory there is *tonal* representation (e.g., program music, onomatopoeia); where they are kinaesthetic there is *mimetic* representation (e.g., the sacred dance). The semantic methexis of which I have spoken seems to be present least in the case of visual imitation and most in the case of mimetic. Wherever a semantic relation is markedly methexic we are inclined to think of its language more as a medium than as a vehicle; thus we find it natural to speak of the sacred dance as a medium of religious expression, but not to speak of a map as a medium.

However, the congruity between vehicle and tenor need not be dependent upon so close a relationship as imitation. The referential relation may more loosely be based on an analogy drawn from general experience: e.g., the symbol of the key to the city. The similarity and imitation here are not between vehicle and tenor, but between the vehicle-tenor relation and some analogous part of general experience. As the actual key opens doors, so the key that is offered symbolically to a distinguished visitor is imagined to open up privileges for him. The symbolic congruity of "fog and filthie air" with the dramatic and moral role of the Weird Sisters offers a subtler and far more significant example of symbolism based on general analogies of experience. While we should not think of the key of the city as a medium, nor its semantic function as methexic, we can readily think of the darkness imagery of *Macbeth* in both of these terms.

2. *Contextual Variation.* An important requirement of steno-language was formulated by Thomas Hobbes over three hundred years ago: "In all discourses wherein one man pretends to instruct or convince another, he should use the same word constantly in the same sense. If this were done (which nobody can refuse without great disingenuity), many of the books extant might be spared."[3] Words, and more specifically what Hobbes calls "names," should be *univocal*, by which adjective he signifies "those which in the same train of discourse signify always the same thing." In contrast to names that accord with this simple honest rule there are *equivocal* names—"those which mean sometimes one thing and sometimes another." And he adds, "Every metaphor is equivocal." His most revealing remark comes

in his next sentence, where he attributes motives to the persons who employ one or the other form of language: "for some employ them [names] properly and accurately for the finding of truth; others draw them from their proper sense, for ornament and deceit."

Hobbes' important half-truth needs to be examined on two levels. Unquestionably there is a large area of discourse ("where one man pretends to instruct or convince another," and more broadly wherever established and rationally justified concepts are foremost) in which the prescription of univocalism is essential. For the alternative would there be that we divert the words from their proper sense, whether "for ornament or deceit" or out of mental sloth—in fanciful literature and playful discourse for ornament, in sophistical argument for deceit, and perhaps most often simply from what Eliot has called "the general mess of imprecision of feeling." Within that definite framework Hobbes is right in proclaiming univocalism as that "which nobody can refuse without great disingenuity."

But language is also needed for dealing with the living flow of experience which is not yet formalized into definite concepts and which cannot be conceptualized without suffering distortion of character. This phenomenological urgency of language, which is the first aspect of its expressive character, has been discussed under the first heading. What invites our attention now is a corollary of it. When we try by language to express presentative immediacy, seeking to express by words the phenomenological object rather than an object that has been largely fixed by conceptual definition, it follows that the semantic character of the language employed must have more flexibility in order to be relatively close to the fluctuating character of the experience in question. Even at best its success must be imperfect; for words are always and only words, a tiny part of experience standing for larger and more receding areas of it. But at all events some language manages better than other language to evoke a lively awareness of the never ceasing flow of things. Since the terms of expressive discourse, unlike those of steno-discourse, cannot be controlled apriori by explicit definition, their referentially intimate meanings must be determined afresh on each occasion of their use—in part by a relatively persistent core of meaning which unites and relates the various semantic occasions together, in part by the entire relevant context which the particular occasion gathers up and partly generates. In poetry the relevant context of a symbol is controlled to a large degree by the poet's individual manipulation of his medium; in religion it appears to depend more upon the elusive factors of social and individual sensibility toward the signatures of divinity as they seem to show themselves in the world.

Consider the Shakespearean tempest, particularly the functional role it plays in *King Lear*, in *Macbeth*, and in *The Tempest*. Regarding stormy weather as a part, and a highly important part, of Shakespeare's dramatic language, we can understand that the dramatic meaning of it, whether it is beheld onstage or reported as occurring offstage or is only presented in the imagery used to describe other events and moods, is not and cannot be quite the same thing in all three plays. There is a partial identity of course, for the tempest in all its manifestations stands opposed in the Shakespearean dialectic to such humanly favorable image-symbols as music, jewels, and feasting. The tempest represents in one way or another those forces, incompletely known, that shake and threaten man's human condition. But man's human condition in its specificity is individually different in each of Shakespeare's plays, and therefore any symbol representing it must allow of semantic shifts and adjustments to the particular dramatic and noetic situation.

Of course the variable possibilities of a word are limited by certain more or less understood conceptual boundaries; these,

however, are not absolute, and it is the poet's task and privilege
to explore ways of conceptual dislodgement that will produce
more gain than loss. To succeed in significant dislodgement is an
act of semantic rejuvenation.

> Essential oils are wrung;
> The attar from the rose
> Is not expressed by suns alone,
> It is the gift of screws.

Emily Dickinson here produces semantic rejuvenation in three
words especially: in "wrung" and "screws" by reason of their
placement and emphasis; in "expressed" most of all, since this
word, by reason of the connotations of physical activity thrown
up by the two emphasized words and by the phrase "by suns
alone," is forced back from its usual more intellectual meaning
into the older etymological meaning of being physically pressed
out.

3. *Plurisignation.* Apart from any question of whether or
not its meanings are altered by shifting context, an expressive
symbol tends on any given occasion of its realization, to carry
more than one legitimate reference—or if not something definite
enough to be called a reference, then at least more than one
legitimate group of connotations and suggestions—in such a way
that its full meaning involves a tension between two or more
directions of semantic stress. Poetically charged language means
mainly this, in fact: that the poetic symbol tends characteristically to be plurisignative, in that its intellectual meanings are
likely to be more or less multiple, yet so fused as sometimes to
defy any attempted analysis into monosignative components,
and always to produce an integral meaning that radically transcends the sum of the ingredient meanings. In these last respects
plurisignation differs from simple punning. A brief example
is Faustus' agonized cry: "See, see where Christ's *blood* streams

in the firmament!" In this case the two semantic aspects of the plurisign have been established independently of the poet's design: the color of the sky is caused physically, and the redemptive power of Christ's blood is an idea drawn from theological tradition. The following, by contrast, is a case where the poet prepares for both referential aspects of the plurisign, by setting up more specific indications within the poem. Hart Crane thus addresses an aeronaut pilot flying over Cape Hatteras:

> Thou hast here in thy wrist a Sanskrit charge
> To *conjugate* infinity's dim marge.[4]

The familiar meaning of "conjugate," having to do with the inflection of verbs, has no general connection with the theme of *The Bridge* but receives its justification locally: from the phrase, "in thy wrist a Sanskrit charge," which might suggest the activity of copying old manuscripts. But "in thy wrist" also goes with the second meaning of "conjugate," the meaning implicit in the word's etymology: "to yoke together"—a meaning associated with the image of the pilot using his wrist to guide the plane toward infinity's dim marge and thereby yoke together far horizons.

The meanings attached to a plurisign in a given poetic context are not necessarily all the meanings of which the word is capable; a skillful poet manipulates his contexts in such a way that the fit reader will think only of the meanings intended. Thus Eliot's manner of contextualizing the Dove imagery in "Little Gidding" directs the reader's mind to take the Dove as symbolizing both a bombing plane and the Holy Ghost; but not the Dove of Peace, although in other contexts that meaning might have been suggested. In the same poem the line, "To be redeemed from fire by fire," unmistakably refers to the opposing fires of hell and purgatory, thereby symbolizing ultimate pain and loss on the one hand, spiritual cleansing on the other; it does not, however, carry another symbolic reference of fire, viz., to the Heraclitean notion of universal change.

The *Concrete Universal* might be numbered "*3a*"; for while it can be regarded as involving a special sort of plurisignation, it develops a set of activities with a special importance of their own. In simple logic a concrete universal is a plurisign in which one of the tensively related meanings is close, immediate, and relatively obvious, while the second meaning has a universal and archetypal character, like the "bright shoots of everlasting-ness" which Henry Vaughan finds in common things. The concrete universal should not be confused either with the abstract universal or with allegory. An abstract universal, which is a universal in the logical sense, is a class-concept, every member of which is an instance of the class and necessarily possesses, by virtue of its subsumption under the universal, such character-istics as are shared by all the other members of that class. In a concrete universal, on the contrary, the universal subsists in the individual not *quâ* abstract but *quâ* concrete. The individual as concretely sensed or imaged or described is the important thing, the bulwark of poetic consideration; the universal is not an-nounced explicitly, but stays implicit in, and yet is strongly affirmed by, the very individuality of the individual.

Since possible illustrations are unlimited, let us be content with a single one: the Shakespearean archetype of False Seem-ing. Outside the Shakespearean framework this archetype has numerous and varied affinities: Plato's darkness of the Cave at once illustrates and largely establishes the Western concept, while the Hindu notion of *maya*, as combined illusion and force, can best mark the Eastern. But remote analogies like these can-not be pursued here. Within the Shakespearean framework there are three main levels of thinking about the archetype in ques-tion; they are those of tragedy, of comedy, and of something intermediate. In *Othello, King Lear,* and *Macbeth* the False

Seeming in one guise or another plays a central dramatic role—as villainous slander, as false show of filial love, and as half-lying supernatural promises respectively, each with its own tragic outcome. In comedy the false show is barely more than a passing moral to adorn a tale, as in the naive lesson of the three caskets in *The Merchant of Venice*. Between these opposed ethico-dramatic conceptions there is the shared idea of the Problem Plays, which elude the division into tragedy and comedy, especially *Measure for Measure* and *The Tempest*. Different as these two plays are from each other, in each of them the dissemblance is neither tragic nor trivial, for it serves functionally in guiding the plot toward a favorable outcome. Hidden Power, whether manifested as the Duke of Vienna's offstage intrigues or as Prospero's magic art, is the shared ideational core of the two themes. But what a pallid, thin idea is the conceptual universal, "hidden power," as compared with the richly developed archetype, a part of whose essential meaning involves in the one case the brothels of Vienna, the hypocrisy of proclaimed purity, the comedy-cliché of the bed-trick, and the uneasy justification of "craft against vice"; in the other case the music that creeps by upon the waters, the ambivalent mystery of sleep and dream, and the three levels (Prospero, Ariel, Ferdinand) of confinement groping for freedom. To speak of the Viennese Duke and Prospero as concrete universals is to recognize that the universality which they share can be known only by analogies drawn from remembered enjoyment of the plays, not by conceptual formulation.

*Indirection* might be considered a special type of plurisignation, an extreme form in which the nearer meaning or set of meanings is either suppressed or accounted as trivial. *Poetic* indirection is not just a "way of saying one thing and meaning another," as Robert Frost called it in one of his familiar bursts of literate Yankee humor. His epigram holds better for innuendo and sarcasm, and also for euphemism, than for poetry. Out-and-out substitution of one semantic vehicle for another is a device that can be employed by steno-language no less than by poetic. Metonymy is the most general form of steno-indirection (there is nothing poetic in the indirective statement that "the pot is boiling"), and euphemism is a functionally differentiated species of it.

Genuinely poetic indirection goes deeper. Its motive is not petty like that behind a euphemistic cliché; it is stimulated by a double desire for greater semantic plenitude and greater connotative precision. For in the more delicate cases of communication one risks both impoverishing and falsifying an intended meaning, especially on its emotional side, by trying to declare it outright. Claude-Edmonde Magny writes: "There are two parts in every book and in every work of art—on the one hand, the author's conscious and expressly intended message, the effect for which he has purposely fitted out his machine . . . ; on the other, the truth which he reveals without realizing it, the aspect of the world which he has discovered almost in spite of himself, in the course of the actual experience of composition; which is doubtless more or less what Gide, in the preface to *Paludes*, speaks of as 'God's share'." Accordingly Mlle. Magny propounds as a law of literary creation: "To the extent that an author is over-successful in communicating his conscious message, the jealous gods refuse him their collaboration." Consequently, she concludes, it is characteristic of the greatest writers that they "find themselves thinking at odds with themselves."[5]

Now there is more than one way of thinking at odds with oneself; and some of the ways, notably that of schizophrenia, are destructive, not creative. Poetic self-division, as distinguished from schizophrenic, is not a breakdown, but a vibrant tension between meanings which are antithetical yet surreptitiously related, or related yet surreptitiously antithetical. One of the most powerfully expressive kinds of poetic tension is that which exists between the story or scenario of a poem and the suggestions thrown off by its imagery—a tension between statement and aesthetic innuendo. Such tensions are dramatic by their very nature, and give a certain dramatic character, an inherent dialectic, to the poem in which they occur. When they occur in a stage-enacted drama, where the casual playgoer is concerned mainly or wholly with spectacle and plot, they offer to more discerning members of the audience indirect hints and clues to the deeper, the more nearly essential, meaning of the presented drama. For they are an organic but semi-independent part of that total movement which Francis Fergusson has called the "tragic rhythm of action,"[6] and to which the joy of a serious reader or auditor consists in responding as adequately and integrally as he is able.

4. *Soft focus.* "The lord whose oracle is at Delphi," said Heraclitus referring to Apollo the god and symbol of wisdom, "neither speaks nor conceals, but gives signs."[7] This gnomic utterance is applicable to indirection and soft focus alike—the former concept pertaining to the manner in which a statement is made and the character of its relation to the tenor, the latter concept pertaining also to the character of the tenor itself. The plain fact is that not all facts are plain. There are meanings of high, sometimes of very highest importance, which cannot be stated in terms strictly defined. "Plain speech is essentially inaccurate," T. E. Hulme remarks; ". . . Always must have analogies, which make an other-world through-the-glass effect, which is what I want."[8] Plain speech may sometimes have conceptual exactitude, but it will be inaccurate with respect to the new thing that one wants to say, the freshly imagined experience that one wants to describe and communicate. For what, after all, is conceptual exactitude? What is strict definition? Conceptual exactitude and the strict definition that at once contributes to it and is made possible by it are possible only to minds which have

agreed (tacitly, no doubt) upon a semantic convention involving the systematic omission of whatever meanings and whatever elements of meaning are such that they cannot be commonly shared. This common nucleus of meaning establishes a denotation to which a given steno-symbol, verbal or otherwise, can refer with shared exactitude—i.e., with demonstrably the same reference for all normal and informed users. But over and above the denotation every symbol carries a connotative fringe, which is not quite the same for everybody, and which is sometimes very different indeed. When a poet tries to express some aspect of this fringe truthfully, the truth will be primarily for himself in a certain mood, which he may not be wholly able to recapture, and secondly for such readers as can most nearly emulate his mood and the pattern of remembered and imagined experiences underlying it. In order to speak to the various members of this loosely unified group of responsibly perceptive readers, the poet must allow a bit of slack in the relation between vehicle and tenor. Besides, he cannot do otherwise, owing to the dubious relation between the common language and the self-creating novelty of the thing he would convey. Since the word "vagueness" carries connotations of reproach, let us speak rather of "soft focus," drawing the metaphor from the photographer's art, which can sometimes reveal the character of a landscape most truthfully by blurring its hard outlines.

The recognition of soft focus as a genuinely semantic characteristic of certain situations (i.e., not just as a psychological characteristic of the poet's response to them) dispels perhaps the main cloud from the problem of obscurity in poetry. Ignoring such instances of obscurity as proceed from either incompetence or snobbishness, we can accept certain poetic utterances as obscure for either or both of two valid reasons: (1) because the subject-matter is too subtle and elusive to allow of exact delineation—as in the portrayal of mature human emotions; or

(2) because the poet can produce his effect more fully by making an ambivalent impression upon the reader's mind. In great as distinguished from merely transient poetry the ambivalence is justified because it corresponds to a real ambivalence in the nature of things; and thus the second valid reason for ambivalence tends to reduce to the first.

Poetry and expressive language in general have, to be sure, their own kind of precision, but it is essentially different from the precision of literal language, even though there is no clear line of cleavage between them. (Analogy: There is an essential difference between moral integrity and cheating, even though actual persons and actions can illustrate all imaginable gradations between them.) We cannot ask whether one type of language is *more* precise than the other, we can only try to understand and accept their different *kinds* of precision. The precision of expressive language is paradoxical, in that it sometimes represents its object (i.e., its subject-matter) most precisely by a sort of controlled vagueness. There have been endless disputes about the character of Hamlet, or, in semantic terms, about what the poetic and dramatic indications of Hamlet's words and actions "really mean." Would Shakespeare have represented Hamlet more precisely by employing indications as definite as he does in the case of Polonius? Obviously not; for the very nature of Hamlet as a "character" or *dramatis persona* is ambivalent—an aura of highly significant obscurity around a brightly focussed center—and one cannot say of him, as one almost can of Polonius, "This, just this and not something more, is what Shakespeare meant."

5. *Paralogical dimensionality.* Steno-language at its best—i.e., when it is most strictly logical—refers to one or the other of two kinds of semantic integration: existential particularity, established by temporal and spatial continuities (e.g., this green book, my present feeling of anger) and conceptual universality,

established by selective abstraction of certain qualities or relations found in certain particulars (e.g., book, green, anger).
These two familiar types of noun-meaning are what Santayana
calls respectively "concretions in existence" and "concretions in
discourse."[9] They produce in speech the familiar grammarians'
distinction between proper and common nouns. From a logical
point of view the distinction is between a particular, which in
one manner or another can be pointed at, and a universal, which
consists of a set of characteristics that are shared by all particulars within a certain group.

Considering existential particularity and conceptual universality as *nodi of meaning,* we can say that a nodus of meaning is
particular when its specifiable references are related by virtue of
some *publicly verifiable space-time contiguity and continuity,*
and that it is universal when its specifiable referencs are related
by virtue of some *publicly verifiable similarity,* of whatever kind
or degree of abstraction. If we examine these two kinds of connection semantically, or perhaps metasemantically, as nodi of
meaning, we discover that they do not exhaust the possibilities
of semantic grouping. They constitute two pragmatically important ways in which here-nows of the experienceable world
(whether sensed, remembered, or imagined) can be grouped
and represented by a symbol. The general concept represented
by the word "horse" results from one kind of such grouping,
based mainly upon publicly understood similarities conceptually
binding one horse to another; the physical horse represented by
the name "Freddy" results from another kind of grouping, based
mainly upon the partly observed and partly inferred spatio-
temporal continuity of the physical parts and temporal moments
of which the horse named Freddy is composed.

But clearly other bases of association are possible. Any aesthetic experience is such an alio-dimensional grouping. An artist's characteristic attempt, in its semantic aspect, is to express

and communicate an experience that involves a new grouping of experiential moments—that is, of perceived and imagined here-nows—for which there is no publicly accepted word, formula, or other symbol already available. In the words of Ezra Pound: "The error of making a statue *of* Night or *of* Charity lies in tautology. The idea has already found its way into language. The function of the artist is precisely the formulation of what has not found its way into language, i.e., any language verbal, plastic or musical."[10] What Pound says of Night and Charity is true both of horseness and of any individual horse: each finds its adequate expression in a language of word concepts—a common noun in the one case, a proper noun (a name) in the other—and an exact undistorted reformulation in terms of painting or sculpture is neither possible nor worth attempting. Horseness shoots through experience in a given direction and "means" a grouping of certain qualities and functions that are conventionally conceived as belonging together to constitute that biological species; the flesh and blood horse now neighing in the stable "means" another grouping—in this case, of physically contiguous qualities; whereas the horses of say Donatello or de Chirico "mean" a more novel and still unconventionalized grouping of qualities, some of which are shared with the dictionary concept "horse," others with the perceptual qualities of live horses that the artist has seen, while still others have closest affinity with subtle forms of feeling and image-making otherwise inexpressible.

Hart Crane's declaration, quoted earlier in Chapter Three, of a poet's concern with "the so-called illogical impingements of words on the consciousness" is relevant here. The so-called illogical—more accurately, *para*logical—impingements are not only legitimate instruments of expressive language, they are a part of its very life. A concrete universal, as I have just observed, fuses a universal idea with some concrete embodiment. That is one way of transcending the logical distinction between universal and particular, but it is not the only one. What a poem, or a passage or a symbol within a poem means, need not be a combination of particular and universal in anything like the logician's understanding of these terms. Poetic meanings can overreach concrete particulars in quite different ways, along quite different lines, as well as by very different techniques, from logical literal meanings. An adequate semantics must recognize and make room for what I have called the principle of Paralogical Dimensionality, otherwise it will be incapable of dealing with poetic meanings in one of their most characteristic aspects.

An expressive symbol, then, transcends the dualism of logical singular ("concretion in existence") vs. logical universal ("concretion in discourse"). For besides the two types of mental association which respectively make these two kinds of meaning possible, there is another important type of association, which we may call, slightly modifying a phrase from William James, *association by emotive congruity*.[11] Our reason for associating a certain man with a grasshopper may not be found in any similarity or relation that we can put a finger on: it may be a "reason of the heart" which eludes all rational formulation and yet has great strength. Association of this kind is esemplastic in a fuller than ordinary sense, and tends to involve a strongly, richly, and freshly imaginative energy-tension. It is present in all art that is anything more than purely formal or purely decorative; for an artist's characteristic attempt, in its semantic aspect, is to express and communicate an experience comprising some grouping of perceived and imagined here-nows for which there is no publicly accepted word, formula, or other symbol already available.

Thus the platitude that great art is universal, although true in a special sense, is misleading. For the integral meaning of a work of art (whatever its component meanings may be) cuts across experience in a different dimension from that of any logical universal whatever, and employs a different principle of grouping. Thereby it establishes its own quality of universality—an eccentric universality, which is to say a more concrete and more alive universality than that which is represented by any dictionary definition whatever. Perhaps an analogous distinction can be observed between the concrete universality of the Cross as an integral symbol for the grouping of certain kinds of acquiescence and implicit valuation that permeate various aspects of experience for a true believer (an "eccentric" or oblique universal from the standpoint of a non-believer) and on the other hand any theological exposition of what the Cross represents. Or again, the difference between the ideal of justice as it appears to men who are sacrificing their comfort and risking their jobs to uphold it, and the idea of justice as it comes up in a discussion of theoretical ethics.

6. *Assertorial Lightness.* Whereas the five foregoing characteristics of expressive language hold true of its elements of meaning and its statements alike, the two remaining characteristics apply to its statements and quasi-statements only. In the context of steno-language the relation between term and statement is easy to define and to illustrate. We can define by saying that a term merely *means* without making or implying any assertion, while a statement both means and *potentially asserts;* that they are non-assertorial and assertorial respectively; that to raise the question of true or false is meaningful in the case of the latter only. We can illustrate by any number of familiar examples: specifying that "cat" and "justice" are terms, but that "Cats practice justice" is a statement, since in the latter case alone it is possible to dispute the truth of the utterance without talking total nonsense, whereas there would be no meaning at

all in either upholding or denying the truth of "cat" or of "justice" taken by itself; if anyone were to seem to do so, he would really be dealing not with the single term but with some unspoken judgment about it.

When logically perfected a statement is a proposition. The sentence in question is too vague to be an authentic proposition, for it does not specify whether the subject term means all cats or most cats or merely occasional cats; moreover the idea of justice and the kind of evidence that would show or refute its effectiveness in feline behavior are likewise vague. On the other hand the sentence "Nine cats are now in this room," is definite enough and verifiable enough to let a "yes" or a "no" be something more than an irresponsible murmur. From a logical point of view every proposition is governed by the Law of Excluded Middle: i.e., the postulated law that any given proposition is either true or false, there being no third possibility. This is tantamount to declaring the postulate of truth-value equivalence: i.e., that any true proposition is equally true with any other true proposition, and that any false proposition is equally false with any other false proposition. "Nine cats are in this room," if true, and "A divine providence rules the world," if semantically determinable and true, are equally true, and the truth-value of each is represented in the vocabulary of logic by the symbol "1." If both of these statements should be false, they are equally false and the truth-value of each would be represented by the symbol "0."

Propositions of probability are not examples of assertorial lightness, since they do not transcend the law of Excluded Middle. For if the degree of probability that is affirmed is justified by the known evidence, and if this is what "probable" is taken to mean by speaker and hearer alike, then the statement that the thing in question "is probably true" will itself be completely true. "It will probably rain before sundown": if this remark is really propositional, and not a mere stopgap for conversational lacunae, it means: "On the basis of the evidence before us (such as black clouds in the sky, published weather reports, etc.) there is a more than fifty per cent likelihood that there will be rain before sundown." In this exactified form the statement is a proposition and the postulate of Excluded Middle must apply to it; for the statement of probability as thus interpreted can only be either true or false. It is not, therefore, an assertorially light statement.

In expressive language, on the other hand, statements vary with respect to the manner and degree to which they are susceptible to affirmation and denial, ranging all the way from *heavy* assertorial tone, which characterizes the literal statement, the proposition, to *light* assertorial tone, which consists in an association or semi-affirmed tension between two or more images or other expressive units. A poetic statement differs from a literal statement not, as Dr. Richards used to maintain, in that the one has a merely subjective, the other an objective reference—at least this is an unnecessary and generally irrelevant difference—but in their manner of asserting. There are differences of what may be called *assertorial weight*. A literal statement (i.e., a proposition) asserts heavily. It can do so because its terms are solid. It must do so because we are all to some degree practical busy creatures who want to know just where we stand. A poetic statement, on the other hand, consisting as it does in a conjunction or association of more or less softly focussed and potentially varying plurisigns, has no such solid foundation, and affirms therefore with various degrees of lightness.

A statement from Carl Rakosi's *A Journey Far Away* offers a syntactical illumination of the principle:

> An ideal
> like a canary
> singing in the dark
> for appleseed and barley

Is the poet making a statement here or is he not? If so, the
syntax is not quite adequate: the copula "is" is needed for its
completion. But try the experiment of inserting it, and see how
fatally that little word destroys the original quality of quasi-
affirmation. "An ideal is like a canary singing in the dark for
appleseed and barley." Note what has been done. Not only has
the reader-response been altered through a lessening of the
pleasure with which the utterance is received: more than that,
the very nature of the affirmation has been changed. The prose
version, we feel, overstates its case, it affirms too heavily: no
ideal can be so much like a canary as all that! Rakosi's way of
phrasing did not belabor the point; it suggested only that between an ideal and a canary there might be a slight and lovely
connection, too tenuous to be expressed by the harsh little word
"is." So delicate an affirmation does not seriously jostle our
other beliefs; we can accept its faint breeze of truth without
mental inconvenience. But the translated literal statement, by
reason of its assertive heaviness, falsifies.

Assertorial weight should not be confused with the strength
or force of a poetic statement. Take, for instance, Christina
Rossetti's well-known quatrain:

> My heart is like a singing bird
>    Whose nest is in a water-shoot;
> My heart is like an apple-tree
>    Whose boughs are bent with thick-set fruit . . .

If some literal-minded reader should object to these comparisons on the ground that the differences separating a joyous heart

from a water-shoot nesting bird and a thick-fruited apple tree are more pronounced than the resemblances, we might justly dismiss him as unduly obtuse, insufficiently imaginative. In terms of the present analysis he would be making an assertorially heavy statement which in this context proves to be ridiculously weak, contrasting painfully with the simple eloquence of the poet's assertorially light statement.

Suppose, again, that the graceful compliment to a lady expressed implicitly by Herrick—

> Her eyes the glow-worm lend thee,
> The shooting stars attend thee . . .

were made more explicit by setting forth the lady's charms with descriptive literalness. Not only the grace, but more subtly the central poetic meaning of the utterance would be destroyed. Herrick's own statement is by indirection. It is offered more lightly than its prose counterpart could be, but partly for this very reason it is all the more forceful and suggestive. Generally speaking, the combination of poetic delicacy and poetic strength is one of the prime distinguishing marks of authentic poetry.

7. *Paradox.* As the principle of Light Statement, or Assertorial Lightness, represents the freedom of expressive statement from being strictly bound by the logical postulate of Excluded Middle, so the principle of Paradox represents the freedom of expressive statement from bondage to that other bulwark of logical discourse, the postulate of Non-Contradiction. Whereas the postulate of Excluded Middle states that $a$ must be either $b$ or $not$-$b$—i.e., must be at least one, there being no third possibility—the postulate of Non-Contradiction makes the complementary statement that $a$ cannot be both $b$ and $not$-$b$ in the same sense and at the same time. Paradox is essentially a challenge to the applicability of this latter postulate to expressive situations.

From a logical point of view paradox is defined as "a seeming contradiction." The definition holds good for such surface-paradoxes as "a pleasing obstacle," "bitter delights," Chesterton's remark that "Darwin was no Darwinian," and Lord Russell's analogy between the paradox of physical ether and the paradox of Homeric authorship: "We know who Homer was—he wrote the *Iliad* and the *Odyssey;* only we don't know whether he existed." The aim of such paradoxes as these is to startle, amuse, and more seriously to jolt the reader or hearer into reexamining the relation between some pair of ideas that he had hitherto taken for granted. Such paradoxes can be cleared up easily enough by anyone who takes the trouble to make the appropriate logical distinctions—between Darwin's views and those of his self-professed followers, and between the abstract conception of "authorship of the *Iliad* and *Odyssey*" and the historical question of whether the two epics were or were not composed by a single author. The same type of paradox is illustrated by the playful-serious oxymoron in Romeo's comment upon the brawl between the two noble houses:

> Why, then, O brawling love! O loving hate!
> O any thing, of nothing first create!
> O heavy lightness! serious vanity!
> Mis-shapen chaos of well-seeming forms!
> Feather of lead, bright smoke, cold fire, sick health!
> Still-waking sleep, that is not what it is!
> This love feel I, that feel no love in this.
> *Romeo and Juliet*, Act I, Scene i

The more important paradoxes of expressive language, on the other hand, are something more than such coy indirections as these. They are depth paradoxes, not merely surface paradoxes. They involve, as I have said, a challenge to the universal applicability of the law of non-contradiction itself. Reality is not natively as clear-cut as logical discourse would represent it, and the strategy of the logician is to stress those aspects of it and those relations within it that *are* clear-cut or comparatively so. When a poet tries not merely to startle by paradox but *to express truth through paradox,* he may do so at either first or second remove: his voice will be either that of the prophet proclaiming the ineluctable paradoxicality of the real or else that of the poet-as-such manipulating the powers of his craft to produce *a paradoxical interplay between statement and innuendo* and thereby to mime linguistically that paradoxicality of the real which underlies, frames, and is presupposed by, all expressive language. For convenience we may distinguish these two forms as *ontological paradox* and *poetic paradox,* recognizing them as the two main species of depth paradox, in contrast to the surface paradox which the foregoing examples illustrate.

An ontological paradox expresses some transcendental truth which is so mysterious and so many-sided in its suggestions of explorative possibilities that neither half of it could be affirmed separately without gross distortion. The great paradoxes of traditional theology are of this kind: God's justice *and* God's mercy; God's foreknowledge of all things to come *and* man's free will. Eliot's *Four Quartets* contains a number of expressive paradoxes which are ontological in the sense here defined:

> Only through time time is conquered.

> So the darkness shall be light, and the stillness the dancing.

> Our only health is the disease
> If we obey the dying nurse . . .[12]

Some of Eliot's depth paradoxes are aided by a serious playfulness which bears a rough analogy to the examples cited from Chesterton and Russell. The line, "To be redeemed from fire by fire," in *Little Gidding* could be logically explained by the distinction between the fire of damnation and the fire of purgatorial cleansing. Yet the paradoxical expression is necessary, not arbitrary here, for it evokes, as an allusive overtone, the archetypal idea of the finding of life through voluntary death ("He who will save his life shall lose it . . ."), and more archetypally still, the idea of the transcendent Oneness that is approached through even the most discrepant particulars.

But the type of paradox most characteristic of poetry is that which occurs when a direct statement—i.e., some part of a poem's scenario meaning—is either mocked or playfully opposed by the suggestions latent in the imagery. The opening lines of Donne's *The Extasie* offer an illustration:

> Where, like a pillow on a bed,
>   A pregnant bank swelled up, to rest
> The violet's reclining head,
>   Sat we two, one another's best.
>
> Our hands were firmly cimented
>   With a fast balm which thence did spring,
> Our eye-beams twisted, and did thread
>   Our eyes, upon one double string;
>
> So to'entergraft our hands, as yet
>   Was all the means to make us one,
> And pictures in our eyes to get
>   Was all our propagation.

The third stanza asserts plainly that there has been no full carnal union and no propagation of new life as yet—a statement which the wooer's plaint is presently to confirm:

> But O alas, so long, so far
>   Our bodies why do we forbear?

The three opening lines, however, had already imprinted on a responsive and uninhibited reader's mind a set of images suggesting in the second line feminine and in the third line masculine fulfillment—a sly and delicately ribald qualification of the outwardly chaste avowal. The intermediate image of twisted eyebeams is more nearly an ontological kind of paradox, although impurely so, for it draws its meaning from a special theory of optics which had a vogue in Donne's day. As the poem progresses its style of paradoxicality becomes more strikingly ontological:

> Might thence a new concoction take,
> And part far purer than he came.

> But as all several souls contain
> Mixtures of things, they know not what,
> Love, these mixed souls, doth mix again,
> And make both one, each this and that.

Such paradoxes as these underline the theme of the inextricable union, in love's mysteries, of oneness and manyness, purity and concoction, spirituality and bodily expression.

The seven foregoing traits of expressive discourse are not categories in any usual sense. Categories, particularly from Kant onwards, have usually been conceived as setting limits to the character of what falls under them, but these seven headings represent ways in which the conventional limits of language and its meanings can be transcended or modified. Thus where categories are closed, our principles of expressive discourse are open; where categories are prescriptive, these are permissive. Unlike Kant's category of causation our group of guiding principles is by no means declared to be equally valid for all phenomena of a certain type. That would be the way of steno-methodology, not of poetic. Rather they represent certain linguistic opportunities for the imagination to explore as it tries to utter and communicate with maximum expressivity. It is quite possible, of course, that this basic aim will strike some readers as needing a larger or differently patterned set of guiding principles than those which I have outlined. Let other solutions be sought, by all means. But if we are not to slip back into pseudo-critical confusion our main approach must be neither grammatical on the one hand nor psychological on the other. The pertinent question is, by what linguistic devices a poem manages to say something fresh and stirring and confirmed by the deepest testimonies of uncorrupted experience. For fresh associations can generate fresh meanings, and the semantic function of poetry consists largely in this: that poetry quickens and guides men's associative faculty, keeps it in athletic trim, and thus actually generates new meanings—meanings that would lose their identity outside the context of the individual poem, but which are authentically real within that context.

# 6

## Metaphoric Tension

Metaphor in its radical, which is to say in its semantic sense, is far more than a grammatical maneuver or a rhetorical stratagem. The essence of metaphor consists in a semantic tension which subsists among the heterogeneous elements brought together in some striking image or expression. Poetic language implicitly crossweaves multiplicity-in-unity and unity-in-multiplicity; it is tensive because of the precarious balance between two or more lines of association which it invites the imagination to contemplate. Of course I do not mean that every poem must be of a highly metaphoric and tensive kind. As the first section of the preceding chapter took pains to declare, a poem can be very direct and must indeed have a sustaining degree of presentative immediacy. Still, whatever else poetic language may be and do, its exploitation of essential metaphor, which is to say of metaphoric tension, properly guided with reference to the poetic context, is one of its most distinctive and triumphant achievements.

Since metaphor is the most important element in expressive language, our ways of thinking about it need to be rescued from misleading habits of thought and particularly from the long tyranny of the grammarians. The familiar textbook definition, descended from Aristotle and Quintilian, is based upon syntactical, not semantic considerations. Both of those ancient masters of rhetorical theory regarded metaphor as little else than abbreviated simile. And since this jejune view of the matter has imposed itself upon readers' minds, it is important to understand the reason for its inadequacy.

Aristotle illustrates his view of the relation of metaphor to simile as follows. "When the poet says of Achilles, 'He sprang on them like a lion,' this is simile. When he says, 'The lion sprang on them,' this is metaphor; for as both animals are brave, he has transferred the name of 'lion' to Achilles." Elsewhere he calls simile "a metaphor with a preface" and declares it inferior to metaphor on two counts: it is lengthier, therefore less pleasing; and "since it does not affirm that this *is* that, the mind does not inquire into the matter."[1] Now it is true that metaphor is often (not, I think, always) preferable to simile on both these grounds, but the grounds are rhetorical not semantic ones. Terseness is more pleasing and more stimulating to thought than verbosity: that is what it comes to. And by no means let us ignore the canons of good rhetoric, whether in poetry or out of it! Poetry is not less than rhetoric, but something more. Nevertheless the rhetorical distinction, whatever its incidental uses, can hardly be said to open up any important insight. It evinces that great vice of bad classification: overstressing an obvious surface difference and ignoring the differences and resemblances that go to the heart of the matter. By Aristotle's rule it is simile to say, "He dances like a clumsy elephant," and metaphor to say, "That clumsy elephant gets in everyone's way." But there is no semantic difference here—no difference, that is to say, in degree of intensity, or in depth of penetration, or in freshness of recombination, or in anything else that matters much. The difference is merely one of rhetorical strategy.

A far more adequate definition is Herbert Read's: "Metaphor is the synthesis of several units of observation into one commanding image; it is the expression of a complex idea, not by analysis, nor by direct statement, but by a sudden perception of an objective relation."[2] Metaphor, by this criterion, could include some instances of what is traditionally designated simile—given the commanding image and the sudden perception of an objective relation. George Eliot writes: "That sudden clang, that leaping light, fell on Romola like sharp wounds"; and while superficially the sentence contains one metaphor ("leaping light") and one simile ("like sharp wounds"), I would say that we grasp the full resident meaning more nearly if we take the entire sentence as projecting a complex metaphoric fusion or metaphoric tension. The tensive quality of George Eliot's figure is clearly something more than that simple terseness and economy which Quintilian finds admirable in the similes of Cicero, such as: "He fled from court like a man escaping naked from a fire." Cicero's simile rests on a plain logical analogy, and the pleasure which it gives, if any, is simply of intellectual recognition. The same may be said of many tropes which have the grammatical form of metaphor, as when Aeschylus calls a harbor the stepmother of ships. This minor piece of wit is not metaphor in the essential and semantic sense of the word, for it makes its connection by analysis and labored comparison rather than by the "sudden perception of an objective relation." One might perhaps call it a tabloid simile. It lacks what Martin Foss calls the "energy-tension" proper to real metaphor. Compare it with Homer's description of the wrathful Apollo: "His coming was like the night." Grammatically considered Aeschylus' trope is a metaphor and Homer's is a simile; semantically and essentially the distinction stands in reverse. Why so? Because of the great difference of semantic energy-tension. Homer's comparison stirs us emotionally as with a sudden revelation of half-guessed half-hidden mystery, whereas Aeschylus' phrase pleases us superficially as a riddle or a joke might do.

## Two Imperfect Theories of Tension

Tension, or tensive relation, is indispensable to living language, and hence *a fortiori* to poetry. For the mutual counterpull of two individual images or ideas, each with its own aura of connotations and implications, is what keeps the rhythm of thought vibrant. Of the critics who have written upon the subject of poetic tension there are two, Allen Tate and Martin Foss, whose ways of handling the problem I shall begin by criticizing. Both are discerning interpreters of poetry, and Tate is also a poet of fine calibre; I make no attempt to do justice to their poetic philosophies as a whole, but confine myself here to pointing out what I find unacceptable in their theories of poetic tension.

Tate explains that he uses the word "tension" in a special sense, "derived from lopping the prefixes off the logical terms *exten*-sion and *in*tension."[3] Consequently when he declares that the meaning of poetry is to be found in its tension he means that it consists in "the full organized body of all the extension and intension that we can find in it." His recipe, however, produces quite a different brew from the one he wants. When "maximum extension" and "maximum intension" are taken in the logician's sense, as signifying respectively the widest applicability and the fullest possession of distinguishing qualities, the tension that results from combining them is not the tension of metaphor, but the tension of concrete universality—of symbolism in the Goethean mode. It is clear, however, from some of Tate's other critical writings, particularly from "Hardy's Philosophic Metaphors," that he does not find or expect much semantic tension in that direction. He has adopted, then, only the logician's pair of words, without their accepted meanings. And he is using that pair of words, evidently, to designate what Richards has more appropriately called tenor and vehicle.

Let us examine the test case which is offered—a stanza from Donne's "Valediction: Forbidding Mourning":

> Our two souls therefore, which are one,
>     Though I must go, endure not yet
> A breach, but an expansion,
>     Like gold to airy thinness beat.

The *tenor* here is the unity of the two lovers' souls, indivisible even when physically separated: such is the "logic" of the passage (Ransom), the "scenario meaning" (Richards); Tate calls it "the abstract form of its extensive meaning." The malleable gold is the spatial and visible *vehicle* by which that meaning is poetically represented: Tate calls it "the intensive meaning." And he declares that "the interesting feature here is the logical contradiction of embodying the unitary, non-spatial soul in a spatial image." Well, in the first place the word "contradiction" is out of place. There is no contradiction between a vehicle which is a spatial image and a meaning which is a non-spatial idea. It is just by such relationship between a concrete vehicle and an abstract tenor that symbolic and metaphoric language characteristically works. The relation here is not the logical one between extension and intension (wherein, if they were both maximized, there *would* be a contradiction from the strictly logical standpoint) but between the expressed and the impressed, between tenor and vehicle, meaning and symbolic image. It is Tate's confusion of these two relations that has led him to ascribe contradiction where none exists.

Furthermore, his use of that questionable pair of terms has misled him, I think, in his exploration of what the vehicle connotes. "Expansion" in the poem he takes as "a term denoting an abstract property common to many objects, perhaps here one property of a gas." From the logician's standpoint the expansion of a gas is included in the extension (the extensive coverage) of the word; but I cannot read Donne's stanza and feel that gas expansion has anything whatever to do with it. Moreover there are two other poetically relevant connotations which I think Mr. Tate might have mentioned but does not—the beauty, richness, and value of gold, and the associations of "airy," appropriate to the souls unhampered by bodily conditions and tending (from the archetypal background of the Four Elements) to heighten the color aspect of gold to suggest the idea of fire. The details of my interpretation are no doubt challengeable, but they should be challenged or accepted within the context of the poem itself; the implications of "extension" and "intension" can prove nothing, and may start us off on false trails.

The other recent view of metaphor that I want to consider here is that of Martin Foss.[4] His stated intention in *Symbol and Metaphor* is to show the place of metaphor among other forms of thought, indicating both its unique and irreducible role and its interrelations with non-metaphorical forms. Metaphor, he declares, is more than Wundt's *Gesamt-Vorstellung;* it is "a process of tension and energy" which has a unique generality of intension involving a sacrifice of the systematic and conventional meaning of the terms, and "it is their mutual destruction in this process out of which a new and strange insight arises." Professor Foss describes this metaphoric process as "energy-tension," and emphasizes that it is a process running through the texture of expressive language and not confined to single words and phrases.

Now the double idea provoked by the epithet "energy-tension" contributes substantially to the discussion of metaphor, but I have certain reservations about Foss's handling of it. In the first place, while "sacrifice" is correctly introduced, "destruction" is surely too strong. If the conventional meanings of the terms drawn into the energy-tension were really destroyed, would not the tension cease to exist? Vasconcelos' idea of vital synthesis should be recalled: a unification of heterogeneous elements in which the heterogeneity is yet paradoxically preserved. With this stipulation in mind it is possible, I would think, to accept "*Gesamt-Vorstellung*" without cavil—translating it "representation of a togetherness [of disparate elements]." To oppose, as Foss does "a process of energy and change" to *Gesamt-Vorstellung* is misleading, for when the radical disparity of the wedded elements is *not* destroyed, an effective energy-tension is the natural result of such togetherness.

The confusion is increased, it seems to me, by Foss's claim to share this promising view of metaphor as energy-tension with Aristotle. Surely if Aristotle had really understood metaphor in such a way it would be a matter of great importance and the only wonder would be that so provocative an interpretation had escaped the notice of his commentators for so many centuries. But has not Foss mistranslated the passage he cites (*Rhetoric*, 1412a)? Aristotle is there discussing a particular employment of metaphor whereby to represent inanimate objects as if animated. His illustrations are such commonplace Homeric ones as "The arrow *yearning* to fly to its mark" and "Down to the valley the boulder *remorselessly* bounded." He is not characterizing all metaphor as *energeia* (which in any case would not quite mean "tension") but is showing how one use of metaphor is to ascribe *energeia* (in the sense of fulfillment of an animate potency, hence quasi-deliberate action) to inanimate things. It is quite certain from Aristotle's treatment of *metaphora*, both in the *Rhetoric* and in the *Poetics*, that he is not thinking in the least of the kind of energy-tension which is generated by a union of heterogeneous elements in one commanding image, but simply of "the transference of a name (from the thing which it properly

denotes) to some other thing." Aristotle's metabiological conception of *energeia*, then, cannot help us in analyzing what
metaphoric energy-tension means and how it operates.

## Simile and Plurisignation

The hypothesis which I should like to put forward is that
metaphor at its best tends to achieve fullness of semantic energy-tension by a merging of two complementary elements—
*simile* and *plurisignation*. In simile, two verbal expressions each
conveying an individual image or idea, are joined; in plurisignation, a single verbal expression carries two or more meanings
simultaneously. That is to say, in simile the vehicle is plural,
the tenor single; in plurisignation the vehicle is single, the
tenor plural. If this contrast appears too simple and gross to
describe most actual poetic situations, that is because there is
a tendency in poetic language for the two tropes to blend into
a metaphoric unity-in-diversity—as the following set of graded
examples, starting first from the side of simile and then from the
side of plurisignation, is intended to show.

### SIMILE

A simple simile without any plurisignative depth is usually
not very interesting. Examples come readily to mind: "He ran
like a scared rabbit"; "He pecks at his food like a canary"; Aeschylus' designation of dust as "the brother of wind" and of a
harbor as "stepmother of ships"; or Coleridge's remark that
"an author's pen, like children's legs, improves by exercise."
Such similes depend in each case upon a single point of resemblance. They offer us no fresh apperception: only, at best,
the amiable surprise of a likeness before unnoticed ("The
majority of husbands remind me of an orangutang trying to

play the violin"—Balzac), or the comedy of one deftly presented ("A simple fellow in gay clothes is like a cinnamon tree: the bark is of more value than the body");[5] at worst a stereotyped mental prop ("as fast as greased lightning").

Consider next the simile, "Shame covered him like a garment." To my sense there is a bit more of poetic expressiveness here (nothing remarkable, to be sure) than in the examples that precede. Why so? There are three reasons, I think. First, the tenor, *shame*, has deeper roots of emotive interest than any of the tenors above except possibly, to some persons, "harbor"— certainly more so than running, pecking, dust (in this context), and pen—and therefore offers more latent possibilities of effective association. Secondly, the vehicle, *garment*, carries unidentified overtones of literary, especially Biblical, association, which most of the other vehicles—scared rabbit, canary, stepmother, and legs—lack. (The vehicle "brother" might evoke a good deal in other contexts; in the one presented, however, it is somewhat prosaically restricted by the general sense.) Finally, the vehicle-idea of a garment covering a man physically and the tenor-idea of shame taking possession of his mind and psyche, are connected by an unmentioned intermediary, which is almost certainly on the verge of presenting itself to the reader's consciousness—namely, the idea of a blush covering the face. The blush is like a garment in being spatial and external, while at the same time it is causally related to and symptomatic of shame. Accordingly the imagination is stirred and enriched by the present simile more than by the earlier ones. The simile has, semantically speaking, a touch of the metaphoric.

There is a more celebrated as well as a more amply poetic use of the garment image in Wordsworth's sonnet, "Upon Westminster Bridge":

> The City now doth like a garment wear
> The beauty of the morning . . .

Here, in addition to the idea of "covering," there are two other characteristics of a garment which were not suggested in the earlier instance. Garments are ornamental, as "beauty" in the next line reminds us; and garments are transient, for the beauty is but the beauty of the morning and will not last. The idea of covering, moreover, would doubtless suggest the physical phenomenon of a morning mist; yet the imagery of the sonnet suggests on the whole a pellucid purity of the early morning scene, so that there is a touch of paradox, never brought to explicit recognition, in the garment image as employed here.

When a simile is stated in very explicit terms there is sometimes danger of overlooking the plurisignative depth which lies beneath it. The following stanza by Emily Brontë appears, on the surface, to depend on a single point of resemblance:

> Love is like the wild rose-briar;
> Friendship like the holly-tree.
> The holly is dark when the rose-briar blooms,
> But which will bloom more constantly?[6]

The analogy, or proportionate equality, which is of the essence of simile, stands out with unusual clarity here. Baldly we could paraphrase: As the rose-briar's beauty blooms earlier and more strikingly than the holly's but fades sooner, so it is with love and friendship respectively. And yet the comparison has an unmistakably poetic quality; it is no mere workaday tool of explication. What produces that quality? Partly, no doubt, melopoeia, the music of the cadences; but there is more to it than that. Much can be attributed to the plurisignative overtones of the component images as well. The main statement which is made about love (implicitly in the final question) is reënforced by the connotation of unpredictability in "wild" and of possible hurt in "briar"; while friendship, on the other hand, is caught up in the associations of cool and green (since the holly-tree blooms through the winter and its green leaves and bright red berries are especially associated with Christmastime) and restfully dark (over and above the logically restricted scenario meaning wherein "dark" refers to the time before the berries have appeared).

In technical contrast to the foregoing examples let us compare two lines from Shakespeare's Sonnets which have the grammatical appearance of metaphors:

[A]  To thy fair flower add the rank smell of weeds.

(Sonnet 69)

[B]  Time's thievish progress to eternity.

(Sonnet 77)

I would judge [A] to be a suppressed, or tabloid simile. Its expressiveness is limited by the implicit analogy: the beauty of the youth likened to a fair flower, and his treachery likened to the rank smell of weeds. On reading [B] I think we feel at once the greater expressiveness of the figure, and I do not believe that this comes merely from the melodramatic evocations of the word "thievish" nor from the quasi-mystical and hyperbolic lift of the word "eternity." The greater interest of it depends more legitimately upon the way in which the word "thievish" functions in the sentence. As connected with "progress" it suggests the kind of progress that a thief might be supposed to make—a sneaking, furtive sort of gait—and thus reminds us of one aspect of time, how it slips away without our noticing it. But "thievish" also connotes the act of stealing; and one of the main themes of the Sonnets is how time purloins and preys upon the beauty of youth. Let us say, then, that there are two images evoked by the word "thievish" in its given context—the image of seizing something that is supposed to belong to another, and the image of sneaking away clandestinely after the deed. But if that double image is the immediate tenor of the linguistic vehicle it is not the ultimate one. The images are not suggested for their own sake, but because they refer to, and evoke a sentiment about, the concretely complex idea of the pang of loss through time's passage. There are the particular losses, such as the beauty of a fair youth, of which time is the perpetrator; and there is the more pervasive loss of time itself, as the present tumbles into the past, and the blaze of the experienced moment fades first into the twilight glow of memory and then into the coldness of a dying image.

The comically ribald may be allowed to offer its own sort of testimony. Aristotle writes:

> Gorgias' rebuke to the swallow when she let drop on him as she flew overhead was effectively theatrical in the best sense. "Shame on you, Philomela!" he said.[7]

What makes the jolt of absurdity possible is the circumstance that vehicle and tenor are drawn together not by any natural likeness but by the traditional story of Philomela's being changed into a bird. In Aristotle's almost painfully explicit exegesis: "It was no disgrace for a bird to have done it, but for a young lady it was. Gorgias' reproach was theatrically appropriate, therefore, in addressing her in her former, not her present character." The idea of a young lady behaving as this bird behaved is plurisignative in its incongruity, since the implications of such behavior for the arrangements of human living could be fairly disruptive; our Freudian censor inhibits a free contemplation of them however, and we are left with an unexplored sense of the mock-scatological.

As a last approach to metaphoric tension from the side of simile consider the problem of poetic synaesthesia—the fusing of imagery drawn from two distant sense-channels. Dante's description of Hell as "there the sun is silent" ( *dove il sole tace* ) and the "Blind mouths!" of Milton's *Lycidas* stand among the great familiar classical examples. Each depends on an inter-sensory analogy. Dante: "The darkness caused by the sun's absence is analogous to the silence caused by the stoppage of its voice if it could speak." Milton: "Mouths (of Christ's vicars) which cannot speak forth boldly to his lost and wandering sheep are analogous to eyes which have lost their power of sight." While such general analogies are perhaps sufficient to account for the impact of these two great cases of synaesthesia upon a normally responsive reader, it is possible in the second case to develop the interpretation more specifically. Professor Leonard H. Frey has pointed out to me that since Milton was a learned and sensitive Latinist he would surely have had in mind, as applicable to Christ's vicars, the Latin words *pastor* and *episcopus* with their respective groups of connotations. *Pastor* means originally a feeder, transitively a feeder of others, hence a shepherd; *episcopus* means overseer. Thus Milton with superbly concentrated irony is able to say in two words that those who should be feeding their flocks have become more concerned with feeding themselves and that those who should oversee have lost their vision—a failure and perversion of the pastoral and episcopal functions simultaneously.

Edith Sitwell has argued that synaesthesia is more needful in contemporary poetry than ever before. "The modernist poet's . . . senses have become broadened and cosmopolitanised," she writes; "they are no longer little islands, speaking only their own narrow language . . . When the speech of one sense is insufficient to convey his entire meaning, he uses another." She then cites a line from her own poem *Aubade*—"The morning light creaks down again"—and observes that "in a very early dawn, after rain, the light has a curious uncertain quality, as though it does not run quite smoothly. Also, it falls in hard cubes, squares, and triangles, which, again give one the impression of a creaking sound, because of the association with wood."[8] This is doubtless an apt enough exposition, as expositions go. But it would be misleading to take the instance as typical of poetry in general. The peculiar brand of *translatio*, the quality of quasi-neurosis and extrapolated nausea, with which Dr. Sitwell so frequently invests her verbs, establishes, after one has read a good bit of it, a sort of aesthetic stereotype of its own; which, however, her spurts of real poetic dedication, as in *Still Falls the Rain*, are sometimes able to overcome. More to the point, her reasons for metaphoric fusion are likely to be intellectually expoundable ones, so that under examination the poetic quality of the fusion tends to wear thin. The splendor of Dante's great synaesthetic metaphor is perduring; once uttered it shows not the least tendency to wear thin; it affirms itself with the authenticity of an age-old archetype, drawn from correspondences that lie deep within the heart of nature herself.

### PLURISIGNATION

Having observed how simile tends to acquire expressivity and depth through the evocation of multiple meanings, fused and latent for the most part, let us now look more specifically at the technique of multiple reference, or plurisignation, starting with instances where it functions entirely by itself.

The readiness of expressive language to carry a plurality of meanings shows itself in such popular and familiar forms as innuendo, *double entendre*, and the pun. In a pun the multiple reference is potentially quite definite; i.e., it becomes explicit and even logically exact when the point of the pun is discovered: two or more clearly distinguishable denotations being joined together as the referends of a single word or phrase. Ordinary popular puns, however, combine the two meanings mechanically, as a joke, without involving any significant emotion, and have therefore no poetic relevance. But when Lady

Macbeth replies to her husband's announcement that King Duncan comes tonight with the question, "And when goes hence?" the double meaning carries an ominous foreboding, functionally related to the movement of the drama.

Marvell's couplet which concludes the second stanza of *To His Coy Mistress* contains two interrelated instances, one of triple reference, the other of double:

> The grave's a fine and private place,
> But none, I think, do there embrace.

On the surface the word "fine" expresses approval of a place so "private" (also in the most obvious sense) where lovers might embrace without interruption, if only they were any longer capable of embracing at all. But the grave is "fine" also in marking the *finis*, the end of all earthly joys, the end of all embracing: an attentive reader thus gets a preview of the counteractive idea even before the second line of the couplet makes it explicit. And thirdly, "fine" carries the added meaning of narrow, constricted: as when we say "a fine line." Meanings two and three of "fine" stir up a second meaning of "private," from the Latin *privatus*, "deprived." Marvell is saying, then, with striking poetical economy, that in one of its aspects, its privacy, the grave would be a welcome refuge for lovers; that the grave marks an end, in that it deprives lovers of the joy of mutual embrace; and that the grave is very cramping.

What strikes us most impressively in the couplet just cited is Marvell's wit. Such is the case in general where a plurisignative expression is effective without any help from simile. Compare the lines in *Romeo and Juliet* where the old nurse promises Juliet

> To fetch a ladder, by the which your love
> Must climb a bird's nest soon when it is dark.

"Bird's nest" is a simile-vehicle here, for which there is no counterpart, in the Marvell couplet, which makes its *main* statement without indirection. But the Shakespeare passage carries plurisignation also. When we ask what is signified by climbing a bird's nest, the uninhibited reader may discover two principal referends, both of them prognosticative of later events. Romeo will use the ladder to climb to Juliet's balcony: that, of course, is the most obvious meaning. But since we have learnt to expect ribald innuendos when the nurse gabbles, and since what she actually says is not "climb up to" but "climb"—i.e., climb the bird's nest itself—we have, evidently, a witty advance notice of love's consummation. The ribaldry is inoffensive, however, not only because of its wit, but also because a profounder idea invites the attentive reader's imagination. Moreover, climbing to the balcony of light ("It is the east, and Juliet is the sun") and its antithesis, descent into the tomb's darkness, furnish the main structure of the play's imagery, as well as evoking the archetypal life-and-death, light-and-darkness pattern which runs through all experience.

Not all cases of plurisignation are as plainly expoundable. Frequently only a single meaning is denotative and capable of literal translation, while the remaining meanings are purely connotative—felt rather than thought—and, although controlled to a high degree by the context, do not have the kind of precision that would enable them to be satisfactorily explicated in analytical language. "Pray you, undo this button"; the request is plain, the denotation single; but the connotative overtones, generated by the context of King Lear's final tragic predicament and vision, have a strange power of suggesting more than can possibly be articulated—not excluding, perhaps, a hushed archetypal reference to some undefined ceremony of preparing for the soul's release from the body.

In most of the greater instances of depth metaphor the elements of plurisignation and simile-analogy are so firmly and naturally harmonized that a reader has no disposition to inquire whether the one or the other predominates.

> DUNCAN: Whence cam'st thou, worthy thane?
> ROSS:                     From Fife, great king;
> Where the Norweyan banners flout the sky
> And fan our people cold.
>
> (*Macbeth*, Act i, Scene ii)

The power of this metaphor comes in part from the tension between the two implicit similes: (1) the Norweyan banners are visually like great fans in the air; and (2) as fans cool our outward parts, so the banners chill our inward parts with fear. But the effect is ambivalent, for the psychological antithesis strikes us more forcibly than the resemblance. Moreover, there is a tension between the fear so indicated and induced by the present metaphor and the fear-*motif* which is dominant throughout the play and which has already been announced by the haggard appearance and ominous words of the Weird Sisters in Scene i. This fear, in turn, moves along in dramatic tension with Macbeth's and his Lady's *hybris*, their over-vaulting ambition, their eventual usurpation and tyranny. The image of banners flouting the sky is perhaps a kind of visual foreshadowing of that sequent rage. These are but clues; the power of the metaphor outruns every expository maneuver.

Homer's "His coming was like the night" shows similar intransigeance. To explain conscientiously that as the darkness of night brings dangers and terrors to men, so Apollo in his anger brings dangers and terrors to the offending Greeks, is beside the mark—as perhaps every attempted explication must be. For night does not invariably bring evil; it may also bring peace and soothing rest. There are different ways in which we can conceive night, and the particular way here appropriate is pointed by the metaphor itself. Thus not only does the simile of night explain the manner of Apollo's coming, but simultaneously Apollo's manner of coming explains the relevant characteristic of night. What we have here is a kind of *floating* plurisignation.

## Latent Metaphor

It has often been remarked that essential, or functional, or radical metaphor, is a chief contributor to the growth and enrichment of language. Friedrich Max Müller, who brought the phrase "radical metaphor" into general use, was especially concerned with just that power of it.[9] Sanskrit, the oldest known member of our Indo-European language group, shows many examples of the process, as Müller demonstrates. The Sanskrit word *arka*, from a root meaning "to shine," comes to signify both the sun and a hymn of praise. The splitting seems to have occurred not by deliberate comparison and transference, but through a mode of experience in which the visible shining and the bursting forth of joy from the heart appeared as two manifestations of one and the same effulgent reality.

Again, as the record of language demonstrates, early Aryan man, in developing the distinct arts of weaving and of setting lines to catch birds, saw enough similarity between the two manual procedures to warrant calling them by a single name. Weaving, says Müller, would thus take the sense of putting snares, and when a new word was wanted for setting snares in a figurative sense—that is, for tricking, cheating, luring, inveigling a person by false words—nothing, again, would have been more natural than to take a word signifying "to weave" and use it in that sense. Thus when Homer speaks of "weaving a plot" he may not have been putting two distinct ideas together, as he was evidently doing in many of his similes; he may have been perpetuating a very old metaphoric fusion of ideas which became intermittently distinct only as practical conditions might require, but which remained more or less fused in the traditional poetic phraseology that was part of the ancient bard's heritage. This particular metaphoric fusion has left its trace in our word "subtle," from the Latin *subtilis*, which in turn (if Müller's view is correct) comes from *subtextere*, "to weave beneath."

The last example is a reminder of the fate that eventually overtakes radical metaphors. They grow old and moribund, losing the vital tension of opposed meanings, dramatic antithesis, paradox, which was theirs at their inception. They become fossilized and enter into everyday speech as steno-symbols which have lost their one-time allusiveness and power to stir. Familiar words like *skyscraper, bulldozer, arm* of a chair, *leaf* of a book and countless others have by now lost all trace of the semantic tension they must have had for their inventors and first users; consequently they are no longer living metaphors, but merely ex-metaphoric corpses, steno-terms, units of literal language. "Three-fourths of our language may be said to consist of worn-out metaphors," A. H. Sayce has remarked.[10] Sometimes, to be sure, the imagination of a poet, or in grosser terms the analysis of a critic, can rejuvenate defunct metaphors, reopening their tensive possibilities. The proem of Hart Crane's *The Bridge* reawakens one's sense of the original meaning of "sky scrapers" and a response to the vivid suggestions of contact between Wall Street's lofty buildings and the sky. In a more pedestrian way the foregoing examination of the meaning of metaphor may have suggested something about the metaphoric backgrounds of the word "metaphor."

Even that most abstract of all concepts, *being*, has grown up and gradually taken conceptual form out of several related metaphoric developments. A century ago Friedrich Max Müller adduced strong evidence that the English word "be" derives from the same Indo-European root as the Sanskrit *bhu,* "to grow, or make grow," and that the English "am" and "is" have divergently evolved from the same root as the Sanskrit *asmi,* "to breathe."[11] The irregular conjugation of the English verb "to be" can thus be regarded as an abbreviated record of a time when men had no independent word for "existence" and could reach toward the idea only by choosing whether to say that something "grows" or that it "breathes." More recently Martin Foss, in his book previously cited, does not confine himself to etymological evidences but maintains that the word "being" *as we now use it* is metaphorical. As I see the matter there is one sense in which his ascription is both true and important, another in which it is both false and trivial, and it may throw some further light upon the nature of metaphor to understand just what these two senses are.

In the one, the trivial sense, Professor Foss asserts that the copula "is" functions metaphorically in the very process of bringing together two distinct concepts, a subject and a predicate. Now surely the idea of metaphor becomes unusably flattened out when it is broadened to such a degree. Are we to allege that "The moon is round" and "The moon is a pancake" are equally metaphorical on the ground that in both cases a meaning other than "moon" is predicated of the moon? But partial otherness is predicated of a subject in *any* significant predication, it does not specifically establish the presence of metaphor. (Let us keep our terms as tidy as the general crepuscule allows.) There is a plainly understood sense in which it is metaphorical to describe the moon as a pancake and not metaphorical to describe it as round. Foss's term "energy-tension," which I adopted earlier, might (although he does not himself use it in this way) help to explain the difference. There is more energy-tension, I would say, in the idea of a pancake moon than in the idea of a round moon, because there are more disparate groups of qualities huddled together and thus an element of paradox, of ambivalence, of tension between astronomical and breakfast-table associations, is introduced.

The other and more valid sense in which "being" is intrinsically metaphorical could be put somewhat like this. When I say "There is (exists) a God" and "There is (exists) an Empire State Building," does the word "is" have the same meaning in the two cases or two different meanings? Operationally the meanings are different, since different procedures of validation would be called for. Shall we say, then, that the word "is"—or better, the phrase "there is," which is roughly equivalent to "exists"—is used metaphorically in both or either of these instances? The answer, again, can be stated with the help of that good term "energy-tension." In our technosophic age the most literal meaning of "exist"—i.e., the most familiar, natural, unreservedly acceptable—is the naturalistic one: a thing exists so far as it has place in the publicly shared space-time continuum which Foss designates "environment," and thus so far as it can be verified by experimental techniques. On this basis it is meaningful and true to say that there is an Empire State Building and it is largely meaningless to say that there is a God—at least some of the indispensable elements of God's meaning are canceled out. From this standpoint, then, the word "exist" is used metaphorically in the statement "God exists"—either as a dead, perfunctory metaphor (which is doubtless how most of us use it most of the time) or as a living paradox, a vibrant, highly charged tension between more or less incompatible meanings— between "being" in the sense of plain empirical existence and "being" in some incompletely defined sense that ploughs up our ordered reality-perspective in struggling for birth. The statement "God exists" is thus inescapably metaphorical and paradoxical in an age like ours where the notion of existence is straitjacketed by experimental and statistical techniques. But it is an inexpungeable expression of what Foss calls our "world," in contradistinction to our "environment"; of the flowing wholeness of things, which we know through the total response of our personhood, and which generates the central divine myth around which our being revolves. The metaphor and the myth are necessary expressions of the human psyche's most central energy-tension; without it and the other expressive energy-tensions that it has engendered during several millenia of cultural history mankind would succumb to the fate that the Forgotten Enemy holds ever in store for us, of falling from the ambiguous grace of being human into the unisignative security of the reacting mechanism.

# 7

## Emblem and Archetype

As man desires not only novelty but also a security of connection with the stable and unchanging, so the imagination operates not only creatively but interpretively—not only by fusing or recontextualizing old ideas in such a way as to generate new ones but also by grasping the particular idea and the transient image in relation to something more universal and perduring. The former is the metaphoric way of imagining, to which the preceding chapter was devoted. The latter may be called archetypal, or (where picture-thinking is stressed) emblematic. The two strategies are natural complementaries in poetic discourse, the one giving liveliness and freshness, the other depth and significance. The expressive imagination is thus, in one aspect, a kind of melting-pot, fusing together diverse elements into a highly individual brew; while in another aspect it is a kind of threshold—a "gateless gateway," as a Chinese philosopher has said[1]—drawing the attention toward truths greater than ordinary.

## The Sun, The Wheel, and the Svastika

There is one daily phenomenon in particular that impresses men repeatedly, and in the most diverse ages and countries, as symbolizing certain attributes of godhead. That is the sun. The solar effulgence arouses men's minds to a sense of power and majesty, while the light of it, in making vision possible, becomes a ready symbol for the spiritual vision which is synonymous with the highest wisdom. A further attribute of the sun, its orderly course through the sky, is symbolically suggestive of the element of law in nature. The stars, to be sure, as distinct from the planets, show equal evidence of order, but the size and radiance of the sun tend to give him clear priority as the cause or guardian of order. These are the most general of the transcendental associations of the sun, supplemented by other more special ones in various localities according to the conditions of living or the accidents of tribal experience. An example of such transcendental particularity is the ancient Egyptian identification of the sun with the scarab, or dung-beetle, which protects its eggs by rolling them up in a ball of dung, which it then pushes along the ground to a proper hatching place. By an obvious step the sun's movement becomes attributed to an invisible cosmic scarab which pushes it slowly each day across the blue sky. Moreover, since the dung-ball contains fertilized eggs, the sun is analogously conceived to possess the germs of life and growth. The Egyptian solar journey falls with equal ease into other imagistic patterns too: notably that of Amon-Ra navigating a boat with the sun as its cargo. In Greece it is not a boat but a chariot that Apollo harnesses up and drives across the vault each morning; and so, with changes of detail, in many other countries.

As an introduction to certain other solar symbols and associations let me cite a more particular and more recent piece of
evidence. In Gloucestershire and Herefordshire, England, according to the testimony of Mrs. Murray-Aynsley,[2] it was a not
uncommon circumstance half a century ago to see on the external walls of some of the older houses one or two pieces of hoop
iron molded into characteristic S-like forms, of which the following are typical:

According to local legend these insignia had the double virtue of protecting the house both from fire and from collapse.
How can this curious combination of ideas be explained?

As a preliminary to explanation let us examine another piece
of evidence, which I take from the same authority. The coat
of arms of the Macleod family of the Isle of Man contains in
its second quarter the three-legged Manx man, or *trinacria*,
described in heraldic terms as "the three legs of a man proper,
conjoined in the center of the upper part of the thighs, placed
in a triangle, garnished and spurred, *or*."

The motto belonging to this fugitive figure is: *Quocunque jeceris
stabit*, "However you throw him, he will stand." Another ancient
family of the Isle of Man, the Stanleys, use the same three-

legged armorial emblem but with a different motto: *Luceo non uro,* "I give light, but I do not burn." Observe how the two ideas associated with the Manxman figure are virtually the same as those associated with the English hoop-iron patterns: the idea of security from collapse, which on the positive side is self-sufficiency and self-sustention; and the idea of security from fire, which now turns out to be connected with the positive idea of light. We seem to be on some kind of a trail.

The *trinacria* and associated forms, grouped under the general term *triskelion*, have been widespread throughout Europe. To mention only a few of many examples, the coat of arms of Sicily includes a *trinacria* fitted out with a face, a beard, and what might be large ears:

And the following figures are found on old coins—the first Lycian, the second Celtiberian, the third from Megara:

Their iconographical connection with the three-legged Manxman is not hard to see, and the Megarian figure appears to be also a symbol of the sun. But the most telling evidence of all is furnished by sun and fire symbols from ancient Denmark:

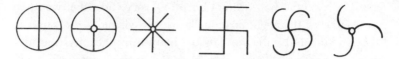

Here we find one of the hoop-iron figures and can see its relation to the svastika, while both in turn are related to the circular figure containing a cross. What is the significance of this latter? Does it represent the Sun or a Wheel? The answer, based on the evidence of ancient Aryan symbols preserved in India, must be—both!

The symbolic significance of the Wheel is well known. A perfect wheel has the property that the circumference moves uniformly while the center, the mathematical axis, stays unmoved. The Wheel thus symbolizes the blessed state of attainment which the great teachers of India—Krishna and Buddha in particular—have taught as man's true goal; to find the pure center, the *atman* or absolute self, at the heart of every action and choice, and thereby to act in perfect harmony and serenity. As Krishna tells Arjuna the troubled warrior, "Act for the sake of good action only, and not for the fruits of action." Circular movement is the one perfect form of movement, both to Hindu thinkers and to Greek, because of its geometrical self-sufficiency. Purity of motive, riddance of all desire for fruits, which is the one secure ground of human self-sufficiency, is symbolized in some Buddhist emblems by a lotus flower at the wheel's hub.

Clearly the Wheel has an iconic connection with the Sun. The spokes of the one are the rays of the other, and in either case they stood to the Hindu for the lines of influence streaming out from the divine center of things to all created beings. The number of rays, or spokes, varies: sometimes sixteen, sometimes eight, sometimes four, and more rarely some other number. The reduction of the outgoing lines to four is hardly a matter of economy; they probably represent the four cardinal directions, as the following ancient Buddhist figure strongly suggests:

Here we can see the process of transition of the Sun-Wheel figure to the Svastika. If you take the figure as a wheel, the broken circumference can be (and has been) taken to represent rotary motion. If you take it as the sun, the arcs probably represent the four winds. For our ancestors were less inclined than we to think of directions abstractly: concretely experienced they are not directions on a map, but directions from which the different types of wind were likely to arise, bringing weal or bane to men. But the motionless sun lives serenely above the moving winds, even as the mathematical axis of the wheel remains unmoved by the circling spokes. Since the wheel, then, symbolizes perfect and self-sufficient motion and since the sun is the primal source and representative of light and fire, we discover in this ancient Aryan symbol-connection the likeliest explanation both of the Herefordshire legend and of the seemingly inconsistent inscriptions on the Manx coats of arms.

Now if we were to think of the svastika as actually having evolved into the *trinacria,* or into other forms of the *triskelion,* we would have to agree with the theory which has been advanced that these are but forms of the svastika as a sun and fire symbol which in process of time has lost one of its arms. There does not appear to be any actual evidence for such a development however; the theory can hardly be anything more than an admission of ignorance. Granted that any theory of the matter must fall far short of certainty, I think that a comparative study of the symbols makes it probable that the three-fold (triskelion) figures and the fourfold (svastika) figures represent independent paths of development from a common source.

For in general it may be said that Three is associated with heavenly, Four with earthly attributes. Stated so baldly the principle is oversimplified and exceptions can be found. Nevertheless the distinction is valid in a broad way, and it has its reasons. Those relating to the mundane character of Four are the more obvious: the importance of the four cardinal directions is sufficient to account for it. The ancient prominence of the svastika confirms this explanation—if the curved form of the segments attached to the points of the cross really did, as some think, represent the winds. For the winds, as I have said, were likely to be associated with the four cardinal directions, or, as we would say, the four points of the compass. The directions themselves were more concretely envisaged then than now. There was the place of the rising sun and there was the opposed place where the sun at the end of his quotidian journey dropped into the caverns of night or dissolved in the circumambient sea of fire. Then there was the direction of the pole star, from which, in the northern hemisphere the wintry blasts come; and there was the contrary direction, where the sun retires in winter ("to escape the cold," as Herodotus reports), bringing the zephyrs back with him when he returns. In Egypt the north-south axis is marked by the Nile River, which notwithstanding its sinuosities, flows generally northward. Anatomically, moreover, it is natural for a man to think in terms of front, back, and both sides—what he sees ahead, what lurks behind, and what moves along in equal-going companionship. The winds, to be sure, do not observe the geometrical requirements of such a conception, but the stylizing imagination supplies that formal pattern which the natural phenomena themselves lack. Fourness is primarily associated with earth, particularly with earth in its geographical rather than in its reproductive and nutritive character.

In Western tradition there are certain more special meanings attached to the number four, by virtue of such influential though culturally restricted doctrines as the Four Elements and the Four Humors. These conceptions would have no archetypal validity to an Easterner, unless affected by Western indoctrination. But that the idea of the Four Elements has achieved archetypal status in the literary consciousness of the West is proved by Shakespeare's symbolic exploitation of it: the immersion of Ariel and Caliban in air-and-fire imagery and earth-and-water imagery respectively, and the contrast between Cleopatra's earth-and-water imagery, concretized also in the crocodile and Nilus' slime—

> Rather a ditch in Egypt
> Be gentle grave unto me! rather on Nilus' mud
> Lay me stark naked, and let the water-flies
> Blow me into abhorring!
> (*Antony and Cleopatra*, Act V, Scene ii)

with her air-and-fire imagery, as the spirit is about to find release—

> Husband, I come:
> Now to that name my courage prove my title!
> I am fire and air; my other elements
> I give to baser life.
> (*ibid.*)

Outside of the West and its sphere of influence, however, the Four Elements doctrine has little or no standing. In the Hindu intellectual tradition its place is supplied by the doctrine of the three *gunas;* in the Taoist by the dyad, *yang* and *yin.* And so far as I can discover, every concrete manifestation of Fourness other than those associated with the cardinal directions is analogously limited.

## The Primal Triad

The number Three tends to be symbolically associated with the religious perspective as Four does with the mundane. But there is no simple factor that will explain the former of these associations as readily as earth's four windways seem to explain the latter. Any phenomenon of a religious sort that may be appealed to, such as the Christian or the Egyptian or the Hindu Trinity, is more plausibly understood as a manifestation or effect of the triadic archetype than as its cause. Of natural phenomena there is one that undoubtedly contributes to the triadic idea in some cultures, and that is the basic family structure of Father, Mother, Child. In Egypt the resultant divine archetype—Osiris, Isis, Horus—was the supreme manifestation of Three-ness to the popular religious consciousness. An analogous family archetype is prominent in Christian iconography, displayed usually in one of two settings—the Manger (or Cave) and the Flight into Egypt. Had the popular elements of primitive Christianity been allowed to follow their natural bent I dare say this family triad might have become a dominant one, molding the structure of Christian thinking—although the ambiguous role of Joseph in the family relationship might have proved a stumbling-block. Historically the Christian Trinity took a different form. Father and Son are present in it, but the place of the Mother is taken by the sexless Holy Pneuma. In ancient Greece, in the Eleusinian Mysteries, the two aspects of womanhood—the fruition of maternity and the desirable femininity ripe for first ploughing—are symbolized by Demeter and Persephone respectively, the father figure remaining in the shadowy background, from which the ancient mythologizers would draw him forth for purposes not of worship but of rationalization. Zeus was needed simply as stud. In that other most prominent of the early Greek chthonic cults, the Dionysian, it is the father-son axis that was emphasized. Dionysus, the divine bull-man child, is the object of worship. Zeus, not involved in the worship, serves as his mythic begetter. In both these cults the family pattern is incomplete and ill-balanced; reflecting no doubt the deficiency (from our point of view) of the actual family relationship in Greek life. It is not through the family pattern but in a religiously deeper and culturally more pervasive way, as will be evident from Chapter Ten, that the Triad manifests itself in Greek religious thought. In Hinduism and Buddhism, too, the most influential forms of triadicity are not those drawn from the pattern of family life.

When we turn from the biological model to the fundamental structure of human thought itself, it seems that there are two primary ways in which the idea of Three-ness tends to impress itself upon man's awareness and enter into his interpretation of situations and events. Geometrizing them for clearer consideration, I will call them the linear and the triangular. The linear triad may take the temporal forms, Beginning-Middle-End and Past-Present-Future. Its chief spatial form archetypally, consists of the three elements: Down-here (Earth), Up-there (Sky), and In-between (Atmosphere). The religious importance of the Linear Triad shows itself in the search for, and mythic imagining of, a meeting-ground between Earth and Heaven. Spirits of the middle air, the *asuras* of Hinduism, the *daevas* of Zoroastrianism, the *daimones* of ancient Greece, and in a more special way the angels of the Lord in Christianity, are among the special forms of intermediary between man and God —between the vicissitudes of Earth and the blessedness of Heaven. A cosmographic form of the idea is represented in ancient Egypt by the combined figures of Nut, the sky-goddess encompassing both Shu, god of the atmosphere, who seems to be holding her up, and Geb, recumbent on the ground:

The triangular form of triadic thinking, on the other hand, is the one by which Hegel has endeavored to systematize all thought and all existence, structuralized as Thesis—Antithesis—Synthesis. There is a firm core of truth in his basic insight, despite the extravagances into which his zeal for system betrayed him. The dialectical movement of thought is fundamental to human living. A says "Yes," B says "No." If they stop there, the outcome must be either indifference or capitulation or war. Can they, however, find a reasonable way of resolving their dispute? In making the characteristically human, because rational, search for a common meeting ground we are declaring in effect that Antithesis, the Dyad, is insufficient as a terminus of thought, and are accepting the triangular Triad as our schematic guide. We are postulating that there shall always be, ideally, a reconciling principle.

Aristotle, in analyzing the principles by which, most basically, nature is to be explained, is insistent on the need of a reconciling principle in all understanding of nature. We cannot simply follow Heraclitus, he argues, and explain the world as a passage from opposite to opposite. If we did so we could apprehend the world kaleidoscopically, but we would have no ground for thinking and speaking of a thing (an *ousia,* in his vocabulary) as changing its qualities while still remaining itself. Yet we obviously cannot get along without this kind of thought-pattern. Hence, he concludes, "the subject of any change is numerically one, but with a duality of form." When wood burns up there is the old form which is destroyed (the wood), there is the new form which is created (the ash), and there is the substance (*ousia*) which persists through the change, enabling us to say not merely that some wood has vanished and some ash has come into existence, but that this ash is the product of that wood.[3]

Aristotle's triadic way of envisioning all natural process is a kind of skeletal reflection of a religious archetype of fundamental importance: the triad of Destruction, Creation, Preservation. In many of the sacraments connected with seasonal worship it is the first two terms that are stressed—the dying and resurrected god. But the third term is usually implicit, for it is the same Tammuz or Attis or Osiris who is born to new life in the new year. The sacred *uraeus* of Egypt, consisting of winged globe and serpent,[4] is a symbol of this triadic relationship:

The dark disc represents the unknown God as the creative source of all things. The wings represent "the brooding and flying and protecting care and goodness of the Spirit." The serpent is symbolically ambivalent. To complete the triad neatly we would have to suppose that the serpent, by reason of its lurking deadliness symbolizes death. Actually, however, all three archetypal elements are recapitulated in the serpent itself. Death it signifies, for familiar reasons. But stretched out straight, the serpent becomes a phallus symbolizing the reproductive power of Godhead—an idea which is reinforced by the serpent's periodic shedding of its skin and thus being born, as it were, to new life. Finally, when coiled into a circle, it symbolizes the self-sufficiency and oneness which are associated with God's preservative power. Thus both the serpent figure itself and the winged figure which includes it represent the divine triad of Creation—Destruction—Preservation.

In India an analogous form of the Triad has attained even greater prominence. The three great gods—Brahma the Creator, Shiva the Destroyer, and Vishnu the Preserver—are, according to the *Mahabharata*, emanations or manifestations (*trimurti*) of the impersonal Atma-Brahman,[5] the supreme principle and World-Ground. In actual worship, however, the three gods receive unequal treatment. Brahma evidently keeps his place in the triad in order to fill out the logical structure—the logic of process, which Aristotle's independent analysis has laid bare—and he has enjoyed a certain emblematic development, as when he is portrayed as a four-headed king riding a white goose; but he has only a minor place in the devotional life of India. Shiva and Vishnu are the gods principally worshipped, and for reasons which appear different on the surface but have an underlying bond of connection. Shiva, like the Egyptian *uraeus*-serpent, is ambivalent in nature. Out of his destructive aspect, classically emphasized in the *Mahabharata*, there has arisen a belief in his reproductive power. His principal emblems are the *linga* and the *yoni*, representing the male and female organs of generation. He is worshiped, therefore, as symbolizing the mystery of reproduction (with its allusive overtone of death passing into new life), and more broadly of creative force in whatever form. The twin ideas of death and new birth, appealing so strongly to our fears and our hopes, carry a strong potential of emotional experience, as every deeply ambivalent idea tends to do.

If Shiva represents the paradox of two-in-one, Vishnu represents the paradox of many-in-one. The difference is not a numerical but a qualitative one. For Vishnu is the god who incarnates himself, who comes repeatedly to earth in one or another heroic or saintly guise (*avatar*)—notably as Rama, the legendary hero of the epic *Ramayana,* and as Krishna, the godlike transfigured charioteer of the devotional *Bhagavad-Gita.* Thus the proliferation of interests and problems breaks up the symmetry of the original triad, without however altogether destroying the sense of triadicity as somehow basic.

In a more intellectualized way the Hindu urge to think triadically shows itself in the doctrine of the *gunas*—the three kinds of quality-substance-action (the three categories are fused here) of which the manifested world is composed.[6] The manifested world (*prakriti*) is not simply the world around us; it includes our psychic states too. Both outwardly and inwardly (unless by disciplined renunciation of the manifested we penetrate to the innermost core of Selfhood, the *Atman*) we find these three tendencies at work, or (from a passive standpoint) these three qualities apparent. They are *sattva*—the bright, serene; *rajas*—the active, intense; *tamas*—the dark, inert. Every human disposition, as every substance and event of nature, contains the three elements in one proportion or another. Members of the Brahmin caste approximate pure *sattva,* it is said; the Kshatriyas (warriors) are a mixture of *sattva* and *rajas;* the Vaisyas (farmers and artisans) a mixture of *rajas* and *tamas;* while the lowly Shudra caste is explained as unleavened *tamas.* By this ingenious set of interlocking correspondences the Hindu thinker has succeeded in harmonizing the triadic principle, whose origin is religious, with the quartic principle, which manifests itself in the differentiation of men in society.

The Platonic triad of mind, energy, and appetite stands in such striking analogy with the Hindu triad of *gunas* as to prompt the question whether they may possibly have had a common Indo-European root. There is no historical evidence for the proposition, although additional analogical evidence may be found in the fact that Plato's symbol of the charioteer driving the spirited and the sluggish horse has a loose analogue in the *Upanishads*. At all events Plato, as most readers know, used that psychologically oriented triad as a basis for understanding not only man but society. Mind (*nous, noesis*) must be the ruler of the energies (which, properly disciplined, support it) and the appetites (which are naturally recalcitrant); in the commonwealth it is those with harmoniously functioning minds, the effective lovers of wisdom, who should similarly have authority over both the energetic citizens (their potential allies) and the sluggishly appetitive (who have mainly to be kept in check).

How does the Christian Trinity relate to these other trinities and triads? An attempt to answer this difficult question can be facilitated by appealing not directly to the theological dogma, which is an intellectual abstraction, but to a triad of Scriptural images which draws us closer to the primitively Christian way of thinking. In the Gospel according to John, Christ is declared to be the Word (John, 1:1), the true Light (John, 1:9), and, in a later chapter, the true Vine (John, 15:1). Of these three symbols it was the Word that became, in Christian history, specifically identified with Christ, the second Persona of the Trinity. What then of the other two? Since our aim cannot be certain proof, but must be content with probabilities or even plausibilities based upon relevant archetypal analogies, I would like to introduce by way of suggestive comparison a triad of emblems from Mahayana Buddhism—the Tree, the Tomb, and the Wheel.[7]

The Tree, in one aspect, represents the *bo* tree under which

*The Tree*

*The Tomb*

*The Wheel*

EMBLEMS FROM MAHAYANA BUDDHISM.
BAS-RELIEF PANELS ON A GATE OF THE
BUDDHIST STUPA AT SANCHI.

Siddhartha Gotoma sat when he experienced the great revelation wherein he knew himself to be a Buddha. But it has developed also a broader significance, as the Tree of Life. The Tomb
represents, of course, Death. But neither death nor life is final;
they are complementaries, ceaselessly conjoined in the world
of *maya*, the illusionistic world of manifold phenomena. Living
and dying are, as it were, convex and concave of the same arc.
Behind them both (or above, or beneath, or at the center of
them) is the Self-Subsistent, the ultimate Ground of all things.
How shall it be represented unless by the most perfect figure of
all, the circle? Its emblem, then, is the Wheel, which (as I have
shown) is often iconographically interchangeable with the Sun,
and the Wheel's spokes with the Sun's rays. The Wheel symbolizes the self-created and self-preservative, the primal and
ultimate form of being, unmoved at the pure center, thereby
causing perfect harmonious movement throughout its parts.
A formalized version of the three emblems is found on ancient
Indian-Buddhist coins:

In Christian iconography the Cross takes the place of the
Tomb as death symbol. As an article of faith the death is followed by a resurrection, but it is the Crucifixion itself that looms
most prominently among the emblems of Christianity. Moreover, if we take the statements in John 14:25-26 in their most
natural signification, it would appear that Christ is about to

depart, and that after he shall have done so the Holy Spirit will
take his place. That such an interpretation is one of the classical
heresies I am well aware, but I am discussing symbolic analogies, not the truth or falsity of doctrines. There does seem to be a
symbolic affinity between Christ and the Tomb, as there is also
between the Holy Spirit and the flourishing Vine of the Invisible
Church. And somehow ontologically prior to them is the ultimate Godhead—at once the self-sustaining Cause (the Wheel)
and the Light that gives meaning to all things (the Sun).

That the Cross symbolizes not only death but new life, would
be admitted and indeed proclaimed by most Christians. It was
the early Christians of Egypt, however, who found a visible
emblem uniting the two conceptions. In place of the familiar
form of the Cross they substituted the *tau*—T—which they called
"the sacred sign" and "the sign of life." The Egyptologist Wilkinson writes that "the early Christians of Egypt adopted it in
lieu of the Cross, which was afterward substituted for it; pre-
fixing it to inscriptions in the same manner as the Cross in later
times, and numerous inscriptions headed by the *tau* are preserved to the present day in early Christian sepulchres at the
great Oasis."[8] Why was there this substitution of an emblem
which to a Christian of the West might appear to be only a
mutilated Cross? The *tau* had already been a potent symbol of
renewed life in pre-Christian Egypt. When a new Pharaoh
assumed the reins of government, the gods presented him with
a *tau*—the presentation being enacted by human representatives
in a sumptuous ceremony. The ceremony was regarded as quickening the life of the kingdom and ensuring health and power
during the new king's reign.

But what lay back of the sacramental importance of the *tau*?
The likeliest theory is that the emblem developed as an icon
representing the key or plug with which the Egyptians closed
and opened the dykes along the Nile—a device for spreading

the periodic inundations more equitably among cultivators. When the river rose to a fixed height the appointed guardians made a T-shaped cut in the dam, releasing the waters. The gift of the *tau* to the Pharaoh at his coronation, Mrs. Murray-Aynsley writes in the work already cited, "may have been intended to signify the bestowal on him by the gods of a typical key of the waters of the Nile, i.e., that it was a token of supreme power; thus it would not unnaturally be regarded as a sign of life, for without it the land could not yield its increase." Thus the *tau* is strongly ambivalent: symbolizing on the one hand Death (by its association with the Cross) and on the other hand more abundant Life (through release of the waters)—an ambivalence altogether appropriate to the Christian archetype, the second Person of the Trinity, which it was designed to express.

## The Threshold and the Melting-pot

How do archetypes enter into the living discourse of poetry? In a great diversity of ways to be sure. But one general principle needs to be reëmphasized: that so far as the poetry is poetically alive, the ingredient universals are somehow concrete, which is to say freshly envisioned and therefore somehow metaphoric, not the static and preëxistent universals which a logical conception involves. Philosophers, trained to think in logical categories (which is not always synonymous with thinking logically) are sometimes prone to ignore this qualification. Filmer S. Northrop, for example, is a philosopher·renowned in both the scientific and the legal field but his published views on poetry err by taking the archetypal element too simply. When poetry goes beyond sheer concrete immediacy, when it does anything more than describe the intuited surface-qualities of experience,

Professor Northrop holds that it must then serve "as the instrument or handmaid for metaphorically and analogically conveying a theoretical doctrine"[9]—where the criteria of the poem's truth and even (if I understand him correctly) of its meaning, reside in some other science or system of thought, independent of the poem. And so he interprets the *Divine Comedy* as taking the philosophic concepts that constitute the *Summa Theologia* ("concepts by postulation," he calls them) and conveying their analogue in terms of what is concretely sensed and imaginable ("concepts by intuition"): because the general public "must have bells rung for them while they salivate, and have vivid images instead of postulationally-prescribed scientific concepts." A prescription more appropriate to advertising than to poetry! What Professor Northrop's view amounts to (despite his undeveloped use of the word "metaphorically") is that all poetry must be either presentationally descriptive or else allegorical.

A modified form of the error, more cautiously qualified, confuses the discussions of poetic meaning in Wilbur M. Urban's *Language and Reality*.[10] A good deal hinges, I grant, upon just what Professor Urban means when he describes poetry as "covert metaphysics." He is wise enough, indeed, to make an important reservation. Although the transition from poetry to metaphysics is "inevitable," he concedes that "the poet, as poet, is not the one to make it." The poet should not depart from his figurative and symbolic way of speaking, "for precisely in that symbolic form an aspect of reality is given which cannot be expressed otherwise." So far I am in full agreement. But Urban unfortunately cannot let a poem stand ontologically on its own. "It remains true," he insists, "that poetry is covert metaphysics, and it is only when its implications, critically interpreted and adequately expressed, become part of philosophy that an adequate view of the world can be achieved." Poetic meanings, so far as they are really meaningful, in Urban's view, must enjoy ultimate membership in the great Philosophical Tradition of the West, as it has received successive expression and formulation at the hands of such master-dialecticians as Plato, Aristotle, Spinoza, Kant, and Hegel.

Now without wishing to claim universal validity for any pronouncement about so fluid and diversified a thing as poetry, I would like to propose the guiding idea that in many of the most heightened passages of poetic utterance the effect comes from a combination of the metaphoric and archetypal modes of envisagement—where what I may call the Melting-pot and the Threshold activities of imagination are in a serene but quickening state of tension. A few illustrative examples follow.

> Golden lads and girls all must,
> As chimney-sweepers, come to dust.

The most obvious expression of the radically metaphoric in these lines from the dirge in *Cymbeline* is the amusing little pun, "come to dust." Taken merely as a pun, however, it becomes, on reflection, distastefully snobbish; for chimney sweeps come to dust in a sordid, plebian, literal way (which we cannot feel very humorous about after reading Blake, for instance), golden lads and girls in a cultivatedly tragic, A. E. Housman, *lacrima rerum* sort of way. The pun, under Shakespeare's hand, passes beyond the antithesis of amusing vs. snobbishly unpleasant; it becomes a serious metaphoric pun, a poetic plurisign, by reason of the deeper meaning which, instead of separating, connects the golden youths and the chimney sweeps. Three main devices give the pun its wider range of inference. The two preceding lines have prepared for it:

> Thou thy worldly task hast done,
> Home art gone, and ta'en thy wages

—where there is a shrewd balance between the universal and

the particular; for while the primary reference is to the human life-cycle, a simple deletion of the word "worldly" will make the lines perfectly applicable to the daily life of a chimney sweep: "You have finished your task, taken your wages, and gone home." The word "worldly" is thus the fulcrum on which the archetypal and presentational elements are delicately balanced. Secondly, there is the ambivalent contrast between *golden* and *dust:* connoting on the one hand life vs. death, on the other (more lightly) the happy estate of more fortunate children vs. the murky life of the chimney sweep. Finally, in Shakespeare's day there appears to have been a third basis of connection; for, as a contributor to *The Explicator* has recently pointed out,[11] it was the practice in parts of rural England for the leader of May Day revels (which celebrated the cyclic return of summer and abundant life) to be dressed as a chimney sweep. The mythic connection here goes pretty deep, for there is a widespread tendency, in rural England as in ancient Eleusis, for spring and summer festivals to develop beyond the stage of agricultural magic, and to symbolize and promote spiritual rebirth, of which the first step is purification. And who, after all, can more aptly symbolize the ritual of periodic cleansing than the chimney sweep? Thus, hidden within Shakespeare's radical metaphor, there is a light suggestion (no more!) of one of mankind's most persistent and indispensable archetypal ideas. We are on a threshold almost without knowing it.

Take now another Shakespearean metaphor, which approaches the threshold of universality somewhat differently. When Cleopatra is dying and Charmian exclaims "O eastern star!" the Queen replies:

> Peace, peace!
> Dost thou not see my baby at my breast,
> That sucks the nurse asleep?
> (*Antony and Cleopatra*, Act V, Scene ii)

The remarkable power with which this utterance affects us seems to derive largely from such elements as the following. There is the idea of quietude connoted by the words "peace" and "asleep," which contrasts satisfyingly with the tumult of environing events. Then there is the reversal of normal order, suggested by the baby's putting the nurse to sleep—a reversal which like Shakespeare's various tempests and tumblings of nature's germens, furnishes a symbolic parallel to the tumbling of empire. At the same time the abnormal idea is counterpointed by a normal one, for the baby is at its usual place on the nurse's breast and seems to perform its usual action of sucking; only the result is opposite, for it is the nurse instead of the baby who is put to sleep in the process. And contrapuntive again is the paradox of life and death: for the very action of nursing which normally furthers life in the baby now brings death to the nurse. Finally, over and above such justifications by immediate context there is the above-mentioned archetypal significance of the serpent as at once the sharp tooth of death and the symbol of new life. This ancient and widespread piece of symbolism appears to have been suggested and perpetuated by the several impressive characteristics of the serpent discussed in connection with the sacred *uraeus* of Egypt: its casting off of old skin, its mysterious arising out of the ground, that is to say out of the womb of Mother Earth; its phallic shape, its electric quickness, its hypnotic stare, and its aptitude of coiling itself into a circle (for, as Heraclitus remarked, "In the circle the beginning and end are one")—all these aspects standing in effective tension with the idea of lurking deadliness. It is impossible to be sure how much of the archetypal meaning Shakespeare and the audience for whom he wrote were aware of, but I should think a good deal.

In poetry at its most heightened moments, then, there is apt to be some fusion of the two imaginative procedures which I have called the archetypal and the metaphoric, the Threshold and the

Melting Pot. The way of the Melting Pot is to create a fresh relationship between two or more images (with attendant ideas or adumbrations of idea) which outside of just that poetic context would be somewhat disparate and irrelevant, but from whose present unexpected combination a nuance emerges which has not hitherto existed. The way of the Threshold is to see a general idea in and through the particular images drawn from the real world, heightened but not radically distorted by the poet's creative imagination. To combine these two ways in a single living act of being, thought, and utterance is to accept the challenge of Wannemunne and sing the full human song.

# 8

# The Mythic Dimension

All is prepared in darkness. Enormous light
is but the foetus of big-bellied night.
The image hatches in the darkened room:
the cave, the camera, the skull, the womb.
Future and past are shut. The present leaps:
a bright calf dropped between two infinite sleeps.
DILYS LAING, "The Apparition"

As a preliminary working definition for the semantic study of myth I propose this from the *Encyclopedia of Poetry and Poetics:* "a story or a complex of story elements taken as expressing and therefore as implicitly symbolizing, certain deeplying aspects of human and transhuman experience."[1] Although the definition is incomplete, since it does not yet raise the necessary question of the relation of myth to ritual and to the rituomythic way of life, it is serviceable as far as it goes. For it specifies the two semantic complementaries of myth: the vehicle which is a story, and the tenor which is some kind of vaguely looming significance. On the surface a myth is a tale, a narrative, either about events believed to have occurred at some significant moment of human history (e.g., the virgin birth of Jesus, his crucifixion and resurrection), or about prehistoric events (e.g., the creation of Adam, the Hesiodic Golden Age ), or about events regarded as taking place outside of human time altogether ( e.g., Athena's birth from the head of Zeus, Lucifer's revolt and expulsion from Heaven). But so far as these events are truly mythic their narrative accounts are not important in themselves but only in their reference to their tenor, which is something perhaps vague but yet of vast importance for the interpretation of human experience. The truly mythic, in short, has archetypal implications.

Nevertheless the mythic is something more than the archetypal which it implicitly embodies. For the mythic involves not only archetypal ideas, but more characteristically archetypally significant events and situations. From a sophisticated standpoint—i.e., where one is an observer, an onlooker, no longer personally involved in the mythic pattern of which he speaks— the mythic can be conceived as the archetypal in action. Thus we can characterize the Good as archetypal but God as mythic, Evil as archetypal but Satan as mythic, Creative Energy as archetypal but Mother Earth as mythic, Alienation as archetypal but Hell and Limbo as mythic. Existentially, however, the mythic came first, the archetypal is a later intellectual offshoot.

Let it be noted, please, that in characterizing certain kinds of sacred story as "mythic" I do not declare them "mythical." The latter adjective, as commonly used, throws sharply into doubt the literal everyday truth of the narrated events. Such questions lie altogether outside the semantic inquiry on which we are engaged. Whether a physical Garden of Eden ever existed, and whether Krishna did actually reveal himself to Arjuna on the battlefield in the guise of his charioteer, I do not know and do not see how anyone can know—unless, of course, "know" is taken to mean "resolved to believe." Judgments of probability are neither here nor there, for they would turn out quite differently according as one's standpoint were Christian, Hindu, or secular.

The important thing is that both the Garden of Eden story and the Krishna-Arjuna story provide and fit in with symbolic patterns of high importance for their respective Christian and Hindu groups of adherents; whether either or both of the stories may be "mythical" in the popular sense is not our concern as semanticists. Hence, bracketing off all questions of literal truth or falsity, we can recognize each of these mythic narratives as embodying an archetypal idea, partly but not entirely translatable into ordinary language—a set of depth-meanings of durable and far-reaching significance within a widely shared cultural perspective.

## Myth as Perspective

Myth, then, is not in the first instance a fiction imposed on one's already given world, but is a way of apprehending that world. Genuine myth is a matter of perspective first, invention second. This radically cognitive function of myth, as a kind of primitive epistemic, is stressed particularly by Ernst Cassirer in his study of "Mythic Thinking," which forms the second part of his three-volume work, *The Philosophy of Symbolic Forms*.[2] Cassirer starts out from the Kantian principle that all knowledge involves a synthesizing activity of the mind; that in the very act of knowing an object the mind contributes those lines of connection whereby the particulars of sense are combined into an intelligible unity. Certain colors and shapes impinge upon our visual awareness and we recognize unhesitatingly, "A tree!" What is involved in such recognition? Something more than the visual data themselves, evidently, for they might equally well be given in dream or delirium. In themselves they are but pictures on the mind's portable movie screen: separate them from mental interpretative response and one's awareness of them would resemble that of the idiot Benjy in Faulkner's *The Sound and the Fury*, whose world consists of bright shapes and uninterpretable fragments of conversation flashing on and off the screen. We are superior to idiots because for us a bright shape is an index of something more permanent and more contextual than the moving kaleidoscope of bare uninterpreted sensations. "It is not merely a bright shape, it is a tree": if the distinction means anything it means at least that the bright shape is connected with other shapes and colors, such as we could espy by circling around the tree, and with possibilities of tactile sensation which we could realize by approaching the tree and touching it. To identify a certain visual configuration as a tree involves at very least a psychic activity—instinctive, immediate, and implicit, not consciously controlled—of combining the present shape-and-color sensations with appropriate subconscious memories and expectancies to form a significant whole object. The expectancies include a confidence that if one continues to look at the tree it will not unaccountably vanish away, Cheshire-cat fashion.

Cassirer, "transposing [as he says] the Kantian principle into the key of myth," inquires how the mind's primary activity of integration—what Coleridge called "the primary imagination"—operates in the condition of pre-civilized living. Such basic categories of thought as space, time, number, quality, cause, and law, he maintains, are conceived in a more flexible, more organic and, one might say, more hospitable manner than would be acceptable to the science-oriented mind. The mythic consciousness "finds its being and its life in the immediate impression, to which it surrenders itself without attempting to 'measure' itself by something else." A Navaho Indian *sees* the clouds in the tobacco pipe smoke, and sees them in a context that includes their desired and expected effect, the rain. The rain is not, to him, something entirely other than the puff of smoke; there is an indefinable coalescence between them.

The coalescence of things in mythic perspective takes also the special form of a coalescence between the individual and the species. "In mythic thinking," Cassirer declares, "the species is immediately present in the particular; in the particular it lives and works." The sacrificed totemic black bear is a representative of its entire species: not a merely numerical instance of it, but a real participant in it, as evidenced by the usual primitive belief that a noble specimen of black bear has *more* of blackbearhood in it than a puny one. The Christian doctrine that every individual man falls from grace through Adam's sin and receives new life through Christ's death and resurrection exemplifies the sense of effective concrete universality on a higher level. The doctrine becomes intelligible when Adam, and when Christ, are understood not as atomically distinct beings but as truly participating in the essence of all mankind and as epitomizing that essence in themselves.

In more subtle ways, too, there is coalescence between the specific tale and the archetypal meaning. A scholar today, studying the ancient Babylonian myth of Marduk's victory over Tiamat, interprets it reasonably as representing the victory of the culture-hero over the monster of daemonic unbridled power. And presumably something like this cosmo-dramatic relationship was felt by the ancient Babylonians as they engaged in ritual acts designed to celebrate and confirm the power of Marduk. But the growth of the idea out of the early cultural matrix requires cautious tracing. Cassirer's tracing of the emergence of mythic law-consciousness out of the proto-mythic Babylonian animatism offers a good model.

Early Babylonian thought involved belief in friendly and baneful powers of nature, daemons of sky and storm, field and forest, mountain and rivulet, confusingly overlapping one another's territory and operating mostly by sheer caprice. As Babylonian wonder and inquiry concentrated more and more on the starry sky (so Cassirer's theory runs) the form of their cosmological beliefs gradually underwent a kind of evolution. The primitive daemon-mythology continued to survive in popular superstition, but the religion of priests and sages began to emphasize holy times and holy numbers, specifically with reference to the movements of the celestial orbs. Out of contemplation of the plain and orderly course of the sun and stars, and the more complex but still orderly courses of the moon and planets, the idea of divine law began to emerge. For it was no longer the particular star as such, but the particular star as exemplifying universal rhythms, that was coming to be the object of attention and to be reverenced as divine. After vanquishing Tiamat, Marduk established the stars in their courses as abodes of the high gods; he divided the year into twelve months, represented by the zodiacal signs, and he set limits beyond which the days were prohibited from wandering. Thereby he established orderly motion and the possibility of life—much as Maui, the racial progenitor and culture-hero of the New Zealand Maori, seized the sun in its falling and gave to it, which had theretofore moved capriciously about the sky, laws governing its motion. Moreover, like most other culture-heroes, Marduk established laws not only for nature but also for man; he was the protector of justice. Such linkage of cosmic and ethical ordering finds lordly expression in the great symbols connoting Justice, Right, the Way, and related ideas in nearly all the more advanced cultures—notably in the *Tao* of ancient China, *Rta* in the Vedas, *Asha* in Zoroastrianism and *Dikê* in ancient Greece. These, says Cassirer, "are expressions of the orderly connection and dispensation of occurrences grasped simultaneously from the standpoint of *being* and *ought*." Nature and right action are seen as two sides of the same mythic reality.

## The Semantics of Ritual

In mythic perspective nature is not merely known, it is enacted. "Nature yields nothing without ceremonies," Cassirer has observed; he might almost have ventured the more radical judgment that nature *is* nothing without ceremonies, for in order to know nature truly in a mythopoeic way one must engage in the gestures and ritual acts which bring oneself into active communion. Nor can such strategies be private. Primitive mysticism is an affair of the forum. Ignoring the special status of magicians, shamans, primitive priests, who in any case play a representative role, we can say that primitive acts of participation in nature must be undertaken tribally, or by a cult or totem group within the tribe. Mythos, then, is not self-intelligible; it has to be studied in the context of rite and ceremony which have engendered it or which at any rate have molded its distinctive form.

A death chant from the islands of Fiji will serve to illustrate this natural interrelation of the ceremonial and the mythic. On the largest island of the Fijian group, some three-quarters of a century ago a British surveying party discovered a road, overgrown and evidently no longer in active use, leading through the wilderness. Further exploration revealed that it ran straight on for fifty miles, often through difficult terrain, from the principal village to the sacred mountain, Nakauvadra, which faces the western sea, and on which is a high ledge, Nai-thombo-thombo, "the jumping-off-place" of ghosts departing for their submarine after-life abode. The road's great length was all the more surprising because at the time when it must have been built the Fijians had possessed no tools to work with other than crudely sharpened stones. What fears or hopes or strange inner compulsions could have urged these savages to so formidable an undertaking?

Because both the road and the mountain were strongly taboo

the explorers' inquiries were nearly always met with silence and evasion. At length, however, after much patient research the following account was pieced together. Some two or three generations ago, the tribal saga ran, the inhabitants of the village were bothered by loitering ghosts, who played such pranks as putting snakes in the cooking-pots, making young women unaccountably pregnant, and turning yams rotten in the ground. The elders took counsel and diagnosed the situation as caused by the ghosts' losing their way to Mt. Nakauvadra. Hence the path was built—laboriously, and with the periodic spur of cannibal feasts—in order to ease and direct their journey.

Formerly when a Fijian died, the funeral rites lasted three days. These three days of sacrament on the part of the survivors were correlated step by step with the events of the three-day journey which the departed one must take along the path to the sacred mountain. Particular chants and ritual acts symbolize particular adventures which the ghost must encounter, and magically aid him as well, for the ghostly path is full of terrors, each in its apportioned place. When the three days have expired the ghost reaches the mountain, and before it comes time for him to dive into the sea he is hospitably received into the mountain cavern, where the spirits of ancient hero-ancestors dwell, guardians of the tribe's morality and well-being. Here, after joining with them in a feast and the singing of tribal lays (enacted also in the actual ritual of the funeral ceremony, where portions of food are laid aside and magically treated in order that their *mana,* or vital essence, may be transported to the sacred cave) the newcomer breaks the last tie with his physical body, and now for the first time clearly realizing his condition, he is overwhelmed with grief. To the accompaniment of native instruments, addressing the ancestors he chants these words:

My Lords! In evil fashion are we buried,
Buried staring up into heaven,

We see the scud flying over the sky,
We are worn out with the feet tramping on us.

Our ribs, the rafters of our house, are torn asunder,
The eyes with which we gazed on one another are destroyed,
The nose with which we kissed has fallen in,
The breast with which we embraced is ruined,
The mouth with which we laughed has decayed,
The teeth with which we bit have showered down.
Gone is the hand that threw the tinka stick,
The testes have rolled away.

Hark to the lament of the mosquito!
It is well that *he* should die and pass onward.
But alas for my ear that he has devoured.

Hark to the lament of the fly!
It is well that *he* should die and pass onward.
But alas! he has stolen the eye from which I drank.

Hark to the lament of the black ant!
It is well that *he* should die and pass onward.
But alas for my whale's-tooth that he has devoured.[3]

The whale's tooth is a peculiarly expressive symbol, carrying the double significance of economic wealth (ivory whales' teeth having been used in Fiji as a standard of exchange) and vital potency (the whale's tooth being also phallic, iconically representing the male organ). The realism of the black ant becomes almost agonizingly clear when it is recalled that Fijian men used to squat or sit on ant-infested ground clad only in a loin-cloth. The ending of the lament is thus dramatically and metaphorically apt; and it marks the climax of the entire mortuary drama— both actually among the survivors and suppositionally in the mountain-cave. When it is over, the ghost ascends to Nai-thombo-thombo and plunges into the sea, while his survivors bring their festivities to a close and bury his now ripe body in the earth.

How are the ritualistic and mythic factors related in the foregoing situation? From a sociological standpoint the festivities and the burial will be taken as the real aspect of the matter, the ghostly adventures as a fictional projection designed to explain and justify them. To the Fijian mourners, on the other hand, the ritual is but an adjunct to a perfectly real supernatural set of occurrences, being designed partly to celebrate and partly by imitative magic to assist the dead man's spectral journey. Probably, to be sure, the mourners do not rationalize in any such distinct way; what they mythopoeically enact in ritual and envision in story being as inseparable as convex and concave in a curve. In any event the dirge I have just quoted serves by its strongly marked rhythms—both the vocal rhythm (so I am assured, although it is lost in translation) and the ideational rhythm which the individuality of the lines preserves—to establish a sense of widened community, whereby, for the duration of the ceremony at least, the chanting survivors, the recently deceased, and the ancient ancestor-spirits are brought into a strongly felt and tersely articulated togetherness. Such reaffirmations of communal participation in the Something Beyond, paced in the tribal calendar according to the occurrence of emotively significant events like births and deaths, puberty, marriage, and war, are the most vitalizing forces in primitive cultural life. And the periodic expression of tribal fellowship tends to find oblique expression in the stories and shapes, the myths and proto-artistic forms, that become, despite their ready inclusion of the fantastic and the grotesque, the treasury of inherited wisdom and cultural cohesion.

## The Role of Magic

A sharply different view of the nature of ritual has received currency from the admirable but too often seductively partisan writings of Sir James G. Frazer, especially in *The Magic Art*, which occupies the first two volumes of *The Golden Bough*. Frazer's theory is that all ritual and all religion have their origin in magic—i.e., in action intended to work coercively upon nature and bring about specific desired effects by exploiting the "sympathetic" connection that subsists between things that have once been joined or that are significantly similar. The coercive motive preceded, he ·thinks, both the petitionary and the celebrative. Men shifted to petitionary tactics only when their evolving intelligence discovered that coercion too often did not work. Ostensibly celebrative ceremonies, like those of the marriage of Zeus and Demeter at Eleusis, of the marriage of Zeus and Hera at Plataea, and the Midsummer Eve festivals of later Europe, he thinks were originally magical rites intended to produce or aid the effects which they dramatically set forth. "If the revival of vegetation in spring," he writes, "is mimicked by the awakening of a sleeper, the mimicry is intended actually to quicken the growth of leaves and blossoms; if the marriage of the powers of vegetation is simulated by a King and Queen of May, the idea is that the powers thus impersonated will really be rendered more productive by the ceremony. In short, all these spring and midsummer festivals fall under the head of homoeopathic or imitative magic. The thing which people wish to bring about they represent dramatically, and the very representation is believed to effect, or at least to contribute to, the production of the desired result."[4] Similarly, since Demeter's anger and self-seclusion after the loss of Persephone is described in myth as causing the failure of the crops, Frazer infers that the ritual connected with her worship is essentially magical in intent, aimed at preventing a recurrence of crop-failure.

Frazer's vast erudition has not guarded him, unfortunately, from an elementary logical mistake. His evidence establishes a strong case for the presence of a magical element in the Eleusinian worship of Demeter; it does not in the least prove that her worship was entirely or even primarily magical. Celebration, veneration, and praise on the one hand, magical incantation and petitionary prayer on the other—who can assign precisely, after this span of centuries, the relative importance of such complementary motives in the Eleusinian Mysteries? Inasmuch as the Mysteries were kept hidden from the profane view and not committed to writing, the known details are sparse. Among other things a sheaf of grain was displayed as a kind of blessed sacrament by the hierophant to the neophytes, and the prominence of that symbol may appear to support the view that we are dealing with a survival of vegetation magic. (Freudians, on the other hand, are more likely to see a phallus in any object so shaped.) But Frazer pays too little heed to the religious tone of the ceremonies. The Eleusinian worship was conducted, according to available testimony, with deep reverence, and the worshiper underwent a genuine purgation of soul, a *katharsis* or *katharmos*, casting off the old self even as Nature discards last year's raiment to be reborn in the new year. Magic is imperious, worship is acquiescent. The magician's aim is to manipulate nature, the worshiper seeks to know her and to become attuned to her pulsations. There may well be magical elements in the Eleusinian as in other religious ceremonies—whether as survivals or as degenerative novelties—and their importance is much greater in some cults and in some ceremonies than in others, but they probably do not lie nearly so close to the heart of the matter as Frazer, with his strong positivistic bias, is disposed to believe.

For although all magic employs ritual as its instrument, it is by no means true that all ritual is primarily or even appreciably magical in intent or in origin. The problem can be understood more objectively if we distinguish ceremonies, from the standpoint of the idea that governs and justifies them, into four main types: the coercive, the contractual, the assimilative, and the confrontative. The first two may be called, in a broad way, magical; the latter two are at least embryonically religious. I ignore such ceremonies as are merely imitative, habitual, and perfunctory, for in them the governing idea has been lost.

Coercive ritual (the adjective connotes the intent and does not prejudge the results) is magical in the most commonly accepted sense of the word. Its magic may work, or be expected to work, either negatively or positively; in the exorcism of troublesome ghosts or in the transformation of natural objects or events at the magician's bidding. In either case such magic is set to work by tapping certain magical potencies, quasi-natural forces which the Melanesians call *mana*, and which the magician can control and exploit by virtue of the superior degree of *mana* in himself or in his magical words or magical instruments.[5]

I will not attempt to estimate, and do not believe that anyone today can possibly do so without bias, how much truth and how much illusion there may have been in the primitive magical belief. At any rate it seems likely that ceremonial magic would have been mixed, even quite early in human evolution, with elements of empirical method, trial-and-error, primitive experiment. Great fundamental inventions, such as the rude necessities of clothing, shelter, and weapons, the discovery of fire and of making food more palatable by cooking it, the first use of the wedge and the wheel, the first sowing of seed and waiting for the harvest: such monumental steps from savage to proto-civilized ways of living, however much attended by magic and ritual, were essentially a kind of infant technology, and thus, despite their aberrations, point at long range to the scientific view of things and to the semantic which is its instrument. In primitive times, however, the earliest technology can hardly have developed much of a semantic of its own: it evolved within a predominantly mythopoeic framework.

Attempts to coerce nature sometimes alternate with, sometimes combine with, attempts to propitiate and persuade her. In its simplest forms propitiation may involve no more than the fear-inspired or awe-inspired sacrifice of some valued possession, to appease either the greed or vengeance or the sheer unexplainable cussedness of the alien forces. At a more sophisticated and consciously deliberate stage it begins to embrace the idea of covenant—the ancient *Do ut des,* "I give in order that you shall give in return."[6] Such an attitude shows an incipient transcendence of the mana-taboo type of consciousness, involving as it evidently does a belief in spirits who can be trusted to uphold their side of the agreement and correspondingly an acceptance of a moral obligation by oneself.

Coercive and propitiatory types of ritual may both be described as magical—the former in the basic and accepted sense, the latter by derivation and analogy. They are alike in two ways. First, they maintain an already developed distinction between self and not-self, between the magician and the natural or supernatural force with which he is concerned; and secondly, the magician's interest in that outer force is utilitarian, he wants to exploit it, turn it to his own uses. The two remaining ceremonial types, the assimilative and the religious, differ respectively on just these two points.

Assimilative ritual consists in reaffirming and attempting to intensify man's continuity and partial oneness with nature, or with the mysterious creative force behind nature. The omnipresent mana-power is conceived not as something separate from oneself and manipulable by one's independent will, but as (so to speak) the womb of reality to which it is a joy to return. Mana tends to be a borderland idea, a mode of existence somehow between and combining the personal and impersonal, the natural and supernatural, the self and not-self. That is not to say that primitive man first thought these antitheses and then blurred them (as our own differently oriented intelligences perhaps oblige us to do) but simply that he did *not* make the distinctions which to us appear logically and experimentally self-evident. His relation to nature was largely one of participation, much in the same way as was his relation to fellow-beings within the tribe.

## Participation and Insight

Accordingly Lévy-Bruhl has declared the Law of Participation to be a governing condition of all primitive thought.[7] "In the collective representations of primitive morality," he writes, "objects and phenomena can be, though in a manner incomprehensible to us, at once themselves and not themselves." Thus when the Bororo tribe of northern Brazil declare that they are red parakeets, they are not merely taking a name or claiming a relationship; they are asserting positive identity with the species of red parakeet. On the basis of our accustomed logic— the logic of Literal Discourse—it is paradoxical to regard them as human beings and as birds of scarlet plumage at the same time, but "to the mentality that is governed by the law of participation there is no difficulty in the matter." Lévy-Bruhl characterizes such mentality as "pre-logical": not implying that it is necessarily antecedent in time to the birth of logical thought, but merely "that it does not bind itself down, as logical thought does, to avoiding contradiction." In practical situations, he observes, like seeking shelter in a storm or capturing a wild beast, where it is necessary to think and act as an individual, the primitive man reasons in much the same way as a civilized one, although with a different fund of information and memories to draw on.

Typically primitive "pre-logical" ideas do not depend on the individual but on the group: "they present themselves in aspects which cannot be accounted for by considering individuals merely as such; they cannot be deduced from the laws of a psychology based upon the analysis of the individual subject." Lévy-Bruhl calls them "collective representations."

Now the element of participation and sympathy, of kinship between society and nature, is not the entire story. It is complemented by a lurking sense of nature's otherness, strangeness, and an ever possible hostility. Man is not only immersed in, he also confronts his world. The typically primitive attitude toward nature is a sort of tension between naïve trust and watchfulness. The former gives men a feeling of membership, of at-homeness, of being comfortably rooted in Mother Earth. The security of the cave, of the family, and subconsciously perhaps of the womb, supplies the primordial ground-plan of human living. Familiar localities, persons, objects, and events confirm the basic sense of belonging; as do the patterned festivities of seasonal and tribal occurrence. But the familiar is not the whole of life, and to bask in it exclusively is to approach the condition of vegetable. Man encounters also, and develops a readiness to encounter, the strange; and this readiness in turn has a double aspect. For the strange can alarm and it can fascinate; it is likely to do both at once, although in different degrees; and the two emotions in combination—terror subdued by wonder—produce awe. Where the effect is more intriguing than frightening, men see fetishes in pebbles, spirits in rocks and rivers, totem-brothers in beasts, and gods in the sun and mountaintops. Where the note of alarm predominates, and where it is not definite enough to arouse the self-preservative instincts by suggesting particular measures of defense—as in the unguessable menace of hurricane and jungle fire, in black night and bottomless pool, in the tiger's sinewy power and the snake's beady stare—men fall into a primal terror of the Wholly Other, of the sheer ruthless mystery of things. The intensity of awe that arises from the simultaneous operation of these two contrary attitudes toward nature's otherness is a fertile breeding-ground of both religion and art.

An instructive instance, if properly understood, is found in the Cro-Magnon peoples who somehow dispossessed the ape-like Neanderthal men in Europe, roughly perhaps some twenty or fifteen thousand years before the Christian era. The Neanderthal savages had reached the ceremonial stage of burying stone weapons with the dead and painting corpses and grave-slabs with red ochre. But their caves appear to have been used only for shelter. Their Cro-Magnon successors, especially in the Aurignacian period, used the caves not only for domestic but also for ceremonial purposes, as the extensive remains of wall-paintings and insignia left in France and Spain bear witness. According to Frazer's theory we would have to suppose that the wall-paintings had originally served a magical intent, and that any purely decorative or purely ceremonial properties therefore represented a later development. Certain particular wall-figures, to be sure, such as the well-known bison pierced with arrows in the cave at Niaux, give strong though limited support to the magical hypothesis. But does magic sufficiently account for the most characteristic types of drawing in the Aurignacian caves?

In *The Gate of Horn*, a recent study of the religious conceptions of the European stone age as suggested by its cave records, Gertrude Rachel Levy gives attention to the problem.[8] She acknowledges that magic has had a large influence; not only paintings of arrow-pierced bison and sculptures of exaggeratedly pregnant females show magical intent, but even the ground-plans drawn on the cave walls at Niaux, La Pileta, La Pariega, and elsewhere she thinks may have served as magical entry permits rather than as mere guides to the actual route. Magical intent does not, on the other hand, explain the remarkable artistry of many of the paintings—the representation of great strength and force in the bison's body together with exquisite grace in the preternaturally thin legs. Dr. Levy concludes that what Aurignacian man wanted even more than magical effects was a condition of reciprocity with living nature, "a participation in the splendor of the beasts which was of the nature of religion itself, and so required this elaborate separation from normal activities." Why did the Aurignacian artist contrive his drawings with such exactitude that the brown bear is still distinguishable from the cave bear and that three distinct breeds of horses can be recognized? She suggests that exactitude may have been desired for the sake of closer attunement with the objects; for to the mythopoeic vision, then as now, there is more of reality in what is more concrete. Consequently, "the perfected forms which flowered in the pitch-dark solitudes were types by which ritual called up the species." And when a drawing is quite explicitly magical, like the one in the cave of Les Trois Frères of two hybrid beasts being commanded by a masked horned magician, she characterizes it as "over-ripe"—a composition in which "the integrity of the animal idea is broken by the intrusion of magic into the domain of religious art."

A further interesting question is raised by the practice of utilizing natural formations of rock and stalagmite deposit, as in the ribs and legs of the horse at Font-de-Gaume and of some of the bison at Altamira, and in the stag's horns affixed to a natural skull-shaped depression at Niaux. Was such practice a mere clever contrivance, a utilization of necessity by the craftsman, analogous to Orozco's ingenuity, when creating the Baker Library Murals at Dartmouth College, in fitting his pattern gracefully around the radiators and his darkest pigments over discolorations of the plaster? But Orozco, like every genuine artist, did more than merely yield to necessity; he turned necessity to effectively expressive purposes, so that the iron gratings of the radiators seem—after repeated acquaintance, at least—to be a part of the total New World pageant, a part of the caustic metallic commentary which the artist is making on the conquest of America. In much the same way that Orozco could enter into such intuitive sympathy with his medium as to see unrealized expressive possibilities in radiators and blotches, so the Aurignacian artist must have felt toward the fissures and depressions and stalagmite protuberances on the wall-surface of the cave. Unlike Orozco he was not obliged to accept them: there was plenty of bare wall-space to utilize if he had preferred. Gertrude Levy (whose area of survey does not include Orozco) concludes that the practice was considerably more than a matter of utilization, that the cave was "a repository of mystic influence," in which nature's markings on the rock appeared as indications of animal souls dwelling there.

May we not see, then, in those early artistic completions of what nature had barely hinted at, a record of the stage at which the human vision was passing from animatism to animism—from a sense of undefined mana-presence to an articulate, figured belief in definite animal souls; and even, at a crude level, in semi-divine presences? The impulse to give visible form to those souls by impressing their shapes upon durable rock would seem to illustrate what Cassirer has called the great revolution of early man—the first necessity of distinguishing the permanent from the transient. Such urgencies are more subtle, more deeply human, and more pregnant with unborn possibilities of meaning than the mere power-drive that impels men to the practice of magic.

These two types of ceremonial attitude toward nature, the assimilative and the confrontational, evolve, in religious context, into mysticism and theism respectively. God can be shadowed forth as that Infinite in which all things find their dwelling, and again as that Presence before whose majesty one's selfhood is at once humbled and reaffirmed. These are complementary aspects of a full-bodied religion. In art the two attitudes find expression in what Nietzsche has identified as the Dionysian and Apollinian components—a self-yielding to the magical power of the musical beat and an aesthetic perception of the balance and bright clarity of plastic form. In poetry the cadences allure us into kinaesthetic identification, while the patterns of image and metaphor confront us quasi-visually. Some such vitalizing tension, between the beholder's intuition of oneness with an object and his intuition of that object's otherness, is what distinguishes genuinely expressive thinking from mere fancy on the one hand and the stereotypes of everyday usage on the other.

## Divine Creation

> God made the cosmos. Why? It was a very odd thing to do.
> DOM JOHN CHAPMAN

Not all myths reveal so evident a relation between mythic content and ritualistic expression. Curiosity, pushed beyond the limits of what is empirically verifiable, moves with great speculative freedom, and among its products are aetiological speculations, attempts to explain how some existing institution or ritual originated. Such inventions will have a mythic character in so far as they reflect any fundamental structures of human experience.

Myths of original creation offer a unique group of examples, since the world is the uniquely absolute institution on which all others depend. Annual creation, the dominant theme of seasonal worship, is myth and ritual at once, since the ideas of propagation and new birth can be socially enacted. But when man tries to cast his imaginative questioning backwards to the absolute origin, the resultant myths are independent of ritual and must take their clues from familiar images of lesser and more par-

ticular creative acts that human experience affords. Three imagistic analogies for the idea of cosmic creation have been especially prominent in human history; I shall designate them the
Love Union, the Craftsman, and the King's Nod.

*The Love Union.* The Maori aborigines of New Zealand tell
that Father Sky and Mother Earth had lain in close-locked embrace for countless years, until in the course of time Mother
Earth became pregnant and bore him children—the brood of
men and animals. At first the offspring lived in darkness and
semi-suffocation between the embracing parents, until at length
they revolted, thrust Father Sky far up overhead and thereby
let in light and air and room for themselves to grow. But the
loving parents weep in endless sorrow over their separation—
the tears of Father Sky falling down again and again as rain
and those of Mother Earth mounting upward as mists.[9]

In this legend the primal Father and Mother appear to have
been distinct beings from the very first. Often, however, the
speculative imagination is unwilling to accept an original duality. There is a type of mind to which Unity seems a more final
explanation than Duality, and where this type of mind prevails,
the myth of an original love consummation presumes a mythic
prologue in which one of the partners emerged out of the other,
or in which the original being was androgynous and split up into
male and female. Aristophanes' quaint fantasy in Plato's *Symposium* transfers the myth of the Androgyne from the original to a
secondary order of creation, but it was probably suggested by
some older and more radically mythic tale.

In Hesiod's *Theogony* the account of origins is somewhat confused; but after the first stage in which wide-bosomed Earth,
snowy Olympus, dim Tartarus, and fair Eros come-to-be out of
Chaos in an unexplained manner, the story begins to fall into
the archetypal pattern of the Androgyne. For "Earth (*Gaia*) first
bare starry Sky (*Ouranos*), equal to herself, to cover her on

all sides, and to be a sure dwelling for the blessed gods for ever."[10] Having then brought forth the hills and the sea "without sweet union of love," she lay with Sky, and one after another she bore him sons and daughters. Earth, then, is both mother and wife to Father Sky: he begets by the same womb from which he emerged, so that the total creative process has a kind of androgynous unity.

A more abstract version of the Love Union is found in the Scandinavian poem *Völuspa*,[11] which describes the phantom-germ of the universe as having lain originally in *Ginnungagap*—the great Cup, or Abyss, or Womb—a region of night and mist (*Niflheim*). Into this world matrix a ray of cold light from the blue vault shot down and froze itself into the Cup. When a scorching wind at length dissolved the icy substance and cleared the mist, the streams of living waters gushed forth, creating a new male principle in the giant Ymir, and a new female principle in the cow Audhumla, from whose udder flowed four streams of milk, marking the four directions of space.

*The Craftsman.* A second analogy for the primal act of creation is *homo faber*, man the maker. Perhaps the universe did not come into existence by biological generation, perhaps a divine artist molded it. If so, it must be that the artist had to work with materials. If we deny this implication we are discarding the craftsman analogy, for an artist works by shaping a preëxistent material into a form, and in doing so he is limited to some degree by the nature of the material. The craftsman analogy thus has the advantage of absolving the Creator from the stain of the world's evil. We can suppose, if we will, that God did the best he could with the materials at hand. Thus Plato writes that the Divine Artificer, the *Demiourgos*, created the world by *persuading* Necessity—evidently with incomplete success.

In that oldest surviving epic of the Americas, the *Popul Vuh*, of the Quiché Mayan Indians of Guatemala, instead of a single divine Craftsman we find a Committee of gods experimentally trying to fashion a race of beings that will be able to honor them with proper worship. The author of the document was a native convert to Christianity, and an apparent mingling of Mayan and Christian ideas is suggested by the opening drama of creation:

> This is the account of how all was in suspense, all calm, in silence; all motionless, still, and the expanse of the sky was empty.
> This is the first account, the first narrative. There was neither man, nor animal, birds, fishes, crabs, trees, stones, caves, ravines, grasses, nor forests; there was only the sky.
> The surface of the earth had not yet appeared. There was only the calm sea and the great expanse of sky.[12]

In the midst of the silence "only the Creator, the Maker, Tepeu, Gucumatz, and the Forefathers were in the water surrounded with light." As a seeming afterthought it is declared that there existed "also the Heart of Heaven, which is the name of God and thus He is called." Tepeu and Gucumatz were great sages and thinkers. They came together in the darkness and united their words and thoughts. They planned the creation of earth and dawn, mountains and valleys, thickets and groves of cypress, perceiving too that in the end, when the dawn appeared, they would have to create man, as ruler of all the creation. As a seeming afterthought: "Thus it was arranged in the darkness and in the night by the Heart of Heaven who is called Huracan."

The second chapter tells how "the Creator, the Maker, and the Forefathers" (this being one of several ways of speaking of the primordial creative alliance) brought the various animals into existence, assigned them their respective homes, and commanded them to speak. But alas, the animals could only hiss or scream or cackle according to their several natures, they could not say the names of their Creators and Makers, hence could not properly adore them. "This is not well," said the Forefathers to each other, and they condemned the animals which were on earth to the fate that ever after they should be killed and eaten. Again the Forefathers deliberated: "Let us try again! Already dawn draws near. Let us make him who shall nourish and sustain us! What shall we do to be invoked, in order to be remembered on earth? We have already tried with our first creations, our first creatures; but we could not make them praise and venerate us. So then, let us try to make obedient, respectful beings who will nourish and sustain us." Thus they spoke. This time they made men's flesh out of mud. But unlike their august Hebraic Anatype they found mud to be poorly suited to the purpose: the resulting creature was limp and had no motive power, its face sagged and its sight was blurred. Although it spoke it had no mind. Presently it soaked away in the water. The Proto-Experimenters had to try again. On the next attempt they made creatures out of *tzité*-wood. The wooden figures looked like men, talked like men, and populated the surface of the earth; but "they did not have souls, nor minds, they had no thought of their Creator, their Maker, and they walked on all fours aimlessly." So the Heart of Heaven sent a great flood, by which the wooden figures were all annihilated.

After a digression into folk-tales concerning the exploits and adventures of Mayan culture-heroes, the narrative resumes the account of the faltering creation of man. Before the dawn appeared, before the sun and moon arose, man was made, with white and yellow maize thoughtfully provided for his nourishment. The first men were able to reason and speak, and as no limits had been set to their sight they knew all things at once. Although they were devout and offered prayers of thanks for the gift of existence, the gods were frightened at the prospect of such admirably endowed beings, and breathed a cloud over the mortals' eyes in order that they might see only a little way and not preen themselves on being divine. Somewhat later moreover, when the race of men had become populous, the gods deprived them of their original language, and gave to each geographic group a language of its own—presumably a further precaution against human cockiness.

At all events, so far as the matter of creation is concerned, there is doubtless a good deal to be said for the Mayan *mythos*. If man, with his conspicuous failings, could be understood as the product not of a single fiat by the Alone Omnipotent One, but of trial-and-error methods by a genially bungling group of Cosmic Powers who admittedly were not sure what the outcome was going to be, the most scandalous of Christian paradoxes would have found its solution.

*The King's Nod.* But neither the Conjugal nor the Craftsman analogy satisfies all worshipers as being sufficiently exalted to symbolize the primal act of Divine Creation. The one seems too much akin to purely natural process to reflect any credit on Deity as its real author; the other seems too effortful and incomplete. How else can the process of original creation be conceived? The classical answer in philosophical terms is given by Aristotle. God causes cosmic process (*kinesis*) not by propagating and not by operating, but simply and completely *through being loved*.[13] That is to say, God is not an Effecting (i.e., propelling) but a Final (i.e., telic) Cause. He does not push things into their changes of state, but draws them toward their highest perfection *simply by virtue of being what he is.* He is "that for the sake of which" in the most radical and purest sense; he thus causes process in all things without undergoing process himself in any respect. He is like, but transcendently more than, a wise father who sets an example for his child instead of continually prodding the child into action.

To most ancient peoples the Father archetype finds its highest mundane expression in the King. Now the more powerful a king, the less effort he has to make in order that his will shall be effective. The perfect king trains his ministers to be so alert to his hidden wishes that the merest nod or frown is a sufficient signal of command. At a nod from the Homeric Zeus a tremor ran through all the universe. The Hebrew Jahveh said, "Let there be light," and there was light. As a limiting ideal the Monarch would not even have to speak or nod; his will, even his implicit will, his being-what-he-is, produces the full effect.

Although the visual form is so different, the King's Nod has close archetypal affinity with the ancient symbol of the Wheel. The King who makes his will effective without utterance or gesture and the perfectly rotating Wheel with an immovable axis are both ideal conceptions; they employ our empirical acquaintance with kings and wheels to construct two different threshold symbols pointing to the idea of the Unmoved Mover. Aristotle's main argument for an Unmoved Mover, as given in the *Metaphysics*, shows that the images are implicitly associated in his mind; for immediately after his declaration that God causes movement or process through being loved, he adds: "The primary kind of process (*kinesis*) is spatial movement, and the primary kind of spatial movement is circular; this, then, is the kind of process that the Divine Whatness directly produces." The pure unmoved Center of the Wheel is to the motion of the spokes and rim as the sheer *being* of God is to the activity of the entire universe.

## Dimensions of Religious Mythos

Running through all mythic experience, giving it character and importance, is the human awareness, however dim and problematical, of somehow standing in a relationship with a reality higher than one's individual self. The metaphor "higher" cannot be fully explicated, for it acquires different specific meanings according to the religious perspective in which it is used;

but it is likely to include connotations of better, more complete, more authoritative, and more enduring. Man's relation to this Something Higher, actual or sought, is what is chiefly and essentially meant by the word "religion."

As a means of ordering and characterizing the principal forms of religious relationship, considered as types of mythic pattern, I offer the schematic Table on the opposite page. The problem needs to be envisaged in terms of man's sense of his own and mankind's most essential deficiency; for it is this sense, together with his search for a viable solution, that gives dynamic and unique character to religion as distinguished from other sociological phenomena. In order to avoid the prejudicial connotations of such familiar words as "sin" and "guilt" I shall employ the neutral Greek word "*hamartia.*" Etymologically "hamartia" connotes "missing the mark," suggesting an archer whose arrow has flown wide of the target; and hence in philosophical context the word can refer to any essential respect in which a man's conduct of his life has erred.

It is easiest to begin with the help of spatial metaphor, thinking in terms of three spatial directions: upwards, downwards, inwards. The upward object of religious attention may be designated *ouranian* (from Greek *ouranos,* the enveloping sky), the downward *chthonic* (from *chthôn,* earth); and these words can also apply to the type of religious interest involved. The third type of religious search—the seeking of God, Brahman, Tao, Absolute Reality, through concentrated attention to one's ultimate inwardness—is the most philosophical of the three; it brings the seeker into confrontation with the relational problem of inner and outer, hence with the question of how reality is to be found and to be discriminated from appearance; it may therefore be designated *ontological.* In practice, however, the threefold spatial schema yields four main religious frames of reference; for the chthonic shows itself in two aspects, cor-

*Dimensions of Religious Mythos*

| Aspects | Typical symbols | Hamartia | Penalty | Solution |
|---|---|---|---|---|
| I. Chthonic: Mortuary | ghosts of the dead | breaking of taboo or tribal mores | vengeful ghosts | exorcism: "do ut abeas" |
| II. Ouranian | father sky, sun | hybris | nemesis | sacrifice, covenant: "do ut des" |
| III. Chthonic: vegetative | mother earth, tree, serpent | pollution | illness, blight | ritual washing; banishment |
| IV. Ontological, mystical | sphere, light | individuation | alienation, blindness | mystical union, new vision |

responding to the two main mythic functions of earth—as the mother of all life and as the recipient of the dead. While the two aspects are intricately related in seasonal worship, they tend to develop different groups of symbols and different ethical philosophies. The four resultant types of religious reference and attitude are here placed in what seems most generally to be the order of advancing maturity, and to each is attached the conception of hamartia, and of its consequences and cure, which is most typical of that religious perspective.

The conceptual simplicity of the schema is not matched by the complex variety of religious phenomena in history. The four types assume various disguises, combine and interpenetrate, and may occasionally lead to higher spiritual developments than the schematic account is capable of showing. Nevertheless I think that the schema, if not conceived too rigidly, can serve as a guiding hypothesis, perhaps throwing some light upon the anthropological components and semantic connotations of man's religious and ethical conceptions.

(1) The mortuary aspect taken by itself is not so much religious as proto-religious. Its emotional tone is determined predominantly by fear; it may occasionally rise to awe, but almost never to the essentially religious emotion of reverence. Its corresponding ethical conception is a respect for taboo, backed by a terror of breaking it. Its mythic symbols are likely to be such figures as Dis, lord of the dead, or Death itself personified, or his ministers, or Hermes conductor of souls to the nether world, or ghostly agents of retribution—either the angry ghosts of those who have suffered injury, such as that of Clytemnestra in the *Eumenides*, or generalized ghost-avengers represented in ancient Greece by the Furies, or Erinyes. Such ghostly antagonists are not easy to placate. Clytemnestra appears to have succeeded in winning the Furies over to her side by rituals of libation, but that is because they are in a vague way mother-archetypes, less

insistently concerned therefore with the murder of a husband. She has more difficulty in placating Agamemnon's individual ghost, as the opening of the *Choëphori* makes evident. Orestes when plagued by the Furies has no chance at all, until at the end he is saved by Athena's divine act of grace.

(2) The ouranian religion, and consequently the ouranian ethic, is an affair of bright space and clear boundaries. Homer tells that when Zeus, Poseidon and Dis drew lots for the world and Zeus won the sky, Poseidon the sea, and Dis the underworld, they swore by the River Styx, the most dreadful of oaths, to respect the fall of chance and *not overstep the boundary*. The broad earth, inhabited by men, remained a common territory, unassigned to one god more than another. Francis M. Cornford has remarked that this cosmic legend appears to reflect what must have been an earthly situation during the years when the Dorian invaders of Greece were consolidating their victory and settling down to the unaccustomed arts of agriculture. A nomadic people, which depends mainly on the luck of the hunt, for its food is likely to regard the food thus obtained as common property, to be distributed according to some accepted principle of rank or need. When such a people becomes stationary and begins to live by planting and reaping, the principle of universal sharing becomes unwieldy and encourages sloth. Boundaries must be set up, and as Hesiod's *Works and Days* records, a new ethical idea must now be insisted on: "Respect your neighbor's boundary!" or, more generally, "Do not overstep the boundary!"[14]

The topographical division on earth and the ouranian myth of the division of the cosmos combine to give great force to that most characteristic of Greek moral principles, the Golden Mean. For the injunction not to overstep the Boundary grows into the more general and humanistic principle of following the Middle Way—"Nothing too much!" "Do not overstep the boundary between courage and cowardice, nor yet the opposing boundary between courage and recklessness": such, in effect, is the intellectualized form which the principle assumes in the ethics of Aristotle. But meanwhile there is an application which has great importance in Greek epic and dramatic literature—the idea of respecting the boundary between man's estate and that of the Olympian immortals. Failure to do this, a wish to emulate the gods by being something more than man, whether in wealth or power or even (like Hippolytus) in virtue, is the hamartia of *hybris*, arrogance. The arrogant man errs by overstepping, yes, but in terms of another metaphorical figure he upsets the natural balance of things, which must then be restored. The divine judgment which tends to overtake such a man becomes half-personified, never wholly so, as Nemesis. The Erinyes, too, are operative in this connection—only secondarily as "Furies," primarily as restorers of the order of nature. Thus Heraclitus declares: "The sun will not overstep his measures [*metra*—i.e., the boundaries of his course]; if he does, the Erinyes, attendants of Justice, will hunt him out."[15]

(3) Vegetation religion can be better understood if we stop to reflect upon the nature of good and evil from a radically organic standpoint. Good is life, vitality, propagation, health; evil is death, impotence, disease. Of these several terms *health* and *disease* are the most important and most comprehensive. Death is but an interim evil; it occurs periodically, but there is the assurance of new life ever springing up to take its place. The normal cycle of life and death is a healthy cycle, and the purpose of the major seasonal festivals was at least as much to celebrate joyfully the turning wheel of great creative Nature as to achieve magical effects. Disease and blight, however, interrupt the cycle; they are the real destroyers; and health is the good most highly to be prized.

What is health? This is a question upon which all schools of medicine in ancient Greece seem to have been essentially agreed. Health is a right proportion of parts and functions in an organism, disease is a corresponding disproportion. Medical schools differed, to be sure, in their identification of the elements to be ordered. But whether the parts were conceived in terms of opposites (as by the Pythagoreans), in terms of the four natural substances: fire, air, water, and earth (as by the doctors of that "ancient medicine" which Hippocrates criticizes), or in terms of "bodily juices" (as by Hippocrates himself), the opinion was general that health consisted in a right relationship among the organic parts, enabling the organism to function well as a whole, and that disease was the lack or loss of such right relationship. How, when lost, was a right relationship to be restored? The logic seemed clear. The simplest way of changing a disproportion into a true proportion is by ridding the body of the superfluous elements, thereby allowing (as the Empedocleans put it) the elements that remain to unite in health-giving love. If the unwanted element was such that it could be cut away, then cautery was indicated; if not—if it was, for instance, an excess of heat as in fever, or an excess of cold as in rheum—then the cure was to be found in purging (*katharsis* or *katharmos*) or, symbolically, in ceremonial ablution (expressed by the same pair of Greek words).

But in the actual manifestations of chthonic-vegetative religion in Greece the ideal was considerably more dynamic than the medical and philosophical concept of health would suggest. The ideal called for a harmony between man and the creative forces of nature, symbolized by the Dionysian dance, by the spirits of grainstalk and vine, the half-animal creatures who roam the woods and fields, and the mysterious figure of the seasonal god himself, who is slain and reborn annually.

> The whole earth bursts into joyous dance
> when Bromios leads his troop toward the hills,
> where the bands of women await him, drawn
> from loom and shuttle in reverent ecstasy.[16]

Murder, from the standpoint here entertained, does violence to the natural order of things. It destroys the right relationship in the social organism. Symbolically, therefore, the murderer is diseased. When his victim is someone in his own family, the disease is the more virulent, for the family is even more compactly an organism than the *polis*. When his method of murder is as unnatural as that of Atreus in serving up Thyestes' children to him baked for dinner, the disease is again the more virulent. The soul of the perpetrator is rendered vulnerable to hostile influences, such as to the curse which Thyestes invoked against Atreus. Moral disease, like physical, spreads by contagion, and the vulnerability was shared therefore by all Atreus' descendants.

Symbolically, murder is a spilling of the victim's blood upon the ground. Since the act is a diseased act, the flowing blood receives the contagion and transmits it to the soil where it is spilt.

> When blood is shed and drunk by Mother Earth
> The vengeful gore congeals immoveable.[17]

The disease spreads through the land, sometimes (as in *Oedipus Tyrannus*) causing a general blight, and eventually its evil effects return upon the murderer or his descendants. Orestes' pursuit by the Furies after he has spilt his mother's blood can also be understood in this manner, and Aeschylus offers imagistic clues that would have enabled the more alert and responsive members of the audience in the City Dionysia to carry an overtone of such interpretation in their minds. The punishment of the murderer is not merely an act of retribution; it is also, from the present standpoint, a means and a symbol of saving the city.

Ablution, which may be effective in removing the stain of ordinary murders, will not serve for the extraordinary ones.

> Though stream on stream should pour
> Their swift-cleansing waters on the hand of blood,
> The old stain shall not be washed away.

Sometimes cautery is the only answer, and as a diseased limb must be lopped off from the parent stem to prevent further contamination, so a murderer must be sent into exile. Such is the situation at the end of *Oedipus Tyrannus*. Orestes, too, suffers a self-imposed exile; and in the third play of the trilogy it turns out that his crime of matricide has contaminated him to the very bone, so that even Apollo, god of healing, is helpless against it. The solution has to await the bestowal of Athena's divine aid.

(4) Ontological religion, so far as it is practiced rather than theorized, tends to become (in a stricter sense than is sometimes attached to the word) mystical. Serious mysticism proceeds from the cardinal faith that individuation is error and illusion, and that therefore we can discover the truth of reality only by entering into union with it.[18] Divinity is to be approached not by confrontation, but by total yielding and assimilation.

But while union through total surrender of one's individuality is the only way to adequate knowledge, the blessedness to come (as a state both of being and of knowing) may be foreshadowed by symbols. An ancient Eleusinian confessional ran thus: "I have fasted, I have drunk the barley drink, I have taken the things from the sacred chest, and having tasted thereof I have put them into the basket and then from the basket back into the chest again."[19] Ceremonial fasting by the worshiper was in mimetic correspondence with the fasting of the grain goddess Demeter when, sorrowing for the abduction of her daughter

Persephone, she tasted neither meat nor drink. Then to partake of the sacred barley drink and of "the things in the sacred chest" (the sacred barley cakes) was a sacrament of communion with the Goddess, whereby the worshiper received an incorporation of the divine substance into himself, symbolized by the assimilation of the sacred food into the body. And just as the sacramental partaking of barley symbolized mystical union with Demeter and the forces of earth, so in neighboring cults the sacramental drinking of wine symbolized mystical union with Iacchos, and thus with earth forces by another route. In the syncretism of the Hellenistic age the symbols of mystical union provided by cakes (or bread, or wafer) and wine became conjoined and adopted into the sacraments of early Christianity.

As the symbolism of barley cakes and wine shows, mystical forms of religion are likely to have closer affinity with chthonic than with ouranian. This is natural, because a band of worshipers enters readily into the rhythms of the chthonic processes of birth, nourishment, and death, whereas the gods of the sky are reverenced from afar as austerely remote.

A more philosophical symbol of mystical religion is Light; and in different contexts the symbol is important not only for mystical-ontological but also for ouranian and chthonic religions. The Olympian gods are bathed in light; and it was the primal creation of the Hebraeo-Christian God. In chthonic perspective the natural succession of day and night provides the principal source from which the symbolism of light is derived. But it is a more philosophical symbol than any of the other symbols employed in chthonic or ouranian thinking, because of the natural and ready analogy between the action of physical light in enabling the eye to see objects and that of "spiritual light" which represents new "spiritual vision," which is to say new insight into truth. The idea of spiritual light vs. spiritual darkness is one of the hardiest of archetypes, for it expresses the most distinctively human of man's characteristics—the desire to know, to be "enlightened." In ancient Greek mystery cults the symbol was further strengthened because it was seen not only as representing new insight but also as heralding the restoration of Persephone after the end of dark winter and the consequent resumption of Demeter's activity and the restoration of life and growth. The passage from a dark chamber, where certain ordeals had to be endured, into a sacred hall of light, was a climactic part of the initiation ceremonies which neophytes to the Greek Mysteries were to undergo.

On the other hand, the symbol of the Sphere, or in flat terms the Circle, belongs more exclusively to the ontological perspective. It is the clearest and simplest symbol of perfection, and any deviation from the perfect shape represents the discord into which human affairs fall when individuals assert their competing individual wills. The symbols of Sphere and Light can jointly serve the ontological point of view, the one representing the perfection of harmony, the other representing the spiritual vision that enables one to see through the sham and frustration of finite concerns. As will be seen in Chapter Ten, the darkness-light imagery in the *Oresteia* is a powerful symbolic instrument for reinforcing the depth-meaning of that great cyclical drama.

## Myth and Belief

The semantic study of myth leads us to a reconsideration of that principle of expressive language which in Chapter Five was discussed as Variable Assertorial Weight and more specifically as Assertorial Lightness. For the question must be faced: Is a mythic statement affirmed quite so heavily as a common-sense statement or, at a later stage of cultural development, as a scientific statement? Reformulating the question in terms of belief: Is a mythic belief held with as much firmness and confidence as an ordinary empirical belief? Of course the differences of belief-attitude are indefinitely numerous, but for the purposes of brief clarity let us glance at certain easily contrasted forms of belief-attitude.

Consider the three statements, (A) "Athena sprang from the head of Zeus," (B) "Jesus was born of a virgin," and (C) "The earth is approximately spherical." Seven hundred years ago an orthodox Christian normally held B to be true, A and C to be false. Today most Christian fundamentalists hold B and C to be true, A to be false. The average contemporary naturalist holds C to be true but dismisses A and B as false. Here are three attitudes which despite their obvious points of difference are alike in one respect, namely that all three of them regard A, B, and C as equally propositional in character—which is to say, as carrying full assertorial weight. Regardless of whether a given one of the statements is believed or disbelieved, it is taken as something to be affirmed or denied with firm assurance that there is a right answer which *should* be the same for everybody.

The poeto-semanticist, on the other hand, confines firm belief to C alone. Only C is propositional, since it alone consists of definite concepts which under ideal conditions are universally sharable, and of an affirmed conceptual relation which under the same ideal conditions is universally verifiable. By contrast the poeto-semanticist regards A and B as mythic (not "mythical"!); for each of them invites belief within the more limited context of the ancient Greek mythic world and the Christian mythic world respectively. In the cases of A and B one's belief-attitude is organically related to the social and spiritual matrix (both adjectives are needed) which has given it birth, growth, and developing significance. This is to say that A and B are not propositional in the sense that C is propositional; they evince and invite varying degrees of assertorial lightness. Thus statements A and B are mythic in that each of them can be significant only within its appropriate mythic context, and within that context the statement will be marked by some degree of assertorial lightness and conceptual flexibility.

These are perhaps difficult ideas for readers newly introduced to them, and a further clarification of assertorial lightness is now in order. In the next chapter, which represents the last step in the present development of my poeto-semantic theory, I shall pursue the problem by reconsidering the idea of assertorial lightness in relation to expressive statement (of which poeto-statement is the most intensive sub-division), metagrammatical analysis, and the idea of poetic truth.

# 9

# Expressive Statement and Truth

A semantics of poetry must allow for the double fact that a poem does say something, does make some kind of statement or statements, and yet that it does not make statements in the same way, nor of quite the same kind, as steno-language does or aims to do. It is therefore reasonable that our examination of meanings in poetry should at length lead to an examination of poetic statement. For statement is not something other than meaning (surely no one would call some group of words a statement if it were altogether meaningless!) but is a special kind of meaning, a special articulation of meaning. The word "statement" signifies that kind of meaningful utterance (spoken or written, it does not matter) to which one can respond with a *yes* or *no*, however qualified, judging it as true or false or perhaps as dubious.

## On Poeto-statement

So far as steno-language is in question the difference between statement and non-statement can be made quite clear. As already pointed out in Chapter Five (pp. 92, f.), "a term merely *means* without having in itself any capacity for assertion, while a statement both means and potentially asserts." A statement such as "The dog has broken loose" is assertorial, whereas the single term "dog" is not. Of course a statement need not actually be employed assertorially. There are several ways in which it can enter into language without being affirmed or denied: it may be held up for contemplation ("What if the dog should have broken loose!") or put forward as a question, or it may be used like a term as part of some larger statement ("*If* the dog has broken loose, we had better search for him"); but the essential point is that the structural meaning of a statement is such that it *can* be affirmed or denied, whereas this possibility does not pertain to what is not a statement overtly or implicitly. Thus a statement is an assertorial type of meaning, and for practical purposes the sentences "It is a statement" and "It can be affirmed or denied" are interchangeable. Moreover, as was further said in that earlier chapter, a statement when logically perfected is a *proposition*. Now poetic language, which does not contain propositions except incidentally, does allow of various statements and approximations to statements. Let us give the name of *poeto-statement* to any statement or quasi-statement that is found in a poem as a legitimate part of it—i.e., having its place there by virtue of, and as contributing to, the poetic activity. Our task in the present chapter is to investigate somewhat further the nature of the poeto-statement.

A poeto-statement should not be confused with what I. A. Richards has defined as a "pseudo-statement." Richards has set up a sharp dichotomy between "statement," which he identifies as "scientific statement, where truth is ultimately a matter of verification in the laboratory," and "pseudo-statement," by which he means a form of words that looks like a statement but whose acceptance or rejection is "entirely governed by its effects upon our feelings and attitudes." Such was the language he used in his relatively early book *Science and Poetry*,[1] but he later ceased to use the word "pseudo-statement" because he found many of his critics taking it to mean "false statement" and thus saddling him with the supposed view that poetry consists largely of statements that are false. Richards has subsequently disavowed the frequent misinterpretation of "pseudo-statement" as false statement, and defines it to be a string of words which in some non-poetic context might be a statement but which in the context of the poem does not function so. A pseudo-statement, according to Richards, is neither true nor false, for the question of truth in the scientifically accepted sense of the word does not arise. Whenever someone applies the words "true" and "truth" to the pseudo-statement he can only mean, by Richards' argument, that the pseudo-statement which is so characterized "suits and serves some attitude or links together attitudes which on other grounds are desirable."

The principal objection to Richards' theory, as I see it, is its unworkable over-simplification. So sharp a cleavage between what can and what cannot be affirmed or denied is inapplicable, or largely so, to the kind of language that constitutes poetic discourse. There are many linguistic possibilities between the fully logical statement, or proposition, and the utter non-statement. A first postulate of the poeto-statement is that it may have any degree of statemental character, ranging between the extremes of fully realized statement, or proposition, on the one hand, and mere pseudo-statement, or phatic collocation, on the other. In the language of logic we can say that the assertorial character of a poeto-statement can range anywhere between 1 and 0.

What makes the question especially difficult is that poeto-statements are by no means always overt, and to bring an implicit poeto-statement into the open is to strip it of its living connections and give it the bare look of a literal proposition. Concealment has semantic values of its own. Moreover, one must differentiate between the partial statements in a poem and the poem's total statement. These two distinctions—of overt vs. implicit and of component vs. total statement—create interesting problems of interpretation by the various ways in which they can be related. The partial statements of a poem can be open or concealed to various degrees; and they can be concealed in more than one sense—notably in that their meaning becomes only gradually apparent as the poem is studied, and also in that the meaning even when seen with maximum clarity resists translation into steno-linguistic terms. Other partial statements in a poem may be quite clear, sometimes misleadingly clear. The total statement, on the other hand, in any serious poem is almost sure to be largely problematic. For even if the poet chooses to formulate his purpose ( e.g., Milton's "to justify the ways of God to man") he never states more than a part or aspect of his total intent, which largely takes shape through the making of the poem itself; and thus his statement of purpose, whether it be made within or outside of the poem, serves in effect as another partial statement, one of the numerous contributing factors by which the full impact and total meaning are to be judged.

Let us take a simplest possible instance to begin with, a playful bit of rhymed nonsense which has the sole merit of setting the double distinction clearly before us:

> We're all in the dumps
> And diamonds are trumps;
> The kittens have gone to St. Paul's.
> The babies are bit,
> The moon's in a fit,
> And the houses are built without walls.[2]

Here are six lines, each of which makes what is syntactically a statement. Each statement, except possibly the first, is sheer fantasy; their crazy-quilt juxtaposition is evidence that the writer does not intend to assert them but merely to offer them for playful momentary contemplation. The assertorial weight of "The kittens have gone to St. Paul's" and "The moon's in a fit" is zero. Each seems to be a pure example of the Ricardian pseudo-statement. But although not firmly asserted each of the six component statements is in clear focus; we understand well enough what it is saying, for we are able to recognize that what it says is indubitably fantastic. Each single unit is clear-cut but carries no assertorial weight whatever.

Does the verse as a whole say anything? Is there a total statement? I should think there probably is. Some idea seems to be vaguely and lightly adumbrated, of which a rough paraphrase might be: "Everything has gone plumb crazy" or "Everything is shot to hell." The total statement is in soft focus, as contrasted with the clear focus of the component statements, but its assertorial weight is not, like theirs, zero. The component statements, which are pseudo-statements, do no more than offer ideas for momentary contemplation; their look of crisp assertion is illusory. What the total statement expresses is not so much an idea as a vague mood; but the mood is not without meaning, and the total statement makes some slight affirmation of the transient perspectival relevance of that meaning. The verse is entirely frivolous, to be sure; but poetic statement can comprehend moods of all kinds, and frivolity is among them. Even in more serious poeto-statement, as distinguished both from scientific discourse and from exhortation, there is a certain take-it-or-leave-it attitude, some limited degree of assertorial weight, of which frivolity is but an extreme form.

In a more significant example, such as Blake's poem beginning "O Rose, thou art sick!" such clear separation as was possible with nonsense verse would be fatally distortive, for there is an organic interplay between the component statements as they are set forth and the total statement which is powerfully but silently connoted by the poem as a whole. To follow Richards in calling Blake's opening line a pseudo-statement, on which the question of truth or falsity has no bearing whatsoever, is to do scant justice to the depth and seriousness, along with the indispensable concreteness, of Blake's metaphysics. Here, expressed through the image of the sick rose, is an implicit judgment about the sickness of the world. If you try a literal translation, such as "That rose is in poor health," the inadequacy is manifest. If you undertake a prose explication of the symbolism, you can hardly stop short of trying to expound Blake's entire philosophy. Such an exposition may perhaps stir fresh insights of its own, but it sidesteps the single direct task of facing up to the meaning of the utterance itself. No two critical expositions of Blake's philosophy are in total agreement of course; the differences, however, concern strategies of analysis, and do not preclude a substantial agreement on an exemplary line such as the one here in question. For the utterance, "O Rose, thou art sick!" appeals to our intellectual and emotive responsiveness at once; and as the two forms of response are not operating separately but are involved together in a single experiential fusion, so (metagrammatically considered) the declarative and exclamatory elements in the sentence are likewise inseparable, scarcely even distinguishable.

A more special problem is posed by the much discussed pair of lines that brings to a close Keats' *Ode to a Grecian Urn:*

> Beauty is truth, truth beauty,—that is all
> Ye know on earth, and all ye need to know.

Here the trio of statements contained in these two lines, or the larger statement embracing the three of them, seems to be specially set apart by reason both of its terminal position and of its speciously logical formulation. For these two reasons the final couplet has been taken by many readers as a virtual summary of the Ode's main purport, and as Keats' final stab at what he meant to say. But Keats said what he meant to say in the poem as a whole, not in an isolated two lines of it. No doubt these two lines come somewhat closer to epitomizing the poem's total statement than any of the other component statements do, but an epitome is an abstraction at best, and the meaning of the poem is concrete, declared in and through the plenitude of images and cadences, and in no other way.

Another thing to note is that Keats puts the couplet in quotation marks: the Grecian urn is their speaker. Momentarily, then, Keats is a dramatist; he is letting his protagonist—the urn—speak for itself. The statement that beauty and truth are identical will not hold up under logical scrutiny; still less will the double statement that follows it. But taken as a half-declarative half-exclamatory utterance which the urn might be imagined to make, the disputed statements seem apt enough. Their truth is a truth in context. And so when Coleridge speaks of "the willing suspension of disbelief" as prerequisite to the proper reading of poetry, he is saying, in effect, that we should be willing to take up residence lightly in whatever poetic situation is offered—willing to accept the partial truth of the insights which are crystallized by a given poetic mood without insisting that their truth must extend unreservedly into all other moods and contexts.

As a last and somewhat different example of assertorial lightness in poetry consider such a passage as this one from Eliot's *Ash Wednesday:*

> Redeem
> The unread vision in the higher dream
> While jewelled unicorns draw by the gilded hearse.

In his Dante essay Eliot says of the pageantry of the *Paradiso* that it "belongs to the world of what I call the *high dream,* and the modern world seems capable only of the *low dream.*" We dream whether we like it or not, and all knowledge, whether in poetry or out of it, involves suspension of disbelief. In our low dreams, our everyday states of consciousness, such suspension takes the form of simple credulity. To combat simple credulity by logical examination and appeal to public evidence may be an act of intellectual virtue, but we do not thereby leave off dreaming; we are merely credulous on a new level of sophistication, credulously ready to accept sophistication as truth. In the low dream we wear a mask without realizing it, in the high dream we put on a mask with stylized grace. The virtue of a poem consists in expressing, promoting, and communicating some phase of the high dream.

## Analysis of Assertorial Lightness

In Chapter Five (pages 92-96) a preliminary account was given of assertorial lightness, as one of the variable possibilities which expressive language, and more especially poetic language, could make use of. In every discourse we employ light statement to different degrees much of the time; and if someone in irritation were to cry, "I wish you'd go to hell!" no one would take him to intend the remark with anything like full assertorial weight. It has the same grammatical structure as "I wish you'd go to the post office"; metagrammatically, however, it is evident that the two remarks are intended in wholly different ways. Mr. Richards would dispose of the matter neatly by calling the former remark a pseudo-statement; and to be sure in this case his interpretative strategy works well enough, for it is evident that the explosive remark "suits and serves some attitude" on the part of the speaker. It is in the intermediate cases that difficulties arise. Suppose, for example, one says to a persistent bore, "I wish you'd get lost." This third remark seems to have neither the firm assertional solidity of the second nor the total assertorial vacuity of the first. Human speech is full of such border-instances, and they are of many qualities and degrees. My postulate, as formulated in Chapter Five as the sixth potential characteristic of expressive language, is that in poeto-statements there are indefinitely many degrees of assertorial weight, ranging between the full heaviness of the literal statement, which is to say the proposition, and the utter lightness of the pseudo-statement and in general of non-referential discourse. We have now to investigate the nature of assertorial weight and the factors that determine its variations.

Our approach is to be metagrammatical. That is to say, although widespread grammatical conventions may offer clues, we do not take them as final, but seek to discover the intelligible forms and relations of which they are imperfect copies.

Let us define a sentence, broadly, as a group of words representing some unified meaning-and-attitude, and let us consider what kinds of sentences there are. Grammarians have handed down a well-known classification of sentences comprising four types: declarative, interrogative, imperative, and exclamatory. Metagrammatically considered how are these four types related? Immediately we see that interrogative and declarative form a pair, since a question invites an answer, and conversely a declarative statement of any significance can be regarded as a reply to some real though perhaps unspoken question. The exclamatory, by contrast, is self-sufficient; it can stand by itself without requiring any further sentence to complete it.

What of the remaining type, the imperative? In the first place the concept must be broadened to include not only command but also exhortation of whatever degree of force or weakness. Probably the best word we can find to signify whatever sentences are included within this range is "hortatory." All forms of hortation have something in common, and what it is can be seen in the kind of response they are designed to elicit. Whereas an interrogative sentence is designed to elicit a cognitive response, which normally falls into declarative sentence form, a hortatory sentence is designed to elicit a response in terms of doing or agreeing to do. In Aristotle's terms the former situation is *theorêtikos*, or cognitive in the broadest sense, while the latter is *praktikos*, or practical in the broadest sense; the former is concerned with what *is*, the latter is concerned with what *to do*. In the former type of situation a question, if successful, elicits a declarative reply; in the latter type a question, if successful, elicits an acquiescence. The proviso, "if successful," is needed; for of course in actuality not every question gets a reply, and not every command or exhortation gets an acquiescence. But conceptually there are the two distinct pairs. Summarily therefore we may conclude: asking and declaring are semantically paired, commanding-exhorting and acquiescing are semantically paired, while exclaiming needs no mate but is complete in itself. These, then, are the five sentential functions: exclamation, interrogation, declaration, hortation, and acquiescence.

But there is a difficulty. If acquiescence is a semantic function on a par with the four others, why (it may be asked) have grammarians taken no account of it? The answer is that although the acquiescent function enters into a great deal of language *as a semantic component*, there are not many verbal expressions which stand out as having a predominantly acquiescent character and therefore it has not seemed worth-while, from the grammarians' standpoint, to think of them as forming a separate class. A few locutions, such as "All right," "O.K.," etc. serve most of our needs in communicating an acquiescent attitude. Usually it is in the commands that the discriminations of meaning are made explicit—"Go!" "Come!" "Hurry!" "Listen!" etc.—while the yielding in each case can be expressed by a single acquiescent expression or even by a gesture. That is to say, when one acquiescent expression stands alone there is often little or nothing to differentiate it from other acquiescent expressions; the differentiation is furnished by the context.

Nevertheless, even isolated acquiescent expressions may be semantically differentiated from one another to some degree, although not so determinately as in the other types of sentence. There are differences of acquiescent tone, most marked perhaps as between secular and sacred modes of envisagement. The difference between "O.K., Joe!" and "Thy will be done!" is more than a matter of linguistic convention. Where the latter phrase is employed honestly and meaningfully its tone is reverent, and to speak with reverence is to ascribe some character of holiness to the object addressed. No such ascription is involved in a flippant or perfunctory or utilitarian colloquialism like "O.K."

The principal difference of acquiescent tone, then, is found in the demarcation between sacred and secular. The Hebrew word *hineni*, usually translated "Here am I," is a Biblical expression of acquiescent reverence, addressed most frequently by man to God. Abraham, addressed twice by God—once to command the slaying of Isaac, and again to remit the command —replies both times *"Hineni"(Gen.* 22:1,11). The boy Samuel hearing God's voice in the temple and mistaking it for Eli's, runs to the priest three times saying *"Hineni,"* and finally when he knows himself to be addressed by the Lord he amplifies his acquiescence into the full sentence, "Speak, for thy servant heareth" (*I Sam.* 3:4-10). The Deutero-Isaiah teaches the comforting doctrine that God, too, may say *Hineni* to his devout worshiper:

> Then shalt thou call, and the Lord shall answer; thou shalt cry, and he shall say *Hineni*.
>
> (*Isaiah,* 58:9)

The word *Amen,* taken over unchanged from Hebrew into English, functions similarly in one of its several uses. Although when used at the end of a petitionary prayer it becomes little more than a devout equivalent of "Please!" yet its sturdier meaning, found frequently in the Bible, is "So be it," "So let it be!"

Now in expressive language, as distinguished from the conventions of steno-language, the five sentential functions tend to merge in various ways, and they are rarely if ever found in complete isolation; a given sentence can usually be found on examination to contain more than one of the functions. Sometimes one of them is sufficiently dominant to establish the sentence as of one type or another; but occasionally two or more functions are so nearly in balance, or let us say so thoroughly blended and interpenetrating, that we cannot be sure just how the sentence should be classified. A hybrid mixture of the exclamatory and interrogative functions is recognized in Spanish by the allowability of using an inverted exclamation mark at the beginning of a sentence and a question mark at the end: e.g., "¡Después?" (combining "Well, then!" and "What, then?"). In English we would have to indicate the secondary function either by tone of voice or twist of phrase. Rubén Darío's sentence, "¡Conque aquel andariego había llegado tan lejos?" might be rendered, "So the wanderer had got as far as that, had he?"[3]

Observe the different shades of meaning-tone in the following sentences, caused by the different degrees to which the interrogative and exclamatory functions are emphasized:

> A. Have you hurt yourself?
> B. Good God, are you hurt?!
> C. Good God, you're hurt!

Sentence A, if uttered in a neutral tone of voice, might be taken simply as a request for information. Or less than that, it might be a phatic way of disposing of the situation ("This is what I am expected to say, so let's get it over with!"). But assuming it to be a real question, its sentential function predominantly interrogative, one could plausibly argue that there are faint traces of each of the other four functions as well: of the imperative-hortatory, insofar as the speaker demands or invites an answer; of the declarative, insofar as he states by implication that he has received enough evidence to justify his question (a question which he would not have asked if there had been no ground whatever for it); of the acquiescent, insofar as his words represent a yielding up of sympathetic attention to the other person's predicament; and of the exclamatory, so far as the speaker's tone of voice may indicate an implicit attitude of shocked or dismayed beholding. Sentence C makes the shocked beholding explicit; it is predominantly exclamatory, although an analogous set of qualifications would have to be made. Sentence B, on the other hand, represents a more or less equal blend of the two functions. Here a conservative grammarian might try to preserve the grammatical amenities by breaking the sentence into two parts and labeling "Good God!" an exclamation and "Are you hurt?" a question. From a semantic standpoint, however, such *ex post facto* maneuvering conceals the real unity of the utterance, whose purport is not first to invoke the Deity and then as a distinct act of thought to pose a question, but to engage in one unified semantic act which is question and exclamation in one. The sentence is virtually the same whether we write it, "Good God, are you hurt?" or "Good God, are you hurt!" or "Good God! are you hurt?" Whichever punctuative convention is chosen, the sentence would normally be taken to express a demand for information and an ejaculation of shocked concern all in one single mental thrust.

Another prominent borderland type of sentence is that which combines the exclamatory and declarative functions. Margaret Schlauch, whose philological writings have done much to liberalize contemporary grammatical theory, uses the term "presentative sentence" for a phrasal locution which, although it lacks a subject and predicate, strikes us as being virtually a complete and self-contained statement.[4] She offers an example from contemporary narrative prose:

> He entered the room quietly. A moment of silence. "Surprise," he said.

No particular verb is understood, and yet we may vaguely feel something to be stated as well as exclaimed. Such presentative sentences, she insists, "cannot be classified according to traditional doctrines about subjects and predicates."

The French words *voilà* and *voici* offer corroborative evidence. "*Me voici*" is usually translated "Here I am!" and may be regarded as mainly declarative (e.g., when spoken in answer to the question, "Where are you?") or as mainly exclamatory, according to context. In a good many cases the French idiom seems to hold the two functions in fairly even balance. In older French, however, the sentential functions were combined differently. Older forms of the phrase "*me voici*" combined the exclamatory and imperative functions instead of the exclamatory and declarative; while the declarative element found expression in the phrase, "*Es mi*." The *voi-* of *voici* still retained much of its original character as an imperative of the verb "to see." When Ronsard writes, "*Approchez, voy me-cy,*" it would seem that the imperative element is still present to some degree, although either or both of the other two elements may be detected also.[5]

The fusion of these same three elements—the declarative, imperative, and exclamatory—is found again in Jesus' words to Mary from the Cross. It is told in the Gospel according to St. John (19:26) that when Jesus looked down and saw his mother and his favorite disciple standing side by side he said: "Woman, behold thy son." These are the familiar words of the King James Version; they are inaccurate, however, because in the Greek text, after the imperative of the word "see," the word for "son" follows in the nominative case. The use of the nominative indicates an element of exclamation in the sentence, and separates the verb from the noun, so that Jesus is represented as saying more nearly: "Look, your son!" St. Jerome in his Latin Vulgate version went so far as to throw the main emphasis upon the exclamatory element by translating: *"Mulier, ecce filius tuus."* Then rather oddly, two recent English translators, a Protestant and a Catholic, Dr. Moffatt using the Greek text as his primary source and Mgr. Knox the Vulgate, both stress the lurking declarative element: "Woman, there is your son" (Moffatt); "Woman, this is thy son" (Knox). Martin Luther scrupulously managed to make two of the elements explicit at once: *"Weib, siehe, das ist dein Sohn"*; but his very scrupulosity seems to have destroyed the exclamatory element almost entirely. The classical French translation, *"Mère, voici ton fils,"* would appear, in view of what was said in the last paragraph, to keep some flavor of the original Greek imperative meaning. Probably none of it survives for the modern French reader, however, to whom the French idiom has lost its connotation of command; and when Louis Segond made a new French version in 1880, his *"Femme, voilà ton fils,"* was no doubt written with the Latin *ecce* in mind and the somewhat imperative flavor of the Greek sentence forgotten.

The foregoing analysis provides a better understanding, I hope, of that character of expressive discourse which I introduced in Chapter Five under the name of *assertorial lightness.* A statement, as I conceive the matter, is *the declarative element in a semantic situation;* and only when a declarative element is present can there be significant assent. But we are prone to think of the declarative function crudely, as something you can turn completely on and off, as operating either in full force or not at all. This conception may be a useful fiction in technical thinking, but at best it represents a limiting case which I do not believe is ever quite attained in any real semantic situation into which a living person enters. An expressive statement tends to assert more lightly than a literal one (i.e., than a proposition) for the reason that it is never quite exclusively a statement, never quite purely declarative, but exercises declarative and other sentential functions in one fused togetherness.

In short, it is the full living situations, not the technical and abstract ones, that are of deepest concern to us; it is in and through them that a serious search for truth must be pursued. But how, in such situations, can we hope to find truth, if truth pertains to the declarative element, and if the declarative element is only a part, and sometimes a minor part, of the total meaning involved? The question is of utmost importance in several major fields. It concerns the very possibility of any religious, ethical, or metaphysical truth, as well as of a truth-function in art. In order to seek and be concerned with truth in these trans-literal fields we shall have to reëxamine, on a broader base than is usual, what truth and falsity essentially mean.

## Is There Poetic Truth?

The concept of a statement naturally raises the question of truth. For a statement, by definition, is something that can meaningfully be affirmed and denied; and if one affirms or denies seriously, of course he intends to do so with proper reference to truth and falsity: he means to affirm what is true and deny what is false. But what can "true" and "false" mean when predicated not of propositions but of poeto-statements?

If, as I have argued, a poeto-statement combines the five sentential factors—declarative, interrogative, hortatory, acquiescent, and exclamatory—it becomes clear on reflection that it is to the declarative element in a poeto-statement that questions of true and false must properly apply. This avowal does not mean, however, that the declarative can be taken separately and apart from the four other elements. All five are organically united into a unified meaningful whole, and if the declarative is pulled out to be examined separately, it thereby becomes treated as a proposition; and when the canons of propositional truth are applied to it, the isolated declarative element may have to be rejected as false, or (perhaps worse) accepted as true in a sense not intended by the poet and not indicated by the poem, or (more wisely in the circumstances) dismissed as a pseudo-statement, a form of words in which true and false do not apply. But the error springs from the initial abstraction.

If Keats' poeto-statement, "Beauty is truth, truth beauty," is ripped out of context and judged propositionally, surely the resultant proposition is quite unacceptable to anyone's critical intelligence. But within the context that Keats provides, in which it is the Grecian urn that speaks, and where the utterance draws its meaning, tone, and force from all that has been said about the urn in the earlier lines of the poem, any assent that a fit reader gives to it is both richer and lighter than the kind of assent or rejection that would be appropriate to a proposition. It is a light assent because the urn's statement is a light statement —a statement that is not exclusively declarative, but in which the declarative factor merges inseparably with the four others, especially, I would think, with the acquiescent and the exclamatory.

Still, one further question remains. Granted that true and false apply to the declarative aspect of a poeto-statement, what is their meaning within that aspect? What is there in common between the truth of a literal proposition and the truth, however qualified, that may be predicated of a poeto-statement? A connection can be found, I think, if we recognize the basic nature of what is being argued about whenever the abstract question of the nature of truth is discussed. When philosophers dispute whether the criterion of truth is to be sought in "correspondence with reality" or in "coherence with a more comprehensive body of significant experience," what is the point of their disagreement? Are they arguing merely about how the *word* "truth" is to be used? Surely there is more to the question than that. They are concerned about finding a method and a criterion. But toward what? The only intelligible reply is: a method and criterion for determining *to what statements we ought to assent.* Inevitably there is an intellectual "ought" in the situation.

For the sake of those tender-minded moderns who squirm when the word "ought" is uttered because they have come to regard it as connoting and threatening outside pressure, let us try another type of vocabulary—axiological instead of deontological. The True, the Good, the Beautiful—that ancient Platonic trio of ideal ends—do they not respectively involve submission of the mind to what seems cognitively truest and therefore intellectually best, submission of the will to what seems morally best, and submission of the sensuous and emotional responses to what seems best in the interplay of feelings and forms? The word "ought" need be no more than a shorthand summation of these three basic types of value-judgment in human experience: of what ought to be assented to cognitively, of what ought to be decided morally, and of what ought to be approved aesthetically. So bare a statement is at most a beginning; much discussion and levelling off will be required. But at least it enables us to maneuver ourselves into a position where we can see as not entirely meaningless the cognitive role of the poeto-statement, even though for reasons already discussed that role is bound to be somewhat blurred (in soft focus), ironic (never quite detachable from the interrogative), manic (ditto from the exclamatory), paradoxical, and inconclusive. Let us not deny or ignore these traits; they are part of the ambiguous delight of poetic statement. And they are useful in restraining a critic and poeto-analyst from the *hybris* of excessive confidence in his own method.

Consider a statement such as the following, which is excerpted from the *Mundaka-Upanishad:*

> This is the truth. As from a blazing fire there fly forth thousands of sparks, like unto fire in substance, so are the various beings brought forth from the Imperishable and they return thither also.[6]

In what sense, and on what grounds, can the opening claim of truth be upheld? I am not now asking whether or not the second sentence is actually true. What I am asking is: *If* that second sentence somehow expresses truth, as adherents of the Hindu philosophy believe it to do, in what sense does it do so? The form of the sentence is declarative, to be sure, and so the principal impact upon a reader is declarative. Some kind of statement is being made. But that is not all. To read the sentence with one's intellectual receptors alert is to be aware that not only the declarative but also the four other sentential factors are implicitly present also. Interrogative, in the mystery suggested by the term "the Imperishable" and by the ungraspable transformation of finite beings out of the Imperishable and into it. Hortatory, or admonitive, because (to borrow a phrase from St. Paul) the words "speak bindingly." Acquiescent, for they speak "prophetically" ("pro-" connoting "on behalf of") as purveyors of the Word from a higher source, a higher authority. And as in all writing that is deeply felt, the exclamatory factor is also present, as direct emotional response to the sheer wonder of the message.

The kind of sentential analysis that I have proposed here for a somewhat typical passage of Hindu religious literature can be attempted, *mutatis mutandis,* for any passage in poetry or imaginative prose where expressive statement is found. Such analysis is never a solution, to be sure, and it should not be pushed to such a degree or in such a manner as to spoil or belittle the direct impact of the poem. Wisely controlled, however, it may offer one conceptual clue for a fresh consideration of the related problems of irony, paradox, and the status of truth in poetry.

Since truth, as I have argued, is "that which ought, by one criterion or another, to be assented to," we can now see a little better the meaning of "poetic truth." A poetic utterance invites our imaginative assent, which is to say our depth assent, to some degree or other and in some context or other. So far as we yield such assent joyfully and gain insight in so doing, there is a real and valid sense in which we can speak of "poetic truth." Even though a certain statement in a poem would be false if taken out of context (as is surely the case with Eliot's "jewelled unicorn" and Keats' "all ye need to know"), the relevant question is, How true is it within that context? And let us not delude ourselves with the hope that there are truths independent of any context whatever. When we think that, and act on it, we become blind to the contextual limitations that condition every judgment and every insight; we fall, so to speak, into a dream within a dream. The poet stakes out his context, the "world" of his poem, with his imagination audaciously alive and responsive; that is the route, if any, toward the regaining of Terrestrial Paradise. Most of us most of the time, with imaginations either stale or running riot, slip into some form of the lower dream, thereby constantly reënacting Adam's fall. The ground-bass of poetic truth is the truth, contextual but real, of man's possible redemption through the fullest imaginative response.

# 10

## Thematic Imagery in the *Oresteia*

There is probably no example of ancient literature on which the foregoing principles can be more suitably tested than the *Oresteia* of Aeschylus.[1] Not only does this single surviving Greek trilogy reveal to an extraordinary degree the interplay of the four types of poetic imagination, but its manipulation of language and imagery to make its points by indirection gives it an allusive richness that no other ancient drama can quite match. What the Choral Leader in the *Agamemnon* says of Clytemnestra's boast of wifely loyalty—"a specious tale to shrewd interpreters"—might apply more generally to the play and the trilogy themselves. Behind the surface-story a shrewd interpreter will discover potent depth-meanings. E. T. Owen does not overstate the case when he writes: "The subject of the *Oresteia* is the creation of a new moral order; Aeschylus depicts the vast chain of events which the death of Agamemnon started in heaven and earth, how it and its results shook the universe to its foundations and altered the spiritual history of the world; he presents the legend as a turning-point in the destinies of mankind."[2] Professor Owen's view is not novel, to be sure, but it is worth reëmphasizing. And the important thing, for an alert reader, is that the indications of this vast theme show forth in several ways at once: through the story, both as dramatically represented and as narrated, through the dark brooding reflections of the Choruses, and, most subtly and most richly of all, through the metaphoric and archetypal associations evoked by the imagery. It is the last aspect, the overtones of meaning which are thrown off by the main images and image-patterns of the play, that will be my subject in the present chapter.

We may begin, in fact, with the very speech to which the "shrewd interpreters" remark is a reply. Clytemnestra had previously foretold King Agamemnon's homecoming from the conquest of Troy, announced to her by the system of island fire-beacons connecting the mainlands of Troy and Argos. Her words had been met with suppressed doubts and suspicions. Now that the news has been confirmed by the Messenger's arrival, she triumphantly reminds the Chorus of Elders how right she was, and then proceeds to boast of her loyalty, her watchdog faithfulness, during her husband's ten-year absence.

> Take this message to my husband:
> that he come with all speed, beloved by his city,
> and may he find a wife within his house as loyal
> as on the day he left her, watchdog of the house,
> good to *him* but fierce to his enemies,
> and in all else as before,
> keeping her pledge throughout that length of time.
> I know no more of adulterous pleasure or scandal
> than I understand the art of dyeing bronze.
> (*Agam.*, 604-612)[3]

Most commentators have been aware of an ominous irony in the speech, and have identified at least some of its elements. But the full power and dark threat of Clytemnestra's words become evident only as we bring the various ironic and ambivalent elements into one focus of attention. "Beloved of his city" (*sotto voce:* but not by me!); "As loyal as when he left her" (but how loyal was that?); "Good to *him*" (the force of *ekeinos* must be rendered either by italics or by "that man"—and which one is meant, Agamemnon or Aegisthus?) The next two phrases, "In all else as before" and "Never having broken her pledge," repeat and reinforce the "loyal wife" ambiguity. Two subtler points of irony call for further analysis: the metal-dyeing and watchdog images. I shall take them as points of departure for the next two sections respectively.

### The Blood Bath

The dyeing of metal, in the usual meaning of the phrase, is a man's work, one of the arts subsidiary to preparing for war, and obviously outside a woman's range of competence. But the hidden meaning is the important one, which the reiteration of the *blood* theme makes sufficiently unmistakable to the audience. It would be wearisome to enumerate all the many references to blood in the *Agamemnon,* direct and oblique; the crimson thread runs through that play much as it does through *Macbeth.* I will confine my observations to some of the most trenchant instances. The most important of them, around which the others may be conceived to revolve, is presented not only in language but also as an iconic symbol upon the stage: the crimson or purple tapestry which Clytemnestra orders spread out for her returning husband to walk on, as a token of his victory. Colors were not classified along the same lines in ancient Greece as they are today. Purple and any of the darker shades of red were joined by a common name, inasmuch as the dye for them had its source in the *murex* or purple-fish (*porphyra*). The sight of the purple-crimson tapestry therefore carries two trains of thought at once: on the one hand it is a sacred color, reserved for certain religious ceremonies, and on which no mortal, not even a king, dare walk in the ordinary manner without committing *hybris;* while on the other it is an iconic symbol of blood and therefore carries some of the potency of blood—the blood in which Agamemnon is to be bathed. Agamemnon at first angrily rejects the over-zealous attentions of his wife (of whose faithlessness his manner suggests that he may have received some report) and twice describes the carpet-tapestry as *poikilos* (*Agam.* 923 and 936), which can mean *elaborately colored* but can also mean *artful, riddling, ambiguous.* At length he yields, although with open misgivings, praying that no god may cast baneful eyes upon his act, and there is deadly irony in his concluding remark, "Treading the crimson-purple I pass into my palace halls" (957).

While Agamemnon thus moves into his palace in the stylized manner of a sacrificial procession Clytemnestra speaks again in double meanings:

> There is the sea, and who shall drain it dry?
> It breeds in inexhaustible plenty
> the crimson ooze which men exchange for silver,
> the wherewithal for dyeing of our garments.
> In these matters, my lord, the gods have well endowed us,
> a royal house that knows no penury.
>
> (*Agam.*, 958-962)

The literal sense is plain enough: "Don't worry about the costliness of the carpet you trample on. There is abundance of crimson coloring matter in the sea, and we are rich enough to buy all we may want of it." But the sinister tone of the opening question puts us on guard. It appears, at one level of meaning, as a cynical echo of the Chorus' repeated plaint, "When will there be an end to all the blood-spilling?"—as an answer, too, appropriate to the dark chthonic powers with which Clytemnestra becomes increasingly allied, that there will never be an end to it, and thus as a denial of the redemptive theme which is central to the trilogy. The House of Atreus, burdened by its evil past and the power of a curse, surely "knows no penury" in the bloody dyeing of garments.

The more furtive meaning of the crimson ooze becomes explicit finally after the murder, when Clytemnestra comes forward to justify her deed before the Elders:

> Then he lay prostrate, coughing up his soul,
> and pouring forth his blood he sprinkled me
> with murky drizzle of the deadly dew;
> while I rejoiced no less than the sown field
> when in the God-given rain the cup
> gives birth to the ear of wheat.
>
> (*Agam.*, 1388-1392)

Clytemnestra here emerges briefly as the hierophant of some bloody sacrificial rite—even, indeed, of two rites merged into one. The image of the priestly sacrificer spattered with the victim's blood is probably derived from the *taurobolium*, the ritual slaughter of the bull-calf sacred to and representing Dionysus. The images of rain (the sperm of Zeus) dropping upon the sown field and of the sacred ear of wheat budding forth from the cup or sheath that enfolds it are probably derived from the mystery cult of the grain-goddess Demeter, which was centered at Aeschylus' birthplace Eleusis. Moreover, while the cup and the ear of wheat by their shapes carry a hint of feminine and masculine symbolism, the Greek word for "cup" (*kalyx*) stems from the verb *kalypto*, "hide," and thus sounds an undertone of religious mystery, as though we should say: "Out of the hidden place, out of the dark womb, is born the sacred bud." And although my botanical friends assure me that the description does not quite accurately apply to the birth of grain, it probably did, by symbolic association, to the mind of the Eleusinian worshiper; for the ear of corn or the sheaf of wheat (no one seems quite sure just what species of grain it was) served him as a symbol of life potency, and, in its deeper meaning, of spiritually restored life. The passage is thus one of concentrated irony, with Clytemnestra blasphemously perverting the religious meaning of the Eleusinian symbols by relating them to her private lust for evil vengeance.

## The Hounds on the Traces

Let us look now at an earlier image in the original quotation—Clytemnestra's boast of having been "watchdog of the house" (*Agam.* 607). The Greek word *kyôn* means simply "dog" or "bitch," its genders not being distinguished; but the added phrase "good to him but fierce to his enemies" leaves no doubt that a watchdog here is meant. The Greek word has, however, three other interwoven meanings.

There is the pejorative feminine sense of the word, as in our slang use of "bitch." When Helen, in the *Iliad*, walks with King Priam along the walls of Troy and is stirred by the old man's goodness to feel compunction at the slaughter which her adultery has caused, she reviles herself as a "bitch." In the *Agamemnon* the prophetess Cassandra hurls the epithet against Clytemnestra with a bit of descriptive elaboration:

> Little does he know what that foul bitch,
> with ears laid back and panting tongue,
> will bring to pass with vicious snap
> of treacherous destruction.
>                    (*Agam.*, 1228-1230)

Still another use of the word is to connote lowliness of condition, though without any ascription of blame. In this sense Electra complains to Orestes that after her father's death she was "kennel ed in her chamber like a dog" (*Choe.* 447); and partly in this sense the Watchman at the opening of the *Agamemnon* complains of having been "couched like a dog on the roof of the House of Atreus." The Watchman functions as a dog also in the first sense I have noted, since he is on the watch for the beacon signal to be flashed from Troy.

But most important of all in the *Oresteia,* and especially in the final play of it, is a fourth connotation of "dog": that of hunting dog or *hound on the scent.*[4] This meaning has more affinity with the first of the meanings enumerated (that of "watchdog") than with the second and third; but it calls for separate examination, not only because of its important symbolic role in the trilogy, but also because of its affinity, through the idea of avenging ghosts, with one of the main elements of Greek religious thought.

Although the greater use of hound-imagery occurs with reference to the Furies, who do not appear until the end of the second play, a preparation has been made in the *Agamemnon.* The Chorus of Elders, half in awe, half in compassion, describe Cassandra as "a hound on scent of blood" (*Agam.* 1093 f), and Cassandra afterward applies less explicitly the same metaphor to herself: "I track down the scent of ancient crimes" (*Agam.* 1184). A like image is applied by the Chorus of Elders to the Achaian warriors following the traces of Helen and Paris over the sea. "Huntsmen down the oarblades' fading footprint" is Richmond Lattimore's translation. Edith Hamilton puts it:

> And a host,
> shield-bearing huntsmen, followed hot,
> tracking the oar blades' unseen footprints.
> (*Agam.,* 694 f)

Both versions indicate the main metaphoric fusion involved, but neither one brings out the full force of κυναγοί. "Huntsmen" is the virtual meaning to be sure, but what the compounded Greek word connotes is *leaders of dogs,* and that connotation helps to build up the gathering momentum of the idea of hounds in pursuit.

The real significance of the hound imagery becomes evident at the end of the *Choëphori*. The Greeks tracking down the fleeing lovers and Cassandra prophetically tracking down the crimes of the palace have been preliminary to the main imagistic movement. Orestes' vision of the Erinyes, the Furies, who begin to pursue him for his deed of matricide, involves both snake-imagery and hound-imagery. The one is pictorially specific, since the creatures have snakes for hair; the other is non-visually symbolic. Orestes cries out:

> What women are those—see!—Gorgon-like,
> dark-robed, their hanging hair entwined
> with many snakes? I dare not stay.
> (*Choe.*, 1048-1050)

And when the Chorus of Bondswomen, not sharing the vision, seek to comfort him, he cries again:

> These are no phantom terrors that I see.
> Full plain they are my mother's hounds of vengeance.
> (*Choe.*, 1053 f)

And a moment later:

> You do not see them, but I see them.
> They drive me on, and I can stay no more.
> (*Choe.*, 1061 f)

Let us avoid the oversimplification of assuming that because Orestes alone sees the Furies they are therefore unreal—that is to say, hallucinatory or "merely subjective." The line between subjective and objective is less rigidly drawn in a mythopoeic than in a technosophic culture, and Aeschylus' audience would, on the whole, have accepted the reality of his supernatural figures to whatever degree the dramatic context required. No special "suspension of disbelief" was needed—at least not to anything like the same degree as with a modern reader. The Greeks could be genially sceptical on occasion, but it was not until the age of the Sophists and the iconoclastic dramas of Euripides that scepticism toward the entire supernatural apparatus began to spread. Even then the beliefs of the large majority were comparatively untouched. And back when the *Oresteia* was first performed (458 B.C.) there was small disposition to doubt that the Furies were effectively and dangerously real. How, then, account for the bondswomen's failure to perceive them? The most natural answer, to the mind of a critical Athenian playgoer who might ask himself the question, was not that Orestes was deluded but that the bondswomen were obtuse.

Even Shakespeare's supernatural figures, it would appear, must often be interpreted in an analogous way. In the first act of *Hamlet* the murdered king's ghost is visible not only to Prince Hamlet but also to Horatio, Bernardo, and Marcellus; in the Queen's closet scene of Act III Hamlet sees it and Queen Gertrude does not. To the Elizabethans there was no inconsistency. Spirits that walk by night, although not grossly corporeal as our living bodies are, yet do affect the air, coagulating it into a vaporous semblance of their sometime physical selves. Such shadow figures, real enough to be sure, are yet not visible to everybody, but only to such as, for one reason or another, are more sensitively responsive to their subtle influence. The royal ghost no doubt stirred the air more cautiously on his second appearance than on his first, mindful of the still loved queen— "But, look, amazement on thy mother sits. / O, step between her and her fighting soul." Nor is it surprising that Hamlet was keyed up to a hyper-perceptiveness in the matter.

Similarly in Orestes' case it is plausible enough that the crime of matricide backed by the ancestral curse should have rendered him vulnerable to supernatural influences, and particularly to those atavisms of matriarchy and jealous defenders of maternal rights, the Erinyes. Their shadow-substance is real and dreadful to him, even though the bondswomen, whose psyches are pitched in a milder key, do not share the perception. Dramatically considered, Orestes' vision is not wholly private. Aeschylus has skillfully prepared for the Erinyes' appearance in the *Choëphori* by at least two occasions in the *Agamemnon* which testify to visionary experience: Cassandra's vision of fiends dancing on the roof of the palace and Clytemnestra's admission that in murdering her husband she was possessed by an evil spirit. But on those occasions the audience sees nothing out of the ordinary; the world of the *Agamemnon* transcends nature by allusion and imagery alone, not yet by direct action. In the *Choëphori* several related forces contribute to breaking through the walls of the natural world and quickening the sensibilities of actors and of audience to the impact of the ghostly: the murdered Agamemnon's unquiet spirit, the command of Apollo by which Orestes is driven, the mounting intensity of the lengthy ritual in which Orestes, Electra, and the bondswomen engage, and at length the power of maternal vengeance which Orestes' deed sets in motion. These forces act magnetically, so to speak, drawing the Erinyes from mythopoeic semi-obscurity into clear dramatic and theatrical focus. In the *Eumenides* their ontological emergence is complete, and they are projected into the action of the play no less realistically than the other characters.

In *The Eumenides* the Furies are first shown in sleep, and as Clytemnestra's impatient ghost prods them out of it their first utterances are a muttering and a whining sound, described in the stage directions by the words *mygmos* and *ôgmos* (*Eum.* 120-129). A student whom I asked what he took these sounds to mean replied, "Well, I guess that's the way Furies talk when they're off by themselves." Maybe it is unwise to go much beyond that modest conjecture; yet it is worth remarking that Diodorus Siculus uses the first word of the pair to describe sounds emitted by dogs. In view of the unmistakable hound imagery that follows I would guess that Aeschylus intended his two problematical words to suggest onomatopoeically the two familiar kinds of sound which dogs awaking from uneasy sleep might make: a muttering suppressed bark, something like *grfff!* and an incipient whine. Doubtless the ancient actors understood what was intended, and the simple directions *mygmos* and *ôgmos* were all the prompting that was required. Our English word *bow-wow* is surely no model of mimetic realism!

Evidently the Furies have been dreaming of pursuing their quarry, for after three such barkings and two such whinings they mutter half in sleep: "Seize him, seize, seize, seize! Don't lose track!" In contemptuous rejoinder the dead Clytemnestra brings the metaphor into the open: "You hunt your prey in a dream, giving tongue like a hound that never rests from his task" (*Eum.* 131 f). The verb which I have translated "give tongue," is regularly used of hounds, according to the lexicon. And later the Furies, who compose the Chorus of *The Eumenides*, take the comparison upon themselves:

> Ha! Here are the clearest traces of the man.
> Follow the trail which the silent witness indicates.
> For as the hound pursues the wounded fawn,
> so do I follow the smell of dripping blood.
>
> (*Eum.*, 245-248)

The imagery of the hunt is further elaborated by the many references to nets and snares, which were habitually employed by ancient Greek hunters. The primary reference of the net imagery is to the manner in which Clytemnestra murdered Agamemnon by entangling him in a crimson-purple robe:

> I so contrived the deed, I'll not deny,
> that he could not avert his doom nor flee.
> Inextricable like a net for fishes
> I cast an evil wealth of robe about him.
>
> (*Agam.*, 1380-1383)

The relevance of the symbol goes far beyond either the visual or functional similarity between a net and the encircling robe. Cassandra in a prophetic vision sees "some net of death" appear and then applies a synonymous word to Clytemnestra (*Agam.* 1115 f): she is a "snare of slaughter." Since beasts caught in a net were sometimes killed by a ceremony of stoning, the lines immediately following, wherein Cassandra invokes the Erinyes, are also germane to the thematic pattern:

> Now let the hellish company, ever insatiate,
> raise a long howl *(ulululu)* over the ritual stoning.
> (*Agam.*, 1117 f)

Two earlier occasions of the net imagery are noteworthy, as preparing the audience's visual imagination for what is to come, and as indicating the force with which the image persists in Aeschylus' own far-ranging mind. After Clytemnestra has announced the fall of Troy to the Elders, they at one point describe its destruction as entanglement in a net:

> O Zeus our Lord! O Night beloved,
> housekeeper of Heaven's bright jewels!
> You have cast on the Trojan towers an enclosing net,
> so that none, adults or children, could overleap
> the trap of capture and bondage.
> (*Agam.*, 355-360)

Later (*Agam.* 1381-1383) Clytemnestra combines the idea of a huntsman's net with that of a net to catch a haul of fish. Moreover there is her application of the image to her husband's own body, when she is hypocritically, but with an innuendo of deadly truth, protesting how she has worried about the rumors of Agamemnon's wounds:

> If he had as many wounds as rumor said,
> his limbs would have been perforated like a net.
> (*Agam.*, 866-868)

Variations of the net imagery continue to be developed in the *Choëphori*, as when, during the invocation of Agamemnon's ghost, Orestes cries, "They snared you in bronzeless fetters"— a metaphor within a metaphor, the bronzeless fetters meaning of course a net; and Electra echoes the idea in a more feminine sort of metaphor: "Ignobly trapped in cunning veils." But these instances are transitional. For in the *Eumenides* the net image is transferred from the slaying of Agamemnon to the Furies' pursuit of Orestes as its new focus of reference, and thus it serves as one of the major poetic devices by which Aeschylus molds the entire trilogy into an aesthetically satisfying unity.

## The Snake and the Omphalos

The action of the *Choëphori*, the middle tragedy of the *Oresteia*, hinges upon an ambiguity. Clytemnestra's supernatural solicitings, like Macbeth's, have brought her a dark prophecy which, though true in one sense, is false in another; and like Macbeth also, her failure to perceive its real import and to guard against the impending ill, leads to her doom. After murdering her royal husband Clytemnestra has been careful to placate the Furies regularly with solemn midnight offerings, and thus for a time has made good her boast on which the *Agamemnon* closed: "You and I (to Aegisthus), now masters of the house, henceforth shall govern it well." But at length, as the exiled Orestes secretly returns to his native land, she is visited by an eerie dream, which is announced by the Chorus of Bondswomen:

> Clear-piercing indeed, causing the hair to rise, was the Phoibos who divines for the house in dreams, when, breathing forth wrath, he caused a shriek from the inner chamber, and terror fell heavily about the women's quarters.
>
> (*Choe.*, 32-36)

The description (which I have translated as literally as possible) is ingeniously duosignative. To a Greek acquainted with the manner of divination at the shrine of Apollo at Delphi such epithets as *clear-piercing, hair-on-end, Phoibos,* and *inner chamber* would carry in addition to their literal meanings a coherent allusion to the sacred Delphic mysteries. On the literal level, *phoibos* can be translated "a spectral vision," the inner chamber is a synonym for the women's quarters, and the other terms are simply descriptive. But Phoibos is also an epithet of Apollo; "inner chamber" alludes to the Inner Sanctum, the Holy of Holies, where the clairvoyant priestess received the dread disclosures; "clear-piercing" alludes to the unearthly tones of the priestess speaking in a trance; and "hair-on-end" to the atmosphere of awe and supernatural terror which surrounded the seance. But these poetic innuendoes, although they enrich the essential drama, do not affect the overt plot. They are followed by an ambiguity which does so.

> Seers, wise in the lore of dreams,
> bound to speak true, do say
> the dead beneath the ground
> are angered sore, and wroth
> at them that slew them.
> (*Choe.,* 37-41)

Clytemnestra, taking the seers' reading of the drama in the likeliest sense, has sent Electra and the bondswomen with offerings to pour on Agamemnon's grave, in hope of placating his angry ghost. Later, however, in the *kommos* between Orestes and the Chorus of Bondswomen, the audience is apprised not only of the dream's content but of its real meaning.

> ORESTES: From what motive did she send the libations?
> Why did she show such tardy regard with so paltry an
> offering? . . . Tell me if you know, for I am eager to learn.

CHORUS: I know, my good youth, for I was there. Because her heart quaked at dreams and night-wandering
alarms the impious woman sent these libations.

OR.: And did you learn what the dream was, so that you
can describe it truly?

CHO.: She thought she gave birth to a serpent. We have
it on her own word.

OR.: And what followed? What is the story's upshot?

CHO.: She dressed the creature in swaddling clothes and
laid it to rest, as one would do to a child.

OR.: How did she nourish the new-born monster?

CHO.: She dreamt that she put it to her breast.

OR.: How could the teat have been unscathed by so
deadly a thing?

CHO.: Scathed it was, for the creature drew curds of
blood with the milk.

OR.: Ah, this is no empty apparition. It means a man.

(*Choe.*, 514-534)

In telling what the apparition signifies Orestes makes explicit
one of the major symbols of the play:

OR.: So then I pray to Earth and to my father's tomb,
that this dream may be a surety of my accomplishment. It
plainly fits my case, as I interpret it. For if the snake issued
forth from the same place as I had done, if it was wrapped
in infant swaddling bands and opened its mouth to the
same teat that once suckled me, if it mingled the kindly
milk with curd of blood so that the pain and fear of it made
her cry out,—why surely it follows that even as she nour-
ished that monster into life, so now she must die a violent
death. 'Tis I, made over into the serpent of her dream,
that shall murder her.

(*Choe.*, 540-550)

Clytemnestra, whatever her vices, did not lack intelligence,
but she was prevented from reading the dream aright since she
still believed Orestes to be dead. On the other hand it might be
remarked that Orestes was in exile, which to the ancients bore

an analogy to death, and the figure of a snake issuing from the womb and taking nourishment at the breast should not have been so very obscure to a people skilled at dream interpretation. However, we need not overstress a small implausibility which the plot required; and in any case Clytemnestra grasps the situation quickly enough when events begin to move and Aegisthus is slain.

> CLYT.: What is happening? Why are you filling the house with such outcries?
> SERVANT: It means that the dead are slaying the living.
> CLYT.: Oho! I take the meaning of your riddle. By craft we perish even as by craft we slew.
>
> (*Choe.*, 885-888)

And Clytemnestra completes her version of the symbolic pattern when on finding herself powerless to soften Orestes' purpose she cries:

> CLYT.: Ah me! so this is that serpent which I brought forth and nourished.
>
> (*Choe.*, 928)

In one set of connections, then, the serpent symbolizes Orestes. But in another it symbolizes Clytemnestra and the dark maternal forces that brood about her. When Orestes first sees the Furies, it is in the guise of wingless Gorgons with coils of writhing snakes, and they retain this character in the *Eumenides*, presumably up to the point of their persuasion and conversion by Athena. Aeschylus makes an effective passage to the feminine phase of serpent symbolism, by introducing it just after the Chorus has been praising Orestes for liberating the land of Argos by "deftly severing the heads of the serpents"— i.c., of Clytemnestra and Aegisthus. It is the same word—*drakon*—with which Orestes immediately after describes his horrid vision. The snake is not directly or primarily a feminine symbol—indeed, its phallic shape tends to give it an iconically masculine imputation wherever the aspect of sex is involved; but as the snake-form is a usual one for *chthonioi*, earth-spirits, to take, it enters into many associations with earth-mother symbolism—especially where, as at the end of the *Choëphori* and the beginning of the *Eumenides*, the mother-figure is also an embodiment of vengeance.

A deeper meaning of the snake-symbolism can be seen in its relation to Delphi. The action of the *Eumenides* opens in front of the temple of Apollo at Delphi, and it is there that the priestess, after praying to representative divinities of both sky and earth, discovers the snake-wreathed monsters. In the pre-classical age it would appear that the worship at Delphi was purely chthonic, and that a snake was the guardian of the ancient oracle-spirit of the place. The legend of Apollo killing the Delphic snake evidently reflects the actual event of an Apollonian cult succeeding the older chthonic one in that place. Chthonian religion had grown up most naturally there, from the physical character of the grotto, within which a deep cleft gave forth vaporous exhalations that seemed to arise from the nether world. At some early period the grotto had come to be conceived as the Omphalos, the world's navel, the umbilical cord by which the children of Mother Earth retain a pristine connection with the older world of vague dark forces which affect human life with blessing or bane. At the coming of Apollonian worship the earlier notion did not disappear; it merely merged, a bit incongruously at first, with the cult of the bright Olympian sun-god, who was also, especially at Delphi, the god of prophecy and healing.

Accordingly the Pythian Priestess' description of Orestes at the Omphalos seeking expiation for his crime acquires an added dimension of significance when it is remembered that Orestes stands as suppliant at the door to the womb of mundane creation.

> PRIESTESS: O horror to behold, horror even to say! . . .
> As I was passing into the laurelled shrine I saw at the
> Omphalos a man in suppliant posture, god-accursed for
> some deed of guilt, his hands all dripping with blood, hold-
> ing a sword newly unsheathed, and the topmost branch
> of an olive tree decently filleted with large white tufts
> of spotless wool.
>
> (*Eum.*, 34, 39-45)

The primary blood-reference is of course to Orestes' deed of matricide, for the Furies, as maternal avengers, lie sleeping about him, presently to be spurred to action by Clytemnestra's restless ghost. But the blood can also represent the bloody state of a new-born babe—which the newly unsheathed sword and the purity of spotless wool might differently indicate. If this interpretation seems lightly allowable, we have here a momentary, iconically suggested prognostic-symbol of Orestes' coming reversal of role. He has cut himself off from the mother-image by murderous violence, thus becoming an exile in more senses than one—not only geographically from the city of Argos, whence the Furies have pursued him, but psychically from all the warmth and naturalness of life which the mother-image properly connotes. The excision was needful because his own particular mother-image had become an embodiment of evil: that was part of the curse upon the royal house. But he cannot find salvation until he has placated the maternal forces of earth which are now taking vengeance upon him. The snakes with which the Furies are semi-identified represent those chthonic powers, potentially both dreadful and beneficent, with which Orestes must eventually make his spiritual peace.

*The Coming of Light*

> CHORUS: Now is the test. Either the murderous blade-
> points will leave their stain and cause the ruin of Agamem-
> non's house forever, or else the son, kindling fire and light
> for freedom, shall reëstablish the duly-ordered rule in his
> city and the prosperity of his fathers.
>
> (*Choe.*, 859-865)

These words, uttered by the Chorus of Bondswomen in the
*Choëphori* just before Orestes' slaying of Aegisthus and Clytemnestra, can be taken in two senses. Paley's paraphrase indicates
the surface meaning: "Orestes will either lose all or gain all by
the present stake; either he himself will be killed, or he will re-
cover the sovereignty, and offer sacrifices for the release of the
Argives from an unjust usurpation."[5] The personal interpretation—what Orestes himself will lose or gain by the immediately
forthcoming contest—is borne out by the athletic metaphor of
the next four lines: "In such a wrestling match the noble Orestes,
the extra contestant, is about to cope with his two adversaries."
The word *ephedros*, which I have translated "extra contestant,"
was applied technically to the third fighter who sat by in a contest between two athletes, prepared to challenge the victor to a
fresh encounter. In terms of this figure Clytemnestra has won the
first bout by slaying Agamemnon, and Orestes the *ephedros* is
accordingly ready to take her on, with Aegisthus as a preliminary. Paley carries out the logic of the interpretation by taking
"fire" and "light" to signify the sacrificial flames which would be
lighted in celebration if Orestes should prove victorious.

Now there is a deeper meaning as well—continuous with the
surface meaning and even reinforcing it, but yet something
more, adumbrating a tragic judgment about the nature and destiny of man in his universal condition. The state of unredeemed

nature is a state of war: of ego against ego, group against group. Life on such terms is a denial of man's high destiny. Parallel to the Christian mythos of Adam's disobedience and loss of Eden stands the mythos around which Aeschylus has built the *Oresteia:* the crime of *hybris*, the curse upon the House, the malign working out of that curse even to the third generation, and the salvation which comes down from above by divine grace in the person of Athena. Forefather Atreus' crime of serving up Thyestes' children to him as baked meats was *hybris* of so extraordinary a degree, doing such dreadful violence to the balanced course of nature (there is balance even in the natural state of war, as Heraclitus keenly perceived), that the entire family of him who committed it became more than usually vulnerable to the curse which the bereaved and outraged father invoked against it. A morality of vendetta follows, a morality of the hunter and the hunted, in which Aegisthus seeks to avenge the cannibalism practised upon his brothers, Orestes to avenge his father by slaying his slayers, and the Furies to avenge Clytemnestra by continuing the deadly pursuit against Orestes. How shall it all end, the Chorus of Bondswomen asks?

> Here, then, upon this royal House
> a third storm has blown and swept along to its end.
> First came the wretched meal of children's flesh;
> next the sad fate of our lord and king,—
> slain in the bath he perished who had led all Greece to war.
> And now a third has come—we know not whence—
> a savior? or shall I say a doom?
> O where shall fulfillment be found?
> How shall the power of guilt be lulled to rest?
>                                    (*Choe.*, 1065-1076)

The tone of these words, with which the *Choëphori* closes, transcends a concern for the fate of Orestes as an individual. It points, although still darkly, toward the fundamental motif of the trilogy: the passage from a morality of vengeance and vendetta to a morality of law.

Aeschylus prepares us for his gradual development of this central theme at the very outset of the *Oresteia*. The *Agamemnon* opens with the great overture which is the Watchman's speech, wherein several of the dominant motifs of the trilogy are announced. I here offer it in as literal a version as English idiom and Aeschylean depth-ambiguity allow, italicizing certain words of symbolic importance:

> Of the *gods* I ask *deliverance from these labors*, watching a year's length now, bedded like a dog on the roof of the house of Atreus. Here I have come to know the assembly of the nightly *stars*—the *shining potentates* which, by their rising and setting, bring *winter tempest and summer harvest* to mortal men.
>
> And now I *keep watch* for the *beacon signal*, the *flame of fire* that bears a tale from Troy, news of its capture. Such is the task commanded me by her whose hopeful woman's heart is joined with a man's strong purpose.
>
> Night after night I keep my dew-drenched couch, never looked upon by dreams, for fear stands at my side in place of sleep, and I cannot close my eyelids in restful sleep. Then when I think to sing or hum a tune, as counter-charm for sleep, I fall to weeping for the fortunes of the house, no longer well labored and administered as of old. But now would that a stroke of luck might bring *deliverance from labors—a fiery flash of good news appearing out of the darkness.*
>
> *(A distant light flares up.)*
>
> Welcome, O torch of night, who givest us *token of the light of day!* inaugurator of many dances which in Argos will celebrate the *happy outcome!* Eeya! Eeya! I *give the sign* to Agamemnon's sleeping queen, that she rise quickly from her bed and raise a joyful *ololugmos* throughout the palace in response to this beacon-fire;—if the city of Troy be really taken, as the torch seems to *announce.*

I myself will dance the prelude. For I shall share in my lord's good fortune, now that this beacon torch has thrown me a triple six. And may it be that I with this hand of mine may grasp my master's beloved hand again when he returns! For the rest I am silent. *A great ox stands upon my tongue.* The House, if it had a voice, could tell a tale all too plainly. *My speech is meant for those who know.* For those who know not—I have forgotten.

(*Agam.*, 1-39)

The opening word of the Watchman's speech is "gods"—*theous,* the accusative plural. The context of star-imagery shows that the invocation is to the gods above—the gods of Olympus, yes, but through and beyond them to a vaguely conceived providential order of things. Such interpenetration of the personal and impersonal elements in religion keeps appearing variously throughout Aeschylus' writings. The Watchman has, of course, no strong or definite theological beliefs, for he makes no further mention of the gods, and in repeating his hope of release some lines later he finds it enough to invoke good fortune. But the watchman moves in symbolic depths of which his limited consciousness has no knowledge. Whereas the *Agamemnon* opens with this brief mention of the upper gods, the *Choëphori* opens with Orestes' more substantial prayer to Hermes, divine attendant of souls on their way to the world of shades below; and finally the *Eumenides* opens with a long formal prayer by the Pythian priestess of Delphi addressed to a number of gods, some of sky and some of earth. The prayer for deliverance from evil times is, in its larger context, not polytheistic but *henotheistic*—an expression of that outreaching of man's heart toward the divine unity which may take the form now of one god now of another, but which transcends every such mythic particularity. The sentiment of henotheism is perhaps more active among early peoples than might be guessed from the multiplicity of their god-names, and the Chorus of Elders in the *Agamemnon* strikes the note of it more than once—as when invoking "Zeus, by whatever name thou art called!" and prophesying, "There is One above, whether called Zeus or Pan or Apollo, who hears the cry of the birds"—i.e., the victims of tyranny—the eagle-chicks molested by the dragon.

Another religious allusion, more oblique but still no less contributory to the undercurrent of religious meaning which gradually widens and deepens as the action proceeds, is the phrase "deliverance from labors" (*apallagê ponôn*). It occurs twice, and the second occurrence is anticipated by the sound and meaning of *pon-* in the verb which I have translated (to keep the full connotation) "labored and administered." The phrase was probably one employed in certain of the mystery religions, although we cannot be sure; in any case it expresses an idea which was central to them. Aeschylus employs the word "deliverance" or "release" (*apallagê*) and its related forms with great care. In the *Agamemnon* they carry dramatic irony. The Watchman speaks of "deliverance from labors" without consciously intending any more than his own hope for release from his irksome vigil. Toward the end of the *Agamemnon* (1289), when Cassandra is prophesying Agamemnon's and her own murder, she charges the word with a more sombre meaning: those who laid waste to Troy are now, in the person of their king, to be "released" from life by the gods' righteous judgment. Then in the *Choëphori*, while Orestes is murdering his mother off-stage, the Chorus of Bondswomen chant a triumphant hymn:

> Raise a joyful ololugmos for the release from evils, from waste of wealth by the two polluters [of the home], and from the rough path.

> (*Choe.*, 942-945)

There are religious overtones to virtually all the main words of this little passage. The ololugmos (found also in the Watchman's Prologue) was the ceremonial outcry of joy and triumph, sometimes combined with agony, on the successful completion of a sacrifice; the rough path could readily symbolize the evils and difficulties of this life from which a release is craved; and the significance of pollution I have discussed in the last section of Chapter Eight. Here the irony is differently oriented but equally strong: the Bondswomen think that the act of matricide will release the House from the curse; but as the audience well knows and as Orestes' pursuit by the Furies will presently confirm, release is not yet possible. Finally, however, in the *Eumenides* the prayer for release becomes intense and direct. Orestes is told by Apollo to make a pilgrimage to Athena's citadel, "and there we shall find means at last to *deliver* you from your trials." (78-83). Apollo's particular expedients (*mechanai*) do not work, to be sure; but Orestes, after making the journey, can declare that having been "taught by suffering" he has learnt the first requirement of a religious initiate, "the occasions when it is right to speak and when to be silent" (276-279). The release is effected in a way that suggests the rites of initiation at Eleusis or Crotona or one of the other religious centers.

The mention of "when to speak and when to be silent" takes us back to another religious symbol in the Watchman's speech. The phrase "A great ox stands (or has trod) upon my tongue" was, to be sure, a colloquialism for "I must be silent." But how did so curious an idiom arise? Generally speaking when the ox (*bous*) or bull (*tauros*) enters into ancient Greek symbolism it is a fair indication that the god Dionysus, whose icons display a bull's or ox's head, lurks in the background. Probably, then, the Watchman's casual phrase (or *was* it so casual?) would remind the Greek audience of the ritual silence imposed upon candidates for purification in the Dionysian and other mystery religions.

The imposition of silence is not a mere negation, either in the *Oresteia* or in the mystery cults to which its imagery so often alludes. Silence is part of the preparation of that essential wisdom which comes through silent suffering—a wisdom that is represented symbolically as a secret imparted only to those who have become ready for it. The idea of a secret fits in very well with Aeschylus' manner of writing upon two levels at once—a public meaning for the "pro-fane" (literally, "those outside the temple") and an esoteric one for the initiates. Such religious ambivalence was practiced universally in the ancient schools of wisdom. Thus the Pythagoreans were taught, "Do not touch beans": which seems to have signified both "Do not violate the organ of generation"—beans symbolizing the testicles, and "Do not participate in politics"—which involves dropping the white and black beans into the ballot-urn. The symbolic meanings were of course the important ones for the followers of Pythagoras; nevertheless, in order that the vulgarly inquisitive might not be led to pry into the secret, the literal meanings were the ones emphasized publicly, and Jamblichus in his *Life of Pythagoras* tells of two Pythagoreans, a man and his pregnant wife, who let themselves be tortured and killed rather than eat some beans at a tyrant's orders, *or even tell why they would not do so.* The Watchman (the first of many "watchers" in the drama) reflects this characteristic of the Mysteries in the closing words of his speech, and the Chorus of Elders conveys its forebodings in dark hints and surmises. Particularly after Clytemnestra's lying but double-edged speech to the Herald, the Chorus tries vainly to warn the unimaginative fellow, in language that might be taken to epitomize the dramatic ambivalence found everywhere: "Thus she has spoken to you, a neophyte, a goodly tale for shrewd interpreters."

Such religious phrases, allusions, and attitudes become important dramatically just so far as they form part of the inner dramatic action, leading to a dramatic consummation. The idea of consummation is itself a religious ideal as well as a dramatic one. A most popular way of invoking Zeus for the success of an undertaking was as *Zeus Teleios,* which connoted at once "Zeus the Perfect One" and "Zeus the Perfecter, the Ripener, the Ful-filler." The word and its cognates occur frequently in Aeschylus' writings. But consummation is of different kinds. Often it means no more than fulfillment of the terms of blood feud, as for in-stance in the *kommos* between Orestes and the Chorus of Bonds-women.

> CHO.: Ye mighty Fates, grant that Zeus send this con-summation, in which justice is on our side. "For word of hate let word of hate be consummated," Justice loudly cries as she gathers in the debt; "and for murderous blow let him pay murderous blow." *Suffering to the doer,*—so speaks an age-old saw.
>
> (*Choe.,* 306-314)

That last maxim represents consummation on the low level. Paradoxically it calls to mind the complementary maxim already met with—*Wisdom through suffering*—which represents the con-summatory process in what Aeschylus regards as its highest hu-man form.

We are now prepared to understand the full import of Clytem-nestra's irony in her final words to Agamemnon as he retires into the palace just before the murder:

> CLYT.: Your coming signifies (*semainein*) summery warmth in wintry storm. When Zeus draws wine from the sour grape, then coolness is already present in the house, with the perfect (*teleios*) master in residence.
>
> (*Agam.,* 969-972)

Look at the second sentence first. Its first two clauses, taken literally, might be simply a way of describing the season, and the last clause might seem just an overstuffed compliment liken-ing Agamemnon to Zeus—a verbal equivalent of making him walk on the sacred crimson carpet. But "coolness" (*psychos*) can also mean "chill," "already" (*tot' hêdê*) can also mean "then straightway," and with these shifts of interpretation the sentence becomes:

> When Zeus draws wine from the unripe grape (*symbolically:* when divine justice spills blood before the victim's normal span of years has ripened), then straightway a chill settles down upon the house, and the resident master is "ripe."

On this level the adjective *teleios,* applied to Agamemnon, is no longer a vapid compliment but a sinister threat. Its related grammatical forms appear three times within the next two lines as Clytemnestra concludes:

> Zeus, Zeus the Ripener, ripen thou my prayers (i.e., bring them to fulfillment) and have a care for all that thou intend'st to ripen.

The ripening-fulfillment-consummatory motif that runs through the *Oresteia* is associated with several characteristic sorts of imagery. The ripening of hunters' and hounds' pursuit of game I have already spoken of. The political metaphor of a successful lawsuit occurs, as does the economic one of profitable exchange. The consummation of childbirth is suggested several times, and in the *Choëphori* it becomes complicated with the idea already discussed of Orestes' symbolical rebirth from the dead. The childbirth idea becomes naturally connected with that of ripening of crops and summer harvest, as in the first sentence quoted from Clytemnestra's words to Agamemnon: "Your coming signifies summery warmth in wintry storm." The surface meaning is an expression of courteous hyperbole, as though the queen were to say, "You have brought summery warmth into my winter"; or, as Conington translates, "Thy coming shows like heat in winter cold." But the statement could also suggest that the summery warmth which the king's return represents is caught up in the wintry blast of violence and evil that overwhelms the house. Similarly, when the Watchman (as quoted earlier) says that the stars by their rising and setting bring winter storm and summer harvest to men, he is expressing more than a fragment of naïve science. The Chorus in the *Choëphori*, in a passage already quoted, uses the word *cheimôn* (which combines the meanings "storm" and "winter") to refer to the misfortunes of the house: "Upon this royal house a third storm has blown." And Clytemnestra uses the word *theros* (which combines the meanings "harvest" and "summer") in a symbolical sense that is also ironical: "the unhappy harvest of our ills" (*Agam.* 1655). The cycle of winter storms and summer harvest becomes a threshold symbol for the cycle of bane and blessing, deprivation and fulfillment, in the human lot.

A more awful theme of consummative symbolism is that of the priestess consummating the sacrifice—illustrated by the ritual blood-bath passage already quoted and by Clytemnestra's earlier double-dealing announcement:

> Go within, Cassandra, you too; since Zeus has auspiciously made it your privilege to stand among the slaves by the altar and share the consecrated pouring of our household sacrifice . . .
> I have no time to idle here outside the door. The sheep stand before the central altar by the hearth awaiting the knife.
>
> (*Agam.*, 1035-1037, 1055-1057)

But the most important consummative image of all, I would say, is the emergence of light out of darkness. Observe that in the Watchman's speech the light-imagery has three phases: the stars, the expectation of the beacon flame, and finally (as consummation of his hopes) the visible appearance of the flame itself. The Watchman speaks of the flame as a *symbolon;* and while it is not certain that the word had acquired in the fifth century B.C. the religious significance it was to carry in the time of Plutarch, one of the meanings which it indubitably did have in the earlier century was "watchword," and thence it could easily have come to mean "watchword for initiates" and therefore "symbol of experiences which only initiates have shared." In any case the contextualization of the light imagery in the Watchman's speech leaves no doubt that it has a symbolic meaning as well as a literal one.

To particularize all the light and darkness images in the *Oresteia* would be tedious for writer and reader alike. But two are especially noteworthy—where Clytemnestra fuses the images of childbirth (with so complex an Oresteian significance of its own) and dawning day:

> CLYT.: Bringing good news, as the proverb says, may dawn come to birth auspiciously out of Mother Night.
> (*Agam.*, 264 f)

> CLYT.: In the night that gave birth to this dawning day.
> (*Agam.*, 279)

These two utterances are followed by the tremendous light-imagery of the Queen's description of the fire-god winging from island pyre to island pyre the news of Troy's fall. Even Aegisthus is caught up in the power of such imagery. When he comes on the scene at the end of the *Agamemnon*, after letting Clytemnestra do the bloody deed whose fruits he will enjoy, he reveals something of his hypocritical character in the cry:

> O kindly light of a day of just reward!
> (*Agam.*, 1577)

With admirable art Aeschylus withdraws light imagery almost entirely in the *Choëphori* and through the early part of the *Eumenides,* and stresses instead the darkness imagery appropriate both to the invocation of Agamemnon's ghost and the appearance of the Furies. For the Furies are children of Mother Night, and until their transformation they must exhibit only sombre associations. As their ancient prerogative of unrestricted vengeance is being stripped away they howl:

> Black Night, my mother! dost thou look on this?
> (*Eum.,* 745)

> Hear my vehement wrath, O Mother Night!
> (*Eum.,* 844 f)

But under the new dispensation which Athena establishes by setting up the Court of the Aeropagus, wherein the rights and wrongs of murder cases will be adjudicated by legal deliberation instead of determined by blind vengeance, the Furies will receive new honors and functions in return for the old "natural rights" of which they are deprived:

> CHORUS OF FURIES: O Queen Athena, what seat dost thou assign me?
> ATH.: One free of all bane: accept it!
> CHO.: Suppose I accept, what honor then is mine?
> ATH.: That no house shall prosper apart from thee.
> (*Eum.,* 892-895)

The Furies, although ceasing to be *mere* agents of vengeance, are to retain enough of their old character so that the well-being of men is unattainable without their good-will.

In political terms the issue might be stated: On what grounds is law enforcement justified? Now law enforcement implies a disposition to punish certain kinds of wrongdoing if and when committed. On what grounds, then, may we punish? The lowest ground, to which a certain bestial instinct sometimes prompts us, is retaliation: "You injured me, so I will injure you." As the concept of retaliation advances, it undergoes two changes. It becomes codified—"An eye for an eye, a tooth for a tooth"—declaring in effect that the punishment should be commensurate with and appropriate to the crime. And it becomes impersonal and at least relatively impartial: the "eye for an eye" formula is meant to apply equally to all persons of a given community—or, it may be, to all of a certain rank within the community. Both of these developments involve some appeal to a principle of justice, but the justice is purely retributive, which is to say backward-looking.

To pass from the retributive to a higher conception of justice requires the raising of two questions: *with what authority,* and *for what purpose.* In a healthily evolving society the two questions will develop in mutual relationship. If every individual pursues his own purposes, or even the common purpose as he privately conceives it, without any respect for the authority of existing rulers and laws, the result is anarchy. On the other hand an authority which issues decrees by rule and rote without any demonstration of its purpose is too brittle to satisfy the human craving for justice; the authorities to which we look up with fervor and willing devotion are those who are concerned for some large common good and who (so we believe) know better than other men how it is to be attained. The one type is authoritarian, the other authoritative. A most important step in the evolution of moral notions can be discovered in the transition from authoritarian codes to authoritative laws—from rules to principles. Ideally speaking, we follow a rule because we are told to; we observe a law because we regard its purpose, or that of the authority that issues it, as good.

The situation, however, is not always ideal. To achieve any purpose, and especially a social purpose, adequate means must be taken, and the means do not usually wear the same look of authenticity as the end. The means, therefore, may have to be enforced if the end is to be achieved. And that is precisely to be the role of the Furies under the new dispensation that Athena establishes. Athena was the Olympian goddess of wisdom; she was also, as her name indicates, the patron goddess of the city of Athens; therefore she was *par excellence* the goddess and symbol of *civic wisdom*. Her great act of civic wisdom, which the *Oresteia* celebrates, was to found the law court of the Areopagus with its institution of trial by jury. Certainly it represents a great advance in public weal that murder cases should be tried so. But public weal cannot be the only consideration. To put men to death simply in the name of public weal is an act of gross and dangerous tyranny. In a state of justice a man may be put to death only if he has done something to forfeit his civic right: thus in the very conception of penal justice there must be an element of implicit retribution *as well as* of civic purpose. The Furies, then, who represent the retributive force in human relationships, must still be retained under the new conception of justice by law. They are to be the "teeth in the law." They will still pursue evil-doers, but now as agents of legally constituted authority. They represent the negative, primitive side of man's social conscience, as Athena represents the positive and constructive.

Thus, the Furies, the Erinyes, are transformed into the Eumenides. Aeschylus here gives symbolic depth to what had otherwise been merely a quirk of Greek idiom. The name *Erinyes* had become so dreadful, and its utterance invited such baneful effects, that people largely refrained from pronouncing it and referred to the dread sisters by a euphemism—as the Eumenides, the Well-Minded Ones. In the *Oresteia* the transformation is not merely verbal but real. They become the *Semnai*, the Holy Ones—beneficent yet still commanding awe. In religious perspective they are thus reconcilers of the light above and the darkness of earth below:

> That so the glorious sun and bounteous earth may unite
> to yield thick burgeoning growth.
>
> (*Eum.*, 925 f)

Thus light imagery is reintroduced at the end, and with great expressive power. When the ex-Furies put on crimson robes and march in the torchlight procession, the symbolism is political and transcendental at once. The ceremony is that of the annual Festival of *Panathenaia*, in which eminent aliens residing in Athens were given honorary citizenship—"the keys to the city," as we would say. Thus in stately analogy the Awful Goddesses, who formerly were alien to men's purposes, shall henceforth enjoy the highest honors among the citizenry. The light and song that mark the procession symbolize the new wisdom and the new harmony which the great transformation has brought into the world. As the Eumenides pass onward to their sacred abodes the Chorus of Citizens chants responsively the verses with which the *Oresteia* closes:

*Strophe*

> Go to your home, ye powers fond of worship,
> Daughters of Night, in auspicious procession.
> Speak only fair words, O countrymen.

*Antistrophe*

> There in the gloomy caverns of earth
> To be worshiped with honors and sacrifices.
> Speak only fair words, O populace.

*Strophe*

> With benign heart and propitious for the land,
> Come, O holy ones, in gladness,
> Follow the torches that light up the way.
> O sing *ololugmos* now to our songs.

*Antistrophe*

Let the drink-offerings flow,
There shall be living in peace for Pallas' children.
Zeus the All-Seeing is thus with Destiny reconciled.
O sing *ololugmos* now to our songs.

(*Eum.*, 1043-1047)

# 11

# Pilgrim in the Wasteland

As a conclusion to these studies in the symbolic possibilities of language I want to explore certain paths of significance in, and approaching, what is perhaps the most fully pertinent single poem of our moment in history, Eliot's *Four Quartets*. It might appear to a circumspective reader, aware of the explorations already made by so many resourceful critics here and abroad, that hardly anything both new and useful remains to be said. And it is true that if systematic exposition were my aim I could not help repeating many of what have become virtual commonplaces of Eliot interpretation. But actually the most I hope to do here is examine several of Eliot's poetic themes which strike me as having certain possibilities of meaning beyond those already suggested. Possibilities only. Whether any particular interpretation is really justified must be left to the gradual discrimination of each devoted and attentive reader.

In discussing the philosophical meaning of any poem it is important to keep in mind how such meanings characteristically show themselves. I am not much concerned (as should be evident by now) with the philosophical propositions that can be screened out of the poem, still less with those that can be imposed upon it as an ideological test; but mainly with the ideas which emerge, or half emerge, from the poetic song and movement and imagery themselves. Philosophical ideas in poetry should be like those sculptures of Rodin's where the unfinished human or animal figure is left continuous with the unhewn stone. In plastic art the power of the representation is increased by a right sense of the medium. Analogously in poetic art the power of the idea should be fused with the rhythmic and imagistic actuality of the poem. Eliot's much quoted testimony "that a poem, or a passage of a poem, may tend to realize itself first as a particular rhythm before it reaches expression in words, and that this rhythm may bring to birth the idea and the image,"[1] needs to be remembered in any discussion of a poet's philosophy. Dionysus skips ahead of Apollo, although it is Apollo who lights the way. Rhythm and ideation, song and vision, collaborate in the poetic act; and their tension motivates—perhaps even *is*—the poem. My earlier emphasis on Assertorial Lightness—the reluctance of a poetic statement to be meant with full logical and epistemological rigor, together with its claim of being yet somehow meaningful—can be restated as an acknowledgment that ideas in a poem must always be understood through the poetic mode of apprehension.

Now the poetic mode of apprehension works very largely through what I have called Compositive or Metaphoric Imagining. It proceeds characteristically (although never exclusively) by fusion of elements; the poem quâ poem is a particular medium in which, as Eliot says, "impressions and experiences combine in peculiar and unexpected ways."[2] This in itself is enough to guarantee that the philosophy of a poem is, at its best, not a doctrinal structure but a pattern of living themes. The poetic Eros, born of Poverty and Plenty, pursues without ever triumphantly grasping the idea; he is always arising from, never quite escaping the debris of the temporal. Accordingly my method will be not expository but perspectival. Any attempt at depth-formulation is always a succession of new beginnings; and in the pages that follow I shall explore, with no compulsion toward a total synthesis, some of the poeto-philosophical ideas and associations that have come into focus during my various rereadings of *Four Quartets*.

## Music, Meaning, and Time

Eliot's published remark that "there are possibilities for verse which bear some analogy to the development of the themes by different groups of instruments; there are possibilities of transitions in a poem comparable to the different movements of a symphony or a quartet; there are possibilities of contrapuntal arrangement of subject matter,"[3] has been sometimes misunderstood. Certain interpreters have overlooked the qualifying force of Eliot's words "some analogy." There is a good deal of misplaced ingenuity in Lloyd Frankenberg's attempt to work out the four voices in strict analogy to the four instruments of a string quartet: the philosophical voice—viola; the lyrical—violin; the narrative—violin; the apocalyptic—cello.[4] A strict analogy with music would require that we be able to distinguish two kinds of shift or transition: a shift from theme to countertheme, and a shift from instrument to instrument. There would have to be a discernible fourfold multiplicity representing the instruments, and a discernible twofold multiplicity representing the themes. Frankenberg believes he has identified a fourfold discrimination running through all four of the Quartets, and he therefore equates it, and presumes that Eliot intended it should be equated, with the four instruments. But this strikes me as a critic's conceptualization of the poem rather than a property of the poem itself.

A more promising attempt at musical analysis has been made by Professor S. Marshall Cohen,[5] who argues that the first movements of three of the Quartets are composed in something like sonata form. In *Burnt Norton* he takes the theme and counter-theme to be deterministic and redeemable time; in *The Dry Salvages*, the imagistic complementation of river and sea; in *Little Gidding*, as seasonal time ("Midwinter spring . . .") and significant place ("If you came this way . . .")—which become integrated in the final coda (he says, less accurately, "chord"):

> Here, the intersection of the timeless moment
> Is England and nowhere. Never and always.

Professor Cohen's interpretation seems to me to approximate the poetic structure somewhat more recognizably than Frankenberg's. His musical analysis of the latter two first movements is plausible enough. But regarding *Burnt Norton* I am a good deal less sure of what the theme and countertheme should be taken to be.

*Burnt Norton* opens with four statements of a formal metaphysical character. Their quaternity can be taken as a structural icon of the quartet-idea, which, however, is offered lightly and then allowed to disappear. But what of their intellectual content? I find that as I reread the statements in different orders, or with different emphases, their logical relationships seem to alter. Nor am I able (except by supplying connectives that are not in the poem) to bring the meanings of all four into logical consistency. Surely that is evidence that we must avoid taking their relationships in a too strictly logical way. Let us begin logically, however, in order to see how far the plain prose method will serve our understandings here.

> (1) Time present and time past
> Are both perhaps present in time future,
> And time future contained in time past.

> (2) If all time is eternally present
> All time is unredeemable.

(3) What might have been is an abstraction
    Remaining a perpetual possibility
    Only in a world of speculation.

(4) What might have been and what has been
    Point to one end, which is always present.

Observe that sentences 1 and 2 are offered tentatively. The first is softened and qualified by the word "perhaps"; the second is stated hypothetically. Regarded logically, which is to say as propositions, they formulate a philosophy of determinism. Sentence 1 might be an impressionistic epitome of Lord Russell's argument that it is theoretically just as possible to remember the future as to remember the past, inasmuch as present, past, and future are all equally and forever fixed. The present has no independent reality on that basis; it dissolves into the remoteness and impersonality of future and past. Sentence 2 declares that if all time is eternally present *in that deterministic sense*, then all time is unredeemable. But there is an altogether different sense that can be given to the phrase "eternally present," and the search for this other sense is one of the main motivations of *Four Quartets*. Sentence 4 announces it. The relationship of time's phases is now reversed. The present is now the "one end" to which all else points. We might say, then (tentatively, as always), that the intellectual movement from sentence 1 to sentence 4 is from a deterministic view of time (future contained in the past) to a more open view of time, offering, if we can but realize them, redemptive possibilities (past contained in, or intelligible only through, the present). The development is neatly paralleled by the transformation in *East Coker* from "In my beginning is my end" to "In my end is my beginning"—the first and last lines, respectively, of that Quartet.

Sentence 3 may be taken as a poetic bridge between the two opposing philosophies, since it is equally a corollary of them both. The truism that the unrealized past is unreal ("no use crying over spilt milk," etc.) would be interpreted differently according as it was based on the one philosophy or the other. Determinism would say: the unrealized past never was more than an unrealizable abstraction, for what has come to pass and what could have come to pass are identical. The redemptive philosophy would say: although other possibilities were real once, they are real no longer. "We cannot revive old factions/We cannot restore old policies/Or follow an antique drum." And yet they may still be real in a sense! And the concrete imagery which comes after indicates what that sense may be:

> Footfalls echo in the memory
> Down the passage which we did not take
> Towards the door we never opened
> Into the rose-garden.

If we are wanting a musical analogy I would be inclined to view the imagery and idea of these four lines as representing the first theme (the four opening sentences being introductory). Then, as the second theme, the doubt, the hesitant retraction, the minor key:

> But to what purpose
> Disturbing the dust on a bowl of rose-leaves
> I do not know.

The two passages have their abstract parallels in opening sentences 4 and 3, respectively. In the main body of the movement the two themes intertwine more freely, and with admirably expressive imagery, as the positive and negative sides of the rose-garden experience. On the one hand, "Quick, said the bird, find them, find them"; on the other, "the deception of the thrush." On the one hand, the main impression of the rose-garden scene ("There they were as our guests, accepted and accepting"); on the other, the counteractive implications of "dead leaves" and "drained pool." In the positive moment "the lotus rose, quietly, quietly"; but "then a cloud passed, and the pool was empty." And finally the music returns, as the movement ends, to the key of the abstract: to a restatement of the "eternal present" theme, now interpreted by the intervening imagery.

### The Masks of Tiresias

The Pilgrim to whom my chapter title alludes can best be conceived as the transcendental spectator, the "I" of the poem, undergoing metamorphoses, sometimes male and sometimes female, now of the present and now of the past, wavering between the concretely personal and the archetypally timeless. But wherein is the Pilgrim different from the mere Wanderer? Evidently in that the one has a sense of direction, the other not. In *Gerontion* and *The Waste Land*, the integrating Figure is identified by a name, but in these poems the purgatorial idea of pilgrimage has not yet taken form, or at best is but vaguely and impotently suggested. Let us consider some aspects of this earlier Poetic Ego, and his changing masks and scenes, before returning to the problems of the *Quartets*.

In *Gerontion* the character of the Ego (or of his major part) is announced in the title: literally, "little old man"; symbolically, the vacant, draughty consciousness of the ageing, sensual unbeliever who has outlived both his sophistication and his desire.

> I have lost my sight, smell, hearing, taste and touch:
> How should I use them for your closer contact?
> These with a thousand small deliberations
> Protract the profit of their chilled delirium,
> Excite the membrane, when the sense has cooled,
> With pungent sauces, multiply variety
> In a wilderness of mirrors.

The paradox of "chilled delirium" is made explicit as a need to "Excite the membrane, when the sense has cooled"—an idea which will reappear in the "trilling wire in the blood" of *Burnt Norton* and (with contrary stress) in the "frigid purgatorial fires" of *East Coker*. The old man's disintegrating mind may be considered the theatre in which the heterogeneous fragments of character and situation are brought together in chaotic union. And simultaneously the old man is the senescence of a disintegrating civilization, drowsily half aware of its lost opportunities and present barrenness.

There is another speaker besides the *geron*, however. Whose is the prophetic condemnatory voice which enters in the seventeenth line?—"Signs are taken for wonders"—and again in the passage beginning "After such knowledge, what forgiveness?" Something distinct from the old man's voice or representing merely another layer of him—his lost and forgotten insights arising like a familiar ghost to confront him? Both, probably. There is a dialectical drawing apart, as in Marvell's *Dialogue between Soul and Body*, along with a substantial and inevitable identity. The judge condemns himself along with the criminal in the dock. For judge and criminal are *per-sonae*—masks which each of us sometimes wears—masks of the chameleon-like Ego which projects the poem, and which sees itself in the end "whirled/Beyond the circuit of the shuddering Bear/In fractured atoms."

In *The Waste Land* the *geron*-figure expands into Tiresias, the blind soothsayer of Thebes. Eliot's note offers two important statements about him: that as all the male characters—the one-eyed merchant, the drowned Phoenician sailor, Ferdinand of Naples—melt into each other, and all the women are essentially one woman, so likewise the two sexes meet in Tiresias; and that "what Tiresias *sees*, in fact, is the substance of the poem." But the role of detached spectator is never pure, and Tiresias himself shares vicariously to some degree, as well as observes, all the scattered experiences past and present, high and low, which the poem semi-dramatizes and brings into precarious community. The various personae of both sexes, including the self-transmogrifying "I," may be conceived on the one hand as constituting the Human Comedy which Tiresias witnesses, and on the other as metamorphosed emanations of him.

One might say there are two levels or layers of metamorphosis in *The Waste Land*—the ontological and the theatrical—symbolized by the respective phrases, "death by water" and "Hieronymo's mad againe." The former and more essential of them I will reserve for comment in the fourth section. The latter might be conceived as its subjective and histrionic correlative. The continual transmutations of all things that exist, the interpenetrating cycles of birth and death that constitute the temporal world, require of the poet their proper *mimesis*. In a classical age the "dramatic reversal" (*peripeteia*) can be unitary and formal without doing violence to a fit audience's idea of what is "necessary, or plausible." But ours is another sort of age. The contemporary dramatic poet's task stands to that of the classical dramatic poet—Eliot's to that of Sophocles, let us say—as the continuum-analysis of the infinitesimal calculus stands to the palpable Greek geometrical conception of number. The difference has a histrionic aspect too. It is probable that the Greek actor, the *agonistes*, changed his physical mask at the moment when the *peripeteia* took place; whereas Eliot's elusive protagonist, Tiresias, exists only through a continuous melting of one mask, one *persona*, into another.

In the coda that brings *The Waste Land* to its close, Tiresias' brief epiphany as Hieronymo ("Why then Ile fit you") makes a terse retrospective commentary upon the meaning of some of the previous action. Thomas Kyd's *The Spanish Tragedy*, in which Hieronymo has his proper being, contains two central image-ideas which reappear slyly and problematically in *The Waste Land:* the pictorial idea of the Hanged Man, with the archetypal figure of the slain Christ in the background; and the dramatic idea of feigned madness, associated with the idea of a drama's author and chief actor merging into one, which in turn carries suggestions of the Incarnation.

In the play the aged Hieronymo, hearing Bellimperia's cry for help, rushes out half dressed into the garden bower, where he discovers his son Horatio murdered and hanging from a tree. His frenzied grief and demand for revenge are expressed in images which carry Christological overtones. The Hanged Man image is associated not only with the card in the Tarot pack which Mme. Sosostris the corrupt soothsayer had been unable to find, but also with the sacrificial death of Christ. "The God of our fathers raised up Jesus, whom ye slew and hanged on a tree" (Acts 5: 30).[6] Hieronymo apostrophizes his dead son as "sweet lovely rose" and exalts him as "pure and spotless." The rose was a recognized symbol for Christ in Elizabethan religious consciousness, and of course the emphasis on "pure and spotless" confirms the haunting overtone (cf. "I find in him no fault at all"—John 18: 38).

The idea of feigned madness, its relation to the idea of the author as actor, and the relation of this latter idea to the theological doctrine of Incarnation, in which Divinity voluntarily accepts embodiment in the world which It has created,—all this offers a set of problems that would reward, I believe, much further study. "I am never better than when I am mad," Hieronymo cries, and he turns the distraction fit into an instrument of the revenge he is plotting. The opportunity comes when he is asked to write a tragedy for the court's entertainment; he replies:

> Why then Ile fit you: say no more.
> When I was young, I gave my mind
> And plied myself to fruitless poetry:

> Which though it profit the professor naught,
> Yet is it passing pleasing to the world.
> (Act IV, lines 68-72)

The play which Hieronymo produces and enacts turns out to be more than a play: for he so casts the roles that Bellimperia, Horatio's bereaved mistress, must pretend to stab Balthazar his murderer; but the pretence is made a reality. And Hieronymo, triumphantly revealing this bloody outcome, boasts himself "author and actor in this tragedy" (IV, 404).

There is a complex irony in the last phrase. Hieronymo thinks himself author of the vengeful deed, but he is more of a mere actor and puppet than he knows. For his bereavement and revenge are all part of a plot set in motion by the ghost of Andrea, a Spanish nobleman whom Balthazar had slain. It is Andrea's ghost, and with him Revenge in person, who open and close the tragedy; and the play which he performs before the court is thus, to Kyd's audience, triply framed.

*The Waste Land* ends (except for the ambiguous Hindu benediction) with a succession of masks, the last of which is Hieronymo's cry, seemingly acquiescent but deadly as it turns out, "Why then Ile fit you"—with, as it were, the stage announcer's comment, "Hieronymo's mad againe." The Tiresias-Hieronymo protagonist confesses here to playacting, even as he had done in the voice of Baudelaire earlier—"You! hyprocrite lecteur!—mon semblable,—mon frère!" But the confession of playacting is itself a bit of playacting, and therefore should not be taken with unguarded assurance. The relation of the poet-protagonist to his masks, as of the doer to his situations, is never fully resolved.

### Sand, Red Rock, and the Vanishing Garden

In the third canto of Dante's *Inferno* the Pilgrim and his guide, on entering the vestibule of Hell, come upon a group of lost souls "whirling through the air forever dark, as sand eddies in a whirlwind, their sighs and loud wailings resounding through the starless air." Vergil the Guide explains to Dante the Pilgrim that these are the wretched remains of those who lived on earth without taking sides, avoiding both praise and blame. Mercy and Justice spurn them alike: "Let us not speak of them, but look and pass on." Dante resumes: "And as I looked, I saw a whirling banner which ran so fast, it seemed as though it could never come to rest; and behind it came so long a train of people, I would not have believed death had undone so many."

The simile of sand eddying in a whirlwind is apt, it would seem, on two counts. Sand is dry and barren; it is also unstable, easily stirred to haphazard movement by every gust of wind. Eliot's allusion to the passage in describing the crowd that flowed over London Bridge—"so many, I had not thought death had undone so many"—thus implies a triple judgment against the typical individuals of our day. And let us not be complacent: the relevant pronoun in such a judgment is not "they" but "we," and more focally "I." The cowardice (*viltá*) that Dante ascribes to Pope Celestine—"him who made the great refusal"—means more strictly, as Sinclair well says, "pusillanimity, littleness of soul, the meanness of nature by which a man refuses his calling and misses his mark." It is what Max Picard has named "the philosophy of flight"[7]—flight from the silent voice that stands always ready, if we will listen, to remind us of our lost direction and of the difficult but imperative way back. As a result of the chronic, unavowed Refusal we become the unstable victims of "pastimes and drugs, and features of the press" —ready to follow any wavering banner, any novel shibboleth that gains passing currency. And thus like dry sand we are barren and unproductive. What we praise as the great productions of our times are, to the undaunted vision, destructions; for to produce in any real and enduring sense would require far more than we are consistently willing to give:

A condition of complete simplicity
(Costing not less than everything).

The antithesis between sand and rock is a natural one, arising from the obvious physical characteristics of the two elements. The similes "firm as a rock" and "shifting as sand" express familiar enough analogies, and do not require a nurtured
tradition to explain them. Yet in a culture that branches from
Christian roots a sensitive mind will hear in the comparison
some echo of Biblical overtones—particularly in Jesus' simile
of the wise and the foolish builder:

> Therefore whosoever heareth these sayings of mine, and
> doeth them, I will liken him unto a wise man, which built
> his house upon a rock:
> And the rain descended, and the floods came, and the
> winds blew, and beat upon that house; and it fell not: for
> it was founded upon a rock.
> And every one that heareth these sayings of mine, and
> doeth them not, shall be likened unto a foolish man, which
> built his house upon the sand:
> And the rain descended, and the floods came, and the
> winds blew, and beat upon that house; and it fell: and
> great was the fall of it.
>
> (Matthew, 7:24-27)

Biblical symbolism of the Rock is abundant and varied. The
Psalmist speaks of the rock of salvation (Ps. 89:26); Isaiah
speaks of God as "the rock of thy strength" (Is. 17:10); Jesus
commissions Peter (*Petros*) as the rock (*petra*) upon which (we
are not told in what sense) the new religious fellowship
(*ekklesia*) is to be founded. More precisely relevant to *The
Waste Land*, as Elizabeth Drew has pointed out, is the later
passage in Isaiah where the prophet is foretelling the blessings
of Christ's kingdom:

> And a man shall be as an hiding place from the wind,
> and a covert from the tempest; as rivers of water in a dry
> place, as the shadow of a great rock in a weary land.
>
> (Isaiah, 32:2)

But the rock symbolizes not only firmness, security, refuge. The first four verses of I Corinthians, Chapter 10, are of peculiar interest to readers of *The Waste Land* because of the co-presence of two significant images—immersion in water (see the "Death by Water" section below) and the drinking of spiritual water from the Rock. St. Paul writes:

> Moreover, brethren, I would not that ye should be ig-
> norant, how that all our fathers were under the cloud,
> and all passed through the sea;
> And were all baptized unto Moses in the cloud and
> in the sea;
> And did all eat the same spiritual meat;
> And did all drink the same spiritual drink: for they drank
> of that spiritual Rock that followed them: and that Rock
> was Christ.

The Apostle's reference, of course, is to Moses' smiting of the rock in Horeb, from which there gushed forth fresh water for his thirsty people.

> And the Lord said unto Moses, Go on before the people,
> and take with thee of the elders of Israel; and thy rod,
> wherewith thou smotest the river, take in thine hand,
> and go.
> Behold, I will stand before thee there upon the rock in
> Horeb; and thou shalt smite the rock, and there shall come
> water out of it, that the people may drink. And Moses did
> so in the sight of the elders of Israel.
>
> (Exodus, 17:5-6)

Why, now, is the rock in *The Waste Land* initially *red* rock? Later, in the penitential mood of *Ash Wednesday* the rock is associated with the color blue and with garden imagery. There the Lady of the Garden, the Lady of Silences

> Made cool the dry rock and made firm the sand
> In blue of larkspur, blue of Mary's color;

and when it next appears the rock itself is blue:

> In the last desert between the last blue rocks.

But that coolness, that *Erhebung* without motion, has not yet been attained in *The Waste Land*. The vision of the Madonna of the Rocks, with a grace-note reminder of Leonardo's painting by that name, is ironically inverted a few lines after the red rock passage, when Madame Sosostris pulls out of the Tarot pack "Belladonna, the Lady of the Rocks"—where Belladonna carries the literal meaning of "beautiful lady" and suggests the Madonna, perhaps also Beatrice; while complementing this is the ironic allusion to the practice of courtesans a generation or two ago of using belladonna to artificially brighten their eyes. The Rock in the wasteland maintains its semantic identity precariously, for it is qualified by such surrounding imagery as dry sand and fear in a handful of dust. On the positive side it is red because the saving grace of Christ's blood streams through all things even in the waste land. But we feel that the symbol is ambivalent, that it carries other connotations balancing the Christian ones, and that those other connotations—as the phrase "fear in a handful of dust" suggests—may well be pagan in character. Can we be any more specific?

I think perhaps we can. My hypothesis, for what it may be worth, is that there is a latent reference here to the ceremony of the Navaho Night Chant. The focal object of the Night Chant is restoration of health to a patient or patients, although this central purpose is surrounded with prayers for abundant rains, good crops, long life, and happiness for all the people. "In this

and other healing ceremonies," according to Washington Matthews,[8] "since the object is to guard against death and prolong
life, it is important that a life element, or what appears to the
Indian mind to be such, should be preserved as much as possible
in all the articles used." The life principle is preserved symbolically: feathers must be obtained from birds captured alive,
and to secure them the Indian must learn to steal upon the nest
in perfect silence at night. Pollen, which is to be sprinkled on the
patient, must have its vital principle preserved by contact with
live birds. The sacred buckskin, which is used for making thongs
and in other ways during the healing ceremonies, must preserve
the deer's life-force. For this reason the animal must be slain
without a wound, and its nostrils closed with pollen, so that a
certain vital element remains even though the animal dies: one
of its souls may depart, but not all.

One of the chief purificatory agencies is the sacred sweat-
bath. As the patient proceeds into the sweat-house, to which
white plumes have been affixed, the Song of the Rock is chanted:

> In the House of the Red Rock
> There I enter;
> Half way in I am come.
> The corn-plants shake.
>
> In the House of Blue Water
> There I enter;
> Half way in I am come.
> The squash-vines shake.

On a floor marked with symbolic designs in sacred pollen
dust the patient sits on spruce twigs. When he has sweated in
silence for some thirty minutes two medicine men approach with
careful ceremony from the east, enacting the roles of two gods,
and apply sacred wands with strong pressure to the essential
parts of the patient's body. A further chant follows:

At the Red Rock House it grows,
There the giant corn-plant grows,
With ears on either side it grows,
With its ruddy silk it grows,
Ripening in one day it grows,
Greatly multiplying it grows.

At the Blue Water House it grows,
There the giant squash-vine grows,
With fruit on either side it grows,
With its yellow blossom it grows,
Ripening in one night it grows,
Greatly multiplying it grows.

The pollen dust pictures are then ceremonially obliterated by being scraped from one end to the other—from head to foot when the figure is a stylized anthropomorph—and the dust from which they were constructed is gathered into a blanket and thrown away a certain number of paces north of the sweat-house.

During the sacred sweat-bath, while the evil is oozing out through the patient's pores, the strictest silence is enjoined upon him. To break silence is to lose all. There is a Navaho story of two boys, one a cripple, the other blind, who sought to be cured. As they entered the sweat-house, which was covered with curtains of blue cloud and mist and adorned on top with pictures of rainbow and lightning, they were strictly charged by the *yei* who conducted them that they must on no account talk. The lodge soon grew very hot and the boys began to perspire; presently the blind one became conscious of a faint light streaming under the curtains, and the cripple felt a stirring in his legs. Their joy was so great that they forgot the solemn warning. "Oh! younger brother," cried the one, "I see." "Oh! elder brother," cried the other, "I move my legs." In an instant the rainbow, the lightning, the curtain of cloud and mist, and the sweat-house itself vanished, and the boys were left sitting on the open ground with nothing but four stones beside them and the spruce twigs under them, the one as blind and the other as lame as ever.

The power of the story goes deeper than pathos, for what I may call the Archetype of the Vanishing Garden draws sustenance from the unplumbed depths of our individual and collective unconscious. Behaviorists have experimentally ascertained that loss of support, even in the plain physical sense, produces fright-reflexes independently of any association-conditionings. Ian D. Suttie, using the methods of depth psychology, has traced the origins of many psychotic ailments to premature or over-violent "psychic weaning."[9] The individual's tragic loss of the womb's security, reënacted psychically at successive stages of childhood, has its mythic counterpart in the Garden of Eden story as well as in the broader Christian theme of mankind's continued self-ejection or self-debarment from Paradise. Even the symbolism of silence, I would suggest, is adumbrated in the Eden myth. The tree of which our first parents ate, in defiance of Jehovah's command, was of the Knowledge of Good and Evil. The Creature, not content with the bounty of the Garden which is freely allowed him, dares to take good and evil into his own hands and to speak in his own way of primal matters, instead of bringing his mind and heart into the stillness of listening and thus into the harmony of universal rhythms. And there is yet a further parallel between the Navaho and Christian versions of paradise lost. The careless boys were upbraided by all the people for having by their untimely chatter broken the efficacy of the cure, not only for themselves but for all Navahos, who thenceforth would have to supplement the healing ritual with gifts. The primal sin, in both religions, infects the entire race; the sinner plays a representative role.

The Vanishing Garden archetype is a major idea underlying both *The Waste Land* and *Four Quartets*. In the one poem the hyacinth garden passage followed by the sombre emptiness of *"Oed' und leer das Meer,"* in the other the rose garden scene followed by "Then a cloud passed and the pool was empty," are among the more explicit representations of it. The closing lines of *Burnt Norton*—

> Ridiculous the waste sad time
> Stretching before and after

—might express a state of consciousness parallel to that of the bereft Navaho brothers left sitting on the open ground. The co-presence of the Vanishing Garden Archetype and the red rock and handful of pollen dust imagery in one mythic pattern strikes me as offering not conclusive but reasonably persuasive evidence that the Navaho Night Chant may have been one of Eliot's sources—whether conscious or forgotten I do not know.

## Death by Water

The brief fourth movement of *The Waste Land* is almost purely lyrical. It contains so little of declarative force, so little assertorial firmness, that any inferences as to its meaning and relation to the poem's total statement must be drawn not from itself but from its context. Phlebas the Phoenician, "entering the whirlpool," is (by Eliot's own testimony) "not wholly distinct from Ferdinand Prince of Naples"; which means that evocations of *The Tempest* imagery are poetically relevant, and especially of the "Full fathom five" lyric. In fact, Shakespeare provides in Ariel's song a text for the redemptive possibilities of death by water as envisaged in *The Waste Land:*

> Nothing of him that doth fade,
> But doth suffer a sea-change
> Into something rich, and strange.
> (*The Tempest,* Act I, Scene ii)

But amid the stony rubbish and dry bones of the wasteland scene, where is the water to be found?

In *The Dry Salvages* the redemptive possibilities of water, although still qualified by ambiguities and dangers, are developed more positively, through the imagery furnished by a more definite locale. Sea, river, rock, tolling bell, wreckage of whale's backbone and shattered lobsterpot, all make their contributions to both the symbolism and the scene. The principal contrast is between the *sea*, whose time is a vast unshapen time measured only by the tolling bell, rung by the unhurried ground swell, and the *river*, "a strong brown god—sullen, untamed and intractable/ ... Unhonoured, unpropitiated/By worshippers of the machine, but waiting, watching and waiting." The river has close symbolic affinity with "the trilling wire in the blood" of *Burnt Norton* and "the fever sings in mental wires" of *East Coker*. Elsewhere I have suggested that it might be regarded as "the physiological correlative of the moment of illumined experience; the pulsebeat by which we respond to the hyacinth ecstasy, to the laughter in the garden, and now to 'the sea howl and the sea yelp.'" For the poem plainly states that "the river is within us, the sea is all about us." Wreckage clutters them both. But it is in the sea that the Rock is to be found—washed by waves, concealed by fogs, a monument on halcyon days, a sea-mark in navigable weather, "but in the sombre season/Or the sudden fury, is what it always was."

In the sestina with which the second movement of *The Dry Salvages* commences, the scene, or metaphoric vehicle, is that of fishermen setting out in their ships or boats upon perilous seas, on an ocean always littered with drifting wreckage and wastage. The opening question, "Where is there an end of it, the soundless wailing ... ?" is plurisignative. The meaning is simultaneously: "When will it stop?" and "What is its purpose?" The question is asked twice, in Stanzas 1 and 4, and answered twice, in Stanzas 2 and 6. As the questions, so the answers too are plurisignative, but with different emphases. The first answer— "There is no end, but addition"—stresses mainly the time aspect: there is no last moment, but a further moment is always superadded. In each individual's life, however, there is an end in the temporal sense—"the final addition"—for we move toward old age "in a drifting boat with a slow leakage" awaiting the bell that announces death. Observe that the word "drifting" sounds an undertone which reminds of the other meaning of "end"; for to drift is to be without a purpose. In the fourth and sixth stanzas the idea of purpose seems to me to become the dominant one; for although the word "forever" in Stanza 5 keeps the temporal meaning alive, the teleological meaning is given greater emphasis by such phrases as "littered with wastage," "no destination," "unpayable," and "drift."

The word "annunciation," which terminates Stanzas 1, 3, and 6, varies its meaning in harmony with the semantic shift in "end." The first two instances, "calamitous annunciation" and "Clamor of the bell at the last annunciation," suggest primarily the tolling bell which announces death; while the third instance, where the word is capitalized, evokes the idea of the historical Annunciation, the tidings brought to Mary, which marked the beginning of the Christian drama. Helen Gardner says of the sestina as a whole:

> Under the metaphor of fishermen setting out on their perilous voyages, over an ocean "littered with wastage," it pictures the lives of individual men, the sum of which makes history. It finds meaning only in the union of the temporal with the eternal, in annunciations: the calamitous annunciation of terror and danger, the last annunciation of death, and the one Annunciation of history. The only *end* to the flux of history is man's response to the eternal manifesting itself in time.[10]

What is "the hardly, barely prayable/Prayer of the one An-
nunciation?" One has only to turn to the account of the Christian
Annunciation in the Gospel according to St. Luke and read the
answer. The angel's last words to Mary, in the traditional King
James Version, are: "For with God nothing shall be impossible."
This, however, is not strictly accurate, for the subject of the
sentence is *rhema*—"that which is spoken"—and the American
Revised rendering comes closer to the meaning: "No word from
God shall be void of power." The most lucid translation, I should
think, would be: "Nothing that God hath spoken shall be in-
capable of fulfillment." The important point is that it is God's
Word which is being spoken about. And either of these latter
renderings gives full relevance, as the older one does not, to
Mary's reply: "Behold the handmaid of the Lord; be it unto me
according to Thy word." Here, then, is the "prayer of the one
Annunciation"—no asking for divine favors, as prayer degen-
erately comes to mean, but a responsive yielding to the Divine
Word, as in Jesus' prayer at Gethsemane, "Not my will, but
Thine, be done." Miss Gardner is doubtless right in connecting it
with "the awful daring of a moment's surrender" in *The Waste
Land*. It is the prayer that we find so "hardly, barely prayable"
today.

## The Fisher King

The prayer, when it does come (as in the fourth movement of
*The Dry Salvages*) is addressed to the Lady in behalf of
"those/Whose business has to do with fish . . ." The mention
of fish and fishermen in the context of sea imagery, with the
ambivalent possibilities of death and restoration which they
imply, revives a memory of the Fisher King in *The Waste
Land*, already recognizable reincarnate as the Wounded Sur-

geon in the fourth movement of *East Coker*. Jessie L. Weston is right in affirming "that the Fish is a Life symbol of immemorial antiquity, and that the title of Fisher has, from the earliest ages, been associated with Deities who were held to be specially connected with the origin and preservation of Life."[11] Two aspects of the fish symbol invite attention: the eucharistic and the baptismal.

There were sacred fish-meals in pre-Christian times. They were evidently an ancient custom among the Jews, for the *Jewish Encyclopaedia* says: "The eating of fish has always been associated with the celebration of the Sabbath. From no orthodox table is fish absent at one or more of the Sabbath meals, however difficult it may be to procure." Cumont mentions the sacramental fish-meal in ancient Syria as a probable source of the Christian fish-symbolism. Among the ancient Greeks, too, it evidently had a place: for Pausanias tells of sacred fish in the waters near Eleusis, which only the priests might catch, and Porphyry says that at the sacrifices of the Eleusinian Mysteries fish were included—which I take to imply that they were also eaten ceremonially by the worshipers. How far any of these practices may have contributed to the Christological fish-symbol is uncertain. Renan thinks that fish were probably cooked and eaten at the suppers of Jesus and his disciples, and offers in support Jesus' question, "Or if he ask a fish, will he give him a serpent?"—arguing that as the serpent had already come to represent Satan, so the fish, by this metaphoric contrast, came to be a type of the Christ. A German scholar, H. Merz, offers a somewhat different theory: that when Jesus commanded metaphorically that men should eat of the Christ's flesh in order to have eternal life, his hearers, who depended on lake fish as a main article of diet, naturally turned to the ceremony of fish-eating as an appropriate way of carrying out the injunction. However, as Professor Rufus Morey remarks, whether we think these speculations plausible or not, positive evidence for them is lacking; he himself explains the eucharistic fish-symbol by the significance given from earliest times to the Multiplication of Loaves and Fishes.[12] Miss Weston goes so far as to declare that orthodox Christianity "knows nothing of a sacred fish-meal." Here, however, I think that the distinguished scholar has overstepped her evidence. She might better have said that little or no literary or iconographical evidence of such a meal survives.

May not the Roman Catholic practice of meatless Fridays have originated in a weekly commemoration of Christ's death by sacramentally eating of the symbolic fish? The orthodox form of the Eucharistic service remained as Jesus had instituted it, of bread and wine. But the Fish as Eucharist may have had its devotees also. Some evidence of such a tradition may be seen in the fragments of the *Abercius-epitaph* which were discovered in 1883, among the remains of the public baths at Hierapolis. Abercius says, describing his pilgrimage to Rome:

> Faith was everywhere my guide and ever laid before me food, the Fish from the Fountain, the very great, the pure, which the holy virgin seized. And this she gave to her friends to eat, having a goodly wine and giving it mixed with water, and bread also.[13]

No sure conclusion can be drawn, for scholars are not agreed on whether Abercius was Christian or not—possibly a follower of some cult involving Orpheus the Fisher. Weston places it "outside the recognized category of Christian belief." Harnack, on the other hand, describes it as certainly Christian, although non-orthodox. A later epitaph, whose Christianity has not been disputed, which a certain Pectorius inscribed in honor of his dead parents and brothers, contains the significant sentences:

> Take the honey-sweet food of the Savior of the saints, eat it with desire, holding the Fish in thy hands.

> Fill thou me with the Fish—this is my longing, O my
> Lord and Savior![14]

The other aspect of Christian fish-symbolism, the baptismal,
may have originated in the metaphor which Jesus employed in
calling his earliest disciple from his occupation as fisher in
Genesareth Lake: "Follow me, and I will make you fishers of
men" (Matt., 4:19; Mark, 1:17). The natural logic of this idea
posits Christ as the Fisher instead of the Fish. Tertullian, who
does not always follow natural logic, writes that "we little fish
(*pisciculi*) are born in water after the model of our Fish (*ich-
thys*) Jesus Christ, nor do we find salvation except by remaining
in water."[15] But earlier than Tertullian is an Alexandrian hymn
of the second century in which Jesus is addressed as the savior
of mankind under two associated similes: as shepherd, and then
as "fisher who entices the little fish with the bait of the blessed
life."

The relation of early Christian fish symbology to the Fisher
King of medieval romance is by no means clear. Yet even if it
be true, as medieval scholars now incline to think, that such
fisher kings as Bron and Manawyd were originally sea gods, the
indubitably Christian complexion of the Grail stories makes it
probable that the older Christological meanings of the fish symbol had become fused with the Celtic and Nordic myth-elements.
A most significant characteristic of the Grail Fisher King is his
mysterious wound (cf. Eliot's wounded surgeon), usually in the
thigh or groin, and the famine or pestilence associated with it.
Roger S. Loomis gives evidence that the wounds of the Other-
world King were conceived as breaking out anew annually, and
argues that "the catastrophe which accompanied the wounding
of the king was rather the desolation of winter; and his infirmity
signifies the low vitality of natural forces, particularly the feeble
winter sun."[16] That is doubtless true enough. But there is also
another dimension of meaning, which Professor Loomis himself suggests in his following chapter, where he identifies

Chrétien's Ile de Voirre with Glastonbury, which was also the traditional site of King Arthur's Isle of Avalon. The wounding of the Fisher King symbolizes both the winter of the calendar and the graver winter of the spirit; the Quest is not only for a return of summer, but for that state of blessedness which the Arthurian legends symbolize variously as Avalon, as the abode of Gwynne the White One, as the Ile de Voirre, as the Castle of Melwas, and so on. The wound can be healed and the life-giving waters released only if one such as Parzival, spending a night in the Castle Perilous with the restorative symbols of Lance and Cup, *can ask the right question*. In *The Waste Land* the attempts of the protean *agonistes* to ask the question (except in the Ezekiel and the Thunder passages) are neurotic, frustrated, and directionless: "Has it begun to sprout?" "What is that noise now?" "But who is that on the other side of you?" In *Four Quartets* Eliot's questions are calmer and more comprehending, for he has passed from the wasteland of the directionless into the purgatory of the Dark Way.

## The Cosmic Dance

> Dancing (bright Lady) then began to be,
> When the first seeds whereof the world did spring,
> The Fire, Air, Earth, and Water—did agree,
> By Love's persuasion,—Nature's mighty King,—
> To leave their first disordered combating;
> And in a dance such measures to observe,
> As all the world their motion should preserve.
> Since when, they still are carried in a round,
> And changing, come one in another's place;
> Yet do they neither mingle nor confound,
> But every one doth keep the bounded space
> Wherein the Dance doth bid it turn or trace;
> This wondrous miracle did Love devise,
> For dancing is Love's proper exercise.
> From Sir John Davies, *Orchestra* (1596)[17]

The Dance serves in *Four Quartets* as the symbolic antithesis of "time on its metalled ways." Its relation to the paradox of the eternal present is clarified by the image of the Wheel, which, like the perfect dance, turns about a central pivot. "Except for the point, the still point,/There would be no dance, and there is only the dance." The still point, "where past and future are gathered," is not fixity. Its symbol is the axle-tree, the firm center about which the wheel turns. The axle-tree is at once still and moving. Being a physical part of the wheel it evidently turns, and yet there is an axis at the center of it, a mathematically pure point, which remains unmoving in relation to the rest—"the still point of the turning world"—and which "reconciles" the contradictions of the surrounding movement. The moral paradox which troubled Lady Julian (or something very like it) is here symbolized by the tapestry image of the boarhound and the boar engaged in their patterned, cyclical dance of pursuit.

The dance about the still point is only a cosmic principle; it must be received into the self. "For dancing is Love's proper exercise." What is Love's dance as a spiritual, not erotic experience? An athleticism of mind is needed here; the Music of the Spheres and the Cosmic Fire are different vehicles for the same spiritual tenor, and I propose that we be at pains to see the essential identity of "the complete consort dancing together," the timeless moment, and the crowned knot of fire in which "the fire and the rose are one."

The doctrine of the Timeless Moment becomes clarified by studying Eliot's amplification of the *Bhagavad-Gita* passage in the third movement of *The Dry Salvages*. In the eighth canto of the *Gita*, Krishna, embodied as Prince Arjuna's charioteer, is teaching his royal pupil about the nature of the transition called death:

> He who, at the time of death, thinking of Me alone, goes forth, leaving the body, he attains unto My being. Have no doubt of this.

O son of Kunti, whatever state of being one dwells upon
in the end, at the time of leaving the body, that alone he
attains because of his constant thought of that state of
being . . .

The majority of beings, coming into birth again and
again, merge helplessly into the unmanifested at the approach of night and become manifest at the approach of
day.

But beyond this unmanifested there is another Unmanifested which is eternally existent and is not destroyed
even when all things are destroyed.[18]

Eliot's version, which at one point becomes literal translation,
is as follows:

At the moment which is not of action or inaction
You can receive this: "on whatever sphere of being
The mind of a man may be intent
At the time of death"—that is the one action
(And the time of death is every moment)
Which shall fructify in the lives of others:
And do not think of the fruit of action.
Fare forward.

Eliot's most significant addition is the clause in the parenthesis,
a reminder of Heraclitus' aphorism, "You cannot step twice into
the same river, for other and yet other waters are ever flowing
on."[19] Departing from the Hindu doctrine of a sequence of
definite incarnations determined by the law of Karma, Eliot
follows Heraclitus in conceiving every moment as a dying and
therefore (since time does not halt) a rebirth. Life and death,
in Heraclitus' central paradox, are "the same"—which is to say,
they are inseparable aspects of every phenomenon, and of every
moment of consciousness. What matters most in this procession
of contradictories is the *quality* of moment-by-moment rebirth—
the degree to which one "attains to My being," as Krishna has
said; the becoming like a dry beam of light, or dry shaft of fire,
in the imagery of Heraclitus. Eliot's sure catalytic instinct here

has been to synthesize the Hindu idea of rebirth through self-disciplined and reverent concentration upon "the Unmanifested beyond the unmanifested" (i.e., the Dark that is sought by the devoted soul, not merely the darkness of the weary round of time) with Heraclitus' idea of the relevance of rebirth to every temporal moment.

And so we are brought back to the relationship of time to the timeless, of past and future to the present—which is to say, in spatial imagery, of the turning world to the still point. The relationship is a complex and largely paradoxical one. The plain statement which concludes the second section of *Burnt Norton,* "Only through time time is conquered," is as central to the philosophical teaching of the poem as any plain statement can be. Again and again it is reasserted, in varying imagery and ever expanding context, until finally, in the four lines that open the coda to *Little Gidding* and hence to the entire *Four Quartets,* it appears for the last time in language simple, strong, and clear:

> We shall not cease from exploration
> And the end of all our exploring
> Will be to arrive where we started
> And know the place for the first time.

The end of the turning wheel is the still axis which is the *archê* of its turning. The end of the cosmic dance is the quietude of love beyond desire. The end of dying is the ever-renewed threshold experience of potential rebirth.

# Notes

## 1. Symbol, Language, Meaning

1. Wannemunne is the Estonian variant of the Finnish Vaina-moinen, the primeval minstrel and culture-hero of the ancient epic *Kalevala*, of which there are English translations by Francis P. Magoon, Jr. (Harvard University Press, 1963) and by W. F. Kirby (Everyman's Library, 1907, 2 vols.). In that epic the hero's status seems to be half human, half divine. Having tarried for an unusual number of years in the maternal womb, he was already mature in years and wisdom at the moment of his birth. Tribute is paid to his matchless minstrelsy. Chief among his gifts to men are fire and agriculture. He is represented as bringing the gift of fire to men by having an attendant eagle strike a flame, and as watering their vegetation by a stream that flowed from his big toe—unfortunately in such abundance as to have caused, at one time, a disastrous flood. In the main he is the great calming influence in nature. Where he has walked all is hushed; and accordingly the Finns used to refer to a calm after storm as *Väinämöisen tie*, "Vainamoinen's way."

In the Finnish version as in the Estonian, the god is associated with music.

> Day by day he sang unwearied,
> Night by night discoursed unceasing,
> Sang the songs of by-gone ages,
> Hidden words of ancient wisdom,
> Songs which all the children sing not,
> All beyond men's comprehension,
> In these ages of misfortune,
> When the race is near its ending.

Far away the news was carried,
Far abroad was spread the tidings
Of the songs of Vainamoinen,
Of the wisdom of the hero.
—Runo 3 (Kirby's translation).

It is said that the spirits of the sun, the moon, and the rainbow sit in the sky weaving as they listen to the song god, and in their delight they let shimmering strands of gold, silver, and the colors of the spectrum fall down through the air to gladden the hearts of men.

Jakob Grimm, *Teutonic Mythology* (Volume III of the English translation, 1883; Dover paperback, 1966), traces the derivation of the god's name to the Finnish word *waino*, "wish, desire, yearning"; which confirms the popular belief that Vainamoinen is the god whose song implants yearning, love, and aspiration in men's souls. Grimm's account of the Finnish version of the tale in my present Chapter One is as follows: "When Wäinämöinen [Grimm's spelling] touches his harp, the whole of nature listens, the four-footed beasts of the wood run up to him, the birds come flying, the fish in the waters swim towards him; tears of bliss burst from the god's eyes, and fall upon his breast, from his breast to his knees, from his knees to his feet, wetting five mantles and eight coats." The goddess Freyja laughs roses and weeps pearls in her delight.

The Estonian version which I have used was originally based upon the account by J. W. Farrar in his *Language and Languages* (London, 1878). Grimm's *Der Ursprung der Sprache* is there mentioned as the source, but in the only edition of that essay known to me the reference to Wannemunne is superficial. However, the same version is given independently by W. F. Kirby, in *The Hero of Esthonia, and Other Studies in the Romantic Literature of That Country* (London, 1895), Vol. II, pp. 81-82.

2. Mary Anita Ewer, *A Survey of Mystical Symbolism* (London, S.P.C.K., 1933), Preface. The primary and most general meaning of "symbol" according to *The Oxford English Dictionary* is: "Something that stands for, represents, or denotes something else (not by exact resemblance, but by vague suggestion, or by some accidental or conventional relation); *esp.* a material object representing or taken to represent something immaterial or abstract, as a being, idea, quality or condition; a representative or typical figure, sign, or token." The ostrich as a symbol of folly, and salt a symbol of friendship (being, on

the authority of Sir Thomas Browne, incorruptible) are cited as seventeenth-century examples. In the eighteenth century the more specialized meaning begins to emerge, and the *O.E.D.* quotes the following statement published in 1727: "Words are the Signs and Symbols of Things: and, as in accounts, Cyphers and Figures pass for real Sums; so . . . Words and Names pass for Things themselves." The reader will perceive that the meanings indicated by these two quotations correspond respectively to what I have called expressive symbols and steno-symbols.

3. Susanne K. Langer, *Philosophy in a New Key* (Harvard University Press, 1942), pp. 30-31. Cf. the statement by A. D. Ritchie: "As far as thought is concerned, and at all levels of thought, it is symbolic process. It is mental not because the symbols are immaterial, but because they are symbolic. . . . The essential act of thought is symbolization." *The Natural History of Mind* (Longmans, 1936). Professor Langer, in quoting this passage, takes issue with the last sentence: "As a matter of fact, it is not the essential act of thought that is symbolization, but an act *essential to thought,* and prior to it. Symbolization is the essential act of mind; and mind takes in more than what is commonly called thought." (Langer, op. cit., p. 41.)

4. The story of the Thunder's Three Commands is translated by Professor Radhakrishnan as follows:

"The threefold offspring of Praja-pati, gods, men and daemons, lived with their father Praja-pati as students of sacred knowledge. Having completed their studentship the gods said, 'Please instruct us, sir.' To them, then, he uttered the syllable *da* and asked, 'Have you understood?' They said, 'We have understood, you said to us *damyata,* control yourselves.' He said, 'Yes, you have understood.'

"Then the men said to him, 'Please instruct us, sir.' To them he uttered the same syllable *da* and asked, 'Have you understood?' They said 'We have understood. You said to us *datta,* give.' He said, 'Yes, you have understood.'

"Then the daemons said to him, 'Please instruct us, sir.' To them he uttered the same syllable *da* and asked, 'Have you understood?' They said, 'We have understood. You said to us *dayadhvam,* be compassionate.' He said, 'Yes, you have understood.'

"This very thing the heavenly voice of thunder repeats—*da, da, da,* that is, control yourselves, give, be compassionate. One should practice this same triad, self-control, giving, and compassion." *Brihad-Aranyaka Upanishad,* Chap. V, Sec. 2, in *The Principal Upanishads,* edited in transliterated Sanskrit with parallel translations, by S. Radhakrishnan (London, Allen & Unwin, 1953).

Probably the syllable *da* is onomatopoeic to the Hindu ear, representing iconically the sound which thunder makes.

## 2.   Man's Threshold Experience

1. The liminal ontology, or metaphysics of the threshold, which is barely sketched in this chapter, provides the philosophical background, or underground, of the entire book. Its basic proposition is roughly: "We are never quite *there,* we are always and deviously on the verge of being there." In the present chapter I have indicated three principal ways in which the liminal character of experience manifests itself. A fuller treatment of the question must await a later occasion. Expressive language, which is the subject of the present book, has its superiority to steno-language principally in its ability to suggest, largely by its overtones and paradoxical indirections, something of that ineluctably liminal character of human experience. Steno-language, and more conspicuously all dogmas whether theological or scientistic in kind, represent man's usual struggle to erect mental barriers against the unsettling fact of that incurably "not-quite" condition of existence. Poetic utterance by contrast can occasionally, with luck, flash through the veil of conceptualities that shape our usual view of the world and of ourselves in it, to stir brief inconclusive hints of ultimate paradox.

2. Julián Marías, *Reason and Life* (Yale University Press, 1957), translated by Kenneth S. Reid and Edward Sarmiento from *Introducción a la Filosofía* (Madrid, Revista de Occidente, 1948). The book gives perhaps the fullest and clearest statement of an enlightened Catholic existentialism. The present reference is to p. 27 of the English version, p. 31 of the Spanish, and *passim.* Cf. José Gaos, "El Mas Allá" ("The Beyond"), in *Filosofía y Letras,* No. 29 (Universidad Nacional de México, 1948).

3. Berkeley easily repels this type of rough-and-ready attack in the first and second of his thirteen answers to objections: Sections 34-41 of his *Treatise Concerning the Principles of Human Knowledge*

(London, 1710), particularly Section 36. An excellent recent edition of the celebrated treatise is in Vol. II of *The Works of George Berkeley Bishop of Cloyne*, edited by A. A. Luce and T. E. Jessop (London, Thomas Nelson, 1948-1953).

4. I have discussed these grounds in my article, "On the Meaning of 'You' " in *Proceedings and Addresses of the American Philosophical Association*, 1966-1967.

5. Ferdinand Ebner, *Das Wort und die geistigen Realitäten* (Insbruck, 1921) in *Schriften*, Vol. I (Munich, 1955).

Martin Buber, *I and Thou* (German original, 1923; Eng. tr., 1937); *Between Man and Man* (German, 1929; English, 1947). What was originally a separate small book, *Urdistanz und Beziehung* (1951) has been published in English as an article under the title "Distance and Relation" in *The Hibbert Journal*, Vol. 49 (1951), in *Psychiatry*, Vol. 20 (1957), and as Chapter II of Buber, *The Knowledge of Man*, edited by Maurice Friedman (Harper Torchbooks, 1965). The translations of all three works are by Ronald Gregor Smith.

Gabriel Marcel, *The Mystery of Being* (London and New York, 1950-1951), especially in Vol. I, Chapters VI, "Feeling as a Mode of Participation," and IX, "Togetherness: Identity and Depth." Cf. the important concept of "disponibility" (*disponibilité*) as developed in *Being and Having*, pp. 69 ff., 73 ff., etc. The meaning of the concept is explained by Gallagher's statement that "The disponible person is hospitable to others, the doors of his soul are ajar."—Kenneth T. Gallagher, *The Philosophy of Gabriel Marcel* (Fordham University Press, 1962), p. 26.

Guido Calogero, *Logo e Dialogo* (Milan: Edizioni di Comunità, 1950); *Filosofia del Dialogo* (same, 1962).

6. The significance of the metaphors of Upward, Downward, and Inward in religious mythology will be examined further in Chapter Eight, in the section entitled "Dimensions of Religious Mythos."

### 3. Four Ways of Imagination

1. Kant conceives the original role of imagination as a synthesizing activity that makes possible our perception of the world—a synthesiz-

ing of the manifold of sensation into intelligibly connected patterns. Kant's word for imagination is *Einbildungskraft*, which connotes by its etymology a power (*Kraft*) of making (*bilden*)—a semantic advantage not shared by the English word.

Hobbes' theory of the imagination as decaying sense can be found in Part I, Chap. II of *Leviathan*, and in Chap. III of *Human Nature* where he defines imagination as the "conception remaining and by little and little decaying from and after the act of sense." The two passages may be found in Vols. III and IV respectively, of *The English Works of Thomas Hobbes*, ed. by Molesworth (London, 1839).

2. Samuel Taylor Coleridge, *Biographia Literaria*, Chapter XIII. Cf. Note 14. There is a lucid and thoughtful treatment of the problem of poetic imagination, with important references to Coleridge, in D. G. James, *Scepticism and Poetry: An Essay on the Poetic Imagination* (London: Allen and Unwin, 1937).

3. A tentative beginning in this direction has been made in the last chapter of the author's *Metaphor and Reality* (Indiana University Press, 1962).

4. Cf. Rémy de Gourmont: "The sole excuse which a man can have for writing is . . . to unveil for others the sort of world which mirrors itself in his individual glass." Translated in *Some Imagist Poets: An Anthology*, Vol. II (Houghton, 1916) from de Gourmont's *Le Livre des Masques* (Paris, 1896). Cf. also William Butler Yeats: "One night I heard a voice that said: 'The Love of God for every human soul is unique; no other can satisfy the same need in God.'" From the essay, "Anima Mundi," in *Essays* (Macmillan, rev. ed., 1924).

5. John Livingston Lowes, *The Road to Xanadu* (Houghton, 1930), especially pp. 131-132.

6. Coleridge, *Biographia Epistolaris*, edited by A. Turnbull (London, 1911), Vol. II, pp. 153-154.

7. Alan Porter, "Song," in *The Signature of Pain* (Day, 1931). Quoted by permission of the publishers.

8. Edward Bullough, "Psychic Distance as a Factor in Art and an

Aesthetic Principle," in the posthumous volume of his essays entitled *Aesthetics* (Stanford University Press, 1957). Cf. also Alfonso Reyes: "If all perception is already a sort of translation, this is even more truly the case when artistic sensibility is the filter." *El Deslinde: Prolegómenos a la Teoría Literaria* (El Colegio de México, 1944), p. 13.

9. José Ortega y Gasset, *La Deshumanización del Arte* (Madrid, Revista de Occidente, 2nd ed., 1928). I have here quoted from the partial translation by Pedro Fernández, published in *The Symposium*, Vol. I (April, 1930), pp. 202-203. Another and more complete translation has subsequently been made by Helene Weyl (Gloucester, Mass., Peter Smith, 1952).

10. Reprinted from *Reflections on the Theatre* by Jean-Louis Barrault, translated by Barbara Wall for the Rockliff Publishing Corporation, London, 1951, and The Macmillan Company, New York, pp. 113-114.

11. T. E. Hulme, *Speculations* (Harcourt, 1924), p. 120.

12. William Butler Yeats, "The Tragic Theatre," in *The Cutting of an Agate* (Macmillan, 1927), p. 35.

13. The declaration of purpose which has come to be known as the Imagist Manifesto was published anonymously as the Preface to *Some Imagist Poets: An Anthology*, Vol. I (Houghton, 1915).

14. Coleridge, *Biographia Literaria*, XIV. He continues: "This power, first put in action by the will and understanding, and retained under their irremissive though gentle and unnoticed, control, *laxis effertur habenis*, reveals itself in the balance or reconcilement of opposite or discordant qualities: of sameness, with difference; of the general with the concrete; the idea with the image; the individual with the representative; the sense of novelty and freshness with old and familiar objects; a more than usual state of emotion with more than usual order; judgment ever awake and steady self-possession with enthusiasm and feeling profound or vehement; and while it blends and harmonizes the natural and the artificial, still subordinates art to nature; the manner to the matter; and our admiration of the poet to our sympathy with the poetry." The word "esemplastic" is

of Coleridge's own coinage, from the Greek εἰς ἕν πλάττειν, "to shape into one": "because, having to convey a new sense, I thought that a new term would both aid the recollection of my meaning, and prevent its being confounded with the usual import of the word, imagination."

The Walter Jackson Bate quotation is from "Coleridge on Art," in *Perspectives of Criticism*, edited by Harry Levin (*Harvard Studies in Comparative Literature*, No. 20; Harvard University Press, 1950).

15. José Vasconcelos, *El Monismo Estético* (Mexico City, 1918); *Estética* (Mexico City, Botas, 1936; 3rd ed., 1945); *Todología: Filosofía de la Coordinación* (Mexico City, Botas, 1952). The article on Eliot, "Un Gran Poeta," appeared in the Mexican weekly *Todo* in the spring of 1951.

16. "A Discussion with Hart Crane," in *Poetry; A Magazine of Verse*, Vol. XXIX, 1926, p. 36. The discussion was apropos of Crane's poem, "At Melville's Tomb," which appeared in the same issue. Crane continues: "Its paradox, of course, is that its apparent illogic operates so logically in conjunction with its context in the poem as to establish its claim to another logic, quite independent of the original definition of the word or phrase or image thus employed. It implies (this *inflection* of language) a previous or prepared receptivity to its stimulus on the part of the reader. . . . It all comes to the recognition that emotional dynamics are not to be confused with any absolute order of rationalized definitions; ergo, in poetry the *rationale* of metaphor belongs to another order of experience than science, and is not to be limited by a scientific and arbitrary code of relationships either in verbal inflections or concepts."

17. Julián Marías, *Reason and Life* (Yale University Press, 1956), p. 21. Accepting Anaxagoras' principle that "in everything there is something of everything else," Marías adds the needed codicil: "but the decisive factor, for us as for him, is the *perspective*, the functional articulation of the elements."

Much the same perspectival idea has been expressed by Leonardo da Vinci, although as a painter and engineer he was more inclined to emphasize the literal meaning of perspective as a physical angle of vision. "Every visible object [he writes in his *Trattato della Pittura*] can be seen from an infinite number of places, which places have a continuous quantity, divisible *in infinitum*. Consequently every human action shows itself in an infinite variety of aspects." And he adds that the creative artist's originality consists in taking a fresh stand amid that variety.

18. Murray Krieger, *The New Apologists for Poetry* (University of Minnesota Press, 1956; Indiana University Press paperback, Midland Books, 1963). While the entire book can be recommended as germane to many of the questions here discussed, it is to Chapters II, "T. S. Eliot: Expression and Impersonality," and IV, "The Requirements of an Organic Theory of Poetic Creation," that my present reference points.

19. Coleridge, *Essays and Lectures on Shakespeare* (Everyman's Library, 1907; Dutton, 1930). In other words, Shakespeare does not abstract the universal from its natural surroundings (dramatic and linguistic), but intuits it within that spontaneous context and offers it to the recipient's intuition in the same way. That such expression of the universal as embedded in the particular has its source in the poet's unified sensibility is suggested by Coleridge's statement that as contrasted with Beaumont and Fletcher who, as it were, "fit together a quarter of an orange, apple, lemon and pomegranate" to make them look like one round diverse multicolored fruit, Shakespeare, like nature, "works from within by evolution and assimilation, . . . by evolving the germ within by the imaginative power according to the ideal." *Coleridge's Miscellaneous Criticism*, edited by Thomas M. Raysor (Harvard University Press, 1936).

20. W. K. Wimsatt, "The Structure of the 'Concrete Universal' in Literature," in *The Verbal Icon: Studies in the Meaning of Poetry* (University of Kentucky Press, 1954).

21. *Conversations of Goethe*, recorded by Johann Peter Eckermann, entry dated October 29, 1823. An English translation is published in Everyman's Library. Cf. Goethe's declaration therein (June 11, 1825): "The poet should seize the Particular; and he should, if there be anything sound in it, thus represent the Universal. English history is excellent for poetry; because it is something genuine, healthy, and therefore universal, which repeats itself over and over again. French history, on the contrary, is not for poetry; as it represents an era that cannot come again. The literature of the French,

so far as it is founded on that era, stands as something of merely particular interest, which must grow old with time."

Cf. also Goethe's reply (July 26, 1826) to Eckermann's question how a play should be constructed in order to be effective in the theatre: "It must be symbolical, that is to say, each incident must be significant in itself and lead to another still more important." Here, as in Goethe's discussion of "the law of required change" (February 1, 1827) and elsewhere, the meaningful outreach of the symbol is seen to be not only upward to a universal but simultaneously forward to the next public situation for which it is already preparing the context.

22. Quoted by Fritz Strich, "Das Symbol in der Dichtung," in his volume of critical essays, *Der Dichter und die Zeit* (Bern, Francke, 1947). Strich comments: "The symbol is thus, in Goethe's sense, the fullest coalescence of a particular instance and a general idea." Again he declares: "In the living experience (*Erlebnis*) of a poem I become a whole man. . . . Spirit and nature, reason and sense, the essence of mankind in me and my own particular ego—these all coalesce in the *Erlebnis* of the poem, being brought together there by the poet's binding hand."

## 4.  *The Limits of Plain Sense*

The chapter motto is taken from Gertrude Stein, *Useful Knowledge* (Harcourt, 1928).

1. Rudolf Carnap, "Logic," in *Factors Determining Human Behavior* (Harvard University Press, 1937), p. 108. The cited passage is reprinted in Irving J. Lee's anthology of earlier writings on semantics, *The Language of Wisdom and Folly* (Harper, 1949).

2. I. A. Richards, *Principles of Literary Criticism* (Harcourt, 1925), p. 267.

3. I. A. Richards, "Between Truth and Truth": *The Symposium*, Vol. II (New York, 1931; not connected with the later journal published at Syracuse University under that name). The article by John Middleton Murry to which Richards refers had appeared in the preceding volume of *The Symposium*.

4. Bertrand Russell, *An Inquiry into Meaning and Truth* (Norton, 1940), p. 294; p. 270 of The Penguin paperback edition.

5. Charles W. Morris, *Signs, Language and Behavior* (Prentice-Hall, 1946). More directly pertinent to the present discussion is his article, "Science, Art and Technology": *The Kenyon Review*, Vol. I (1939).

6. Cf. W. K. Wimsatt, Jr., and Monroe Beardsley, "The Affective Fallacy" in W. K. Wimsatt, Jr., *The Verbal Icon* (University of Kentucky Press, 1954).

## 5.  *Traits of Expressive Language*

1. *Metaphor and Reality* (Indiana University Press, 1962), p. 95. Although for the most part I am keeping the two books quite distinct, both in their methods of approaching the problem of poetic meaning and in their illustrations, I am making this one example do double service because it strikes me as unusually apt for the purpose.

2. Two most significant uses of *"methexis"* ($\mu\acute{\epsilon}\theta\epsilon\xi\iota\varsigma$) in Plato occur in his dialogue *Parmenides*. At 132d the word refers to the participation of individual things in the timeless "Ideas," the self-subsistent meanings which Plato postulates as making intelligible existence possible. At 151e (cf. 141e) the reciprocal aspect of the relation is in view, for the reference now is to the participation of Being in time and becoming. My own use of "methexis" is not restricted by Plato's doctrine of established Forms ("Ideas").

3. Hobbes' declaration is confirmed by this distinction between univocal and equivocal names. "*Univocal* are those which in the same train of discourse signify always the same thing; but *equivocal* those which mean sometimes one thing and sometimes another. . . . Every *metaphor* is by profession *equivocal*. But this distinction belongs not so much to names, as to those that use names, for some use them properly and accurately for the finding out of truth; others draw them from their proper sense, for ornament or deceit." *The English Works of Thomas Hobbes of Malmesbury*, edited by Sir William Molesworth (London, 1839): First Section, "Concerning Bodies," Part I, "Computation or Logic," Chapter II, "Of Names." It is not without sig-

nificance that Hobbes treats logic as a subdivision of the topic, "Concerning Bodies."

4. From Hart Crane, *The Bridge:* Section IV, "Cape Hatteras." *The Collected Poems of Hart Crane* (Liveright, 1933). Quoted by permission of the publishers.

5. Claude-Edmonde Magny, *Les sandales d'Empedocle: essai sur les limites de la littérature* (Neuchâtel: Baconnière, 1945).

6. Francis Fergusson, *The Idea of a Theatre* (Princeton University Press, 1949). The phrase "tragic rhythm of action" is applied (p. 39) to *Oedipus Tyrannus*, and through it to drama in general, since Professor Fergusson sets himself "to use *Oedipus* as a landmark, and to relate subsequent forms of drama to it."

7. The fragment is numbered 93 in Diels, 18 in Wheelwright, *The Presocratics* (Odyssey Press, 1966), p. 70. Cf. "Nature loves to hide" (D 93, W 17). When Aristotle waxes indignant against this aspect of Heraclitus' doctrine—"It is logically impossible to suppose that the same thing is and is not, as some thing Heraclitus said" (*Metaphysics* 1005b 24) he misses the dark glimmer of truth in the Heraclitean paradox—namely that logical language is too gross to give more than a skeletal residue of truth.

8. "Notes on Language and Style," republished in T. E. Hulme, *Further Speculations* (University of Minnesota Press, 1955).

9. George Santayana, *The Life of Reason*: Vol. I, *Reason and Common Sense*, Chap. VII (Scribner, 2nd ed., 1922).

10. Although "tautology" is the word Pound uses here, "redundancy" would be more accurate. The remark was made in an article, "Epstein, Belgion and Meaning,' in *The Criterion*, Vol. IX, Serial No. 36 (April, 1930), p. 470. Some months earlier *The Manchester Guardian* had interviewed Jacob Epstein regarding his sculptures in the London Underground House, and had quoted him as saying: "It was my idea to make 'Day' and 'Night' the subjects of two groups over the entrances to the building. . . . It is difficult to describe a sculptural idea, for any art has to speak its own language. Well, 'Night' is a mother-figure with her child-man exhausted and sleeping under her protection and benediction. The curved horizontal lines

of the group are expressive of sleep and rest descending on tired mankind . . ." In the January, 1930, issue of *The Criterion* Montgomery Belgion made these remarks the target of an attack which drew much of its ammunition from H. W. B. Joseph's *Logic.* This was the occasion for Ezra Pound's counter-criticism in the article from which I have quoted. Pound then adds:

"When Mr. Epstein says 'Night' is the subject he means rather more. Everybody knows what 'Night' is, but Mr. Epstein or Mr. Phidias or whoever, is presumably intent on expressing a *particular* and definite complex (ideas, emotions, etc.) generally oriented by a rather vague concept already mapped out. The difference is as great as that between firing a bullet in a generally easterly direction and hitting a particular bird."

11. William James, *Principles of Psychology* (Holt, 1890), Vol. II, pp. 576-577. A one-volume reprint has been issued by Dover Publications (1950). Although James is abstractly right in stressing the factor of *"congruity of emotional tone* between the reproduced idea and our mood," his illustrations of the principle—"the same objects do not recall the same associates when we are cheerful as when we are melancholy"—are too elementary for the purposes of poetic criticism. Such a truism needs to be supplemented by a recognition of the unpredictable emotional affiliations—sometimes hardly congruous by ordinary standards—which may erupt from unconscious sources.

12. From T. S. Eliot, *Four Quartets,* published both separately and in Eliot, *The Complete Poems and Plays* (Harcourt, 1952). The first excerpt is from Part II of "Burnt Norton," the second and third from Part III of "East Coker," and the last from Part IV of "East Coker." Quoted by permission of the publisher.

## 6.  *Metaphoric Tension*

1. Aristotle, *Rhetoric,* Bk. III, Chap. 4 (1406 b, 20 ff.). Cf. Quintilian, *Institutio Oratoria,* VIII. vi. 8. There is, to be sure, a good deal of sound sense in Aristotle's discussion of metaphor, despite its limitations. "Metaphors must be drawn from things that are related to the original conception, without being *obviously* so related. . . . Because the hearer expected something quite different, his acquisition of the

new idea impresses him all the more. His mind seems to say, 'Yes, to be sure; I never thought of that.' " (Bk. III, Chap. 11.) So far, excellent. But when he declares, "Those ideas which can be expressed well as metaphors will obviously succeed as similes also; and similes, when the explanation is omitted, will appear as metaphors," (III, 4) he is conceiving the difference between metaphor and simile superficially as a stratagem of grammar, instead of as a difference of semantic quality.

2. Herbert Read, *English Prose Style* (new edition, Pantheon Books, 1952). Elsewhere I have employed Max Müller's word "diaphor" to signify metaphoric fusion in the sense that Read intends, but it may sound too technical to be appropriate for a discussion of poetry. Ezra Pound appears to have meant much the same thing as Read by his self-styled "doctrine of the image": "The Image is more than an Idea. It is a vortex or cluster of fused ideas and is endowed with energy."—"The Image is itself the speech . . . beyond formulated language."—"An 'Image' is that which presents an intellectual and emotional complex in an instant of time." See Stanley K. Coffman, Jr., *Imagism* (University of Oklahoma Press, 1951), where a number of such utterances by Pound have been collected from various sources.

The German word *Bild* ("picture," but with an overtone of meaning from the verb *bilden* "to form") has had a roughly parallel usage. Hermann Pongs, in *Das Bild in der Dichtung* (Marburg, 1927) observes that the word *Metapher* has hitherto not been so alive in German idiom as the related words *Symbol* on the one hand and *Bild* on the other.

3. Allen Tate's essay, "Tension in Poetry," was first published in 1938, and later republished in his volume, *On the Limits of Poetry* (Morrow, 1948), and in *The Man of Letters in The Modern World* (Meridian, 1955). Tate's definition of "tension" is on p. 71 of the latter volume. Cleanth Brooks' essay, "The Language of Paradox," was first published in *The Language of Poetry*, edited by Allen Tate (Princeton University Press, 1942); republished in *The Well Wrought Urn* (Harcourt, 1947).

4. Martin Foss, *Symbol and Metaphor in Human Experience* (Princeton University Press, 1949), Chap. IV, especially p. 60. Al-

though I have found much to admire in this little book, I regret that Professor Foss has chosen, misleadingly for some readers, to follow the semantic positivists in linguistic strategy although not in doctrine; for he restricts, like them, the term "symbol" to the logically explicable kind of linguistic unit that "has as its goal the ordering of the world into clear and convenient patterns." In short, he identifies symbol with steno-symbol, and sets over against it metaphor, myth, and prayer. The works of Wilhelm Wundt to which he refers are *Sprachpsychologie, Völkerpsychologie,* and *Die Sprache.*

5. The orangutang and cinnamon tree similes I picked out of a dictionary of similes which I found in a library. This prompts the reflection that while a dictionary of similes is possible, a dictionary of metaphors is not.

6. *The Complete Poems of Emily Jane Brontë,* edited by Charles William Hatfield from the manuscripts (Columbia University Press, 1941). The stanza quoted is the first of three, but to my mind it constitutes a sufficiently complete poetic statement by itself.

7. Aristotle, *Rhetoric,* Bk. III, Chap. 3 (1406 b, 15 ff.).

8. Edith Sitwell, *Poetry and Criticism* (Holt, 1926).

9. Friedrich Max Müller, *Lectures on the Science of Language,* seventh edition (London, 1873), Vol. I, Lecture VIII, "Metaphor." The entire chapter (which is missing from the earliest editions of the book) is of great interest concerning the relations of metaphor to the growth of language and to myth. The phrase "radical metaphor," connoting chiefly the role of metaphor in the early growth of language, appears on pp. 388, 393, and 417.

10. Archibald Henry Sayce, *Introduction to the Science of Language* (London, 1880; 4th ed., 1900), Vol. II, p. 181. Sayce continues: "In no other way can terms be found for the spiritual and the abstract. *Spirit* is itself 'the breath'; the *abstract,* that which is 'drawn apart.' Our knowledge grows by comparing the unknown with the known, and the record of that increase of knowledge grows in the same way. Things are named from their qualities, but those qualities have first been observed elsewhere. The *table* like the *stable* originally meant something that 'stands,' but the idea of standing had been noted long before the first table was invented."

11. Friedrich Max Müller, loc. cit., esp. p. 384. The Oxford English Dictionary distinguishes also a third ingredient of our irregular conjugation of the verb "be." There is the verb stem *wes-*, from which have been derived the Sanskrit root *vas-*, the German past participle *gewesen*, and the English "was."

## 7. Emblem and Archetype

1. *The Gateless Gate*, translated from the Chinese by Nyogen Sanzaki and Saladin Reps (Los Angeles, John Murray, 1934). The translators state that the *Mu-Mon-Kwan* (literally, "no-gate barrier") was recorded by Mu-Mon E-Kai, who lived A.D. 1183-1260.

2. Harriet (Mrs. John C.) Murray-Aynsley, *Symbolism of the East and West* (London, 1900). I am indebted to this volume for much of the information concerning the *trinacria*, as well as for several of the smaller visual designs employed in Chapter Seven. The empirical basis of some of Mrs. Murray-Aynsley's views on Eastern Symbolism is disclosed in her earlier and slighter work, *An Account of a Three Months' Tour from Simla through Bussahir, Kunowar and Spiti, to Lahoul* (Calcutta, 1882).

3. Aristotle, *Natural Science (Physica)*, Bk. I, Chap. VI. The basic syllogism on which Aristotle's principle of triadicity is based in this chapter is as follows: "Accordingly, if we accept both the previous argument [that opposites are in some way the basic principles of nature] and the present one [that opposites presuppose a substance in which they inhere, and of which they may be predicated], must we not, in order to reserve the truth of both, postulate the existence of a third something [besides the pair of opposites, and on which they act]?"—*Aristotle: Containing Selections from Seven of the Most Important Books*, translated by Philip Wheelwright (Odyssey Press, rev. ed., 1951), pp. 9-10.

4. The *uraeus* was, in secular context, the deadly asp. In Egyptian belief it was one of the scourges of those unfortunate ghost-souls (*ka*) who had not been properly instructed in the rules of other-worldly procedure which have been preserved in *The Book of the Coming-Forth-by-Day* (the so-called Egyptian Book of the Dead). From these natural and supernatural beginnings the uraeus-figure under-

went a good deal of symbolic development. The Pharaoh, according to Maspero, would make his claim to universal dominion by putting on the many-colored diadems of the gods, the head-dresses covered with feathers, and white and red crowns; while "the viper or uraeus, in metal or gilded wood, which rose from his forehead, was imbued with a mysterious life, which made it a means of executing his vengeance and accomplishing his secret purposes."—*History of Egypt* (London, 1891), Vol. II, p. 31. As a religious symbol the uraeus appears to have acquired reference, by synecdoche, to the winged disc figure as a whole, although still referring more specifically to the aspen part of it.

5. Such is the doctrine put forth in the *Mahabharata*, Bk. XII, "The Book of Consolation." In Book III, "The Forest Book," it is Krishna to whom ultimate godhead is ascribed, and the three members of the Hindu Trinity are said to have sprung from different parts of his body. The archetypal pattern is evidently the same through all this. On the polarity of natures in Shiva, the Cosmic Dancer, see Heinrich Zimmer, *Myths and Symbols in Indian Art and Civilization* (Bollingen Series, No. VI; Pantheon Books, 1946), pp. 154-157. On the *lingam* and *yoni* see p. 127 and *passim* in the same volume.

6. The classical account of the three *gunas* is found in Chapter (or Canto) XIV of the *Bhagavad-Gita*. There are over forty distinct English translations of this Hindu devotional scripture. Those of Professor S. Radhakrishnan (Harper, 1948), Swami Nikhilananda (New York, Ramakrishna-Vivekananda Society, 1944) and Franklin Edgerton (Harvard University Press, 1946) can be recommended for analytic study; those of Swami Prabhavananda and Christopher Isherwood (Harper, 1952, and Mentor Books) and of Swami Paramananda (Boston: Vedanta Centre, 1913) can be recommended to the general reader.

7. The plate on page 139 represents the three panels in bas-relief belonging to the western gate of the great Buddhist *stupa* at Sanchi. They are reproduced from Alfred Foucher, *The Beginnings of Buddhist Art* (London: Humphrey Milford, 1917), where they had in turn been reproduced from photographs taken about 1908 by the archeologist J. H. Marshall.

8. John Gardner Wilkinson, *The Manners and Customs of the*

*Ancient Egyptians* (London, 1937). A posthumous edition, revised by Samuel Birch, was published in 1878. Wilkinson's own abridgment of the original work was published in 1854 under the title, *A Popular Account of the Ancient Egyptians.*

9. Filmer S. Northrop, "The Functions and Future of Poetry," originally published in *Furioso,* Vol. I (1941); reprinted as Chapter IX of F. S. Northrop, *The Logic of the Sciences and the Humanities* (Macmillan, 1948).

10. Wilbur M. Urban, *Language and Reality: The Philosophy of the Language and Principles of Symbolism* (Macmillan, 1939).

11. W. W. Main, in *The Explicator,* Vol. IX (March, 1951): Item 36, citing James G. Frazer, *The Golden Bough,* abridged edition (1949), p. 129, in the chapter on "Relics of Tree-Worship in Modern Europe."

## 8.   *The Mythic Dimension*

The poem which stands as headpiece to this chapter, "The Apparition" by Dilys Laing, was originally taken, with the late Mrs. Laing's permission, from her book *Birth Is Farewell.* The poems of that and of her other volumes, as well as a number of poems found stuffed away in bureau drawers and elsewhere after her death, have been assembled by her husband the poet Alexander Laing and published as *The Complete Poems of Dilys Laing* (The Press of Case Western Reserve University, 1967).

1. *Encyclopedia of Poetry and Poetics,* edited by Alex Preminger (Princeton University Press, 1965): article, "Myth." Alan C. Bouquet, in his article "Myth and Literature" in *Cassell's Encyclopaedia of Literature,* puts the matter somewhat differently: "A myth is a story which for those who tell it and for those who receive it has a kind of cosmic purpose. It professes to relate some happening in which supernatural beings are concerned and probably in doing so to offer an explanation of some natural phenomenon." The last sentence is unduly limiting, applying to many myths but not to all. The remark about supernatural beings needs to be taken flexibly. Mr. Bouquet explains that while a myth may include elements of

folklore dealing with men and animals, "it is really concerned with them only in so far as they form part of a world which has to be explained in terms of the sacred or the supernatural."

An interested reader may wish to compare the present chapter with my independent approach to the relations between literature and myth in the seventh chapter of *Metaphor and Reality* (Indiana University Press, 1962).

2. Ernst Cassirer, *The Philosophy of Symbolic Forms*, translated by Ralph Manheim (Yale University Press, 3 volumes, 1953-1957). The second volume, to which alone my present discussion refers, is entitled *Mythisches Denken* in the original and *Mythical Thinking* in the published translation. Here, as throughout the chapter, I have changed the misleading word "mythical" to "mythic." Cassirer's own abridgment of the second volume has been translated by Susanne K. Langer under the title *Language and Myth* (Harper, 1946).

3. The Fijian death chant and most of the attendant information are taken from Basil H. Thomson, "The Kalou-Vu (Ancestor-Gods) of the Fijians": *Journal of the Anthropological Institute of Great Britain and Ireland*, Vol. XXIV (London, 1895). I have modified the translator's English wording, in a few superficial respects, for the sake of better rhythm and readability. His account of the customs and beliefs connected with Fijian burials, while authentic so far as it goes, is not the entire story. Other manifestations, sometimes quite different, are described by the Rev. Lorimer Fison in "Notes on Fijian Burial Customs," in Vol. X (1881) of the same journal.

4. James G. Frazer, *The Magic Art*, Vol. II (which is also Vol. II of the entire *Golden Bough*), p. 142.

5. It was R. H. Codrington who, in *The Melanesians* (Oxford University Press, 1891) first emphasized the effective presence, among the Melanesian islanders, of a proto-animistic, vaguely differentiated power which was there termed "*mana*." Subsequent investigators have come to regard some such phenomenon as characteristic of many, perhaps most, primitive cultures. A good comprehensive account of the idea is offered by Irving King, *The Development of Religion* (Macmillan, 1910), Chap. VI, "The Mysterious Power."

The Iroquois Indians appear to have meant much the same thing by *orenda*, and the Sioux tribes by *wakonda*. J. B. N. Hewitt, an eminent student of the Iroquois, explains the former word as referring to the "force, principle, or magic power" which was assumed by the Iroquois to inhere in every thing and process which displayed energy or a seeming potency of energy, "in any manner affecting or controlling the welfare of man." It was conceived to operate in a manner at once impersonal and mysterious although always embodied in particular objects; to be limited in its efficacy and not at all omnipotent; local and not omnipresent; capable of being "transferred, attacked, acquired, increased, suppressed, or enthralled by the orenda of occult ritualistic formulas endowed with more potency."

The Omaha tribe of the Sioux nation, according to Alice C. Fletcher, employs the corresponding word, *wakonda*, with a double meaning. They apply it to particular objects or phenomena regarded as mysterious and therefore sacred; while in a deeper sense "it is the name given to the mysterious all-pervading and life-giving power to which certain anthropomorphic aspects are attributed." Miss Fletcher reports that the two aspects are never confused by thoughtful Omahas. When an Omaha addresses Wakonda in prayer during a fast, his address is to *the power that causes motion*, which is to say, the power that gives life; for the ability to produce motion is synonymous to the Omaha mind with life. "To an Omaha (she writes) nothing is without life: the rock lives, so do the cloud, the tree, the animal . . . There is to him something in common between all creatures and all natural forms, a something which brings them into existence and holds them intact; this something he conceives as akin to his own conscious being. The power which thus brings to pass and holds all things in their living form he designates as *wakonda* . . . He is taught that when he fasts and prays he must not ask for any special favor or gift: that which he is able to receive will be given him."

J. B. N. Hewitt's article, "Orenda," and Alice C. Fletcher's article, "Wakonda," are both published in *Handbook of the American Indians North of Mexico:* Smithsonian Institution, Bureau of American Ethnology, Bulletin 30, 2nd imp., 1912.

6. Jane Ellen Harrison, *Prolegomena to the Study of Greek Religion* (Cambridge University Press, 2nd ed., 1908), esp. pp. 3-4.

Miss Harrison finds the exorcistic and propitiatory types of magico-religious attitude indicated respectively by the two early Latin inscriptions. *Do ut abeas* and *Do ut des;* and again by the two Greek words, δεισιδαιμονία ("fear of spirits") and θεραπεία ("service to and tendance of the Gods").

7. Lucien Lévy-Bruhl, *How Natives Think* (Allen & Unwin, 1926). Chapter II is most specifically on "The Law of Participation," but illustrative and confirmatory materials are scattered throughout the book.

8. Gertrude Rachel Levy, *The Gate of Horn* (London, Faber & Faber, 1948).

9. James Izett, *Maori Lore* (Wellington, New Zealand, Government printing press, 1904), pp. 27-43. Andrew Lang, in *Custom and Myth* (London, 1888), recounts a variant of the Maori legend: that Heaven and Earth were originally united but were separated by a serpent, and that the mission of the Seer (who "sees all things in one") and of the Poet-Minstrel (who "makes things one through song") is to reunite them. However, as Izett shows, the marital drama is sometimes conceived as the second, not the first step in the scheme of creation. First of all there was *koru*—which can be translated, with striking ambivalence, both "potency" and "the void." That is to say, there was empty space from eternity, but within it were the potencies of all things as yet unborn (Izett, op. cit., p. 11).

10. Hesiod, *Theogony*, lines 126-128. Earth bore some of the primordial gods and natural forces "without sweet union of love"; others after connubial union with Sky.

11. *Völuspa:* done into English out of the Icelandic of the Elder Edda, by Ananda K. Coomaraswamy (2nd ed.; London: D. Nutt, 1909).

12. *Popol Vuh: the Sacred Book of the Ancient Quiché Maya;* English version of Delia Goetz and Silvanus J. Morley, from the Spanish translation by Adrián Recinos (University of Oklahoma Press, 1951).

13. Aristotle, *Metaphysics*, Bk. XII (Lambda), Chap. vii. A somewhat different account of the Divine Mover in relation to cosmic motion is found in the *Natural Science (Physica)*, Bk. VIII, Chaps. vi,

vii, ix. Cf. pp. 97-104 and 57-62 of the volume cited in Chapter Seven, Note 3.

14. Francis M. Cornford, *From Religion to Philosophy* (London, 1912): Chap. I, "Destiny and Law," Sec. 6, "Moira as a system of provinces."

15. Where the Erinyes are seen in ouranian perspective their punitive function becomes subordinate to that of establishing cosmic order. This accounts not only for Heraclitus' remark but also for the strange tale near the end of Book XIX of the *Iliad*. The goddess Hera bestows on Achilles' horse Xanthus the power of speech, which it retains long enough to prophesy its master's death; but then an *erinys* came and silenced its voice, thereby restoring the natural order of things. Aeschylus' *Oresteia* symbolically traces, in the form of tragic drama, the evolution from the guardians' more primitive to their more civilized role.

16. From the first choral stasimon of Euripides, *The Bacchae*.

17. This and the following excerpt are from Aeschylus, *Choëphori*. Their significance will come forth more fully in the context of the next chapter.

18. Let us use the words, "mysticism" and "mystical" accurately, and not (as unhappily is often done) merely to connote mystification. Basically the philosophy of mysticism holds as its cardinal truth that individuation is error and illusion, and that therefore we can know the truth of anything only so far as we enter into union with it. John Wright Buckham, writing in Vergilius Ferm's *Encyclopaedia of Religion* (Philosophical Library, 1945), defines mysticism as "the intuitive and emotive apprehension of spiritual reality." I would accept this with the important qualification that the intuitive rather than the emotive aspect is the one to be stressed. Mystical emotions are sham if they are sought for their own sake; the genuine mystic's desire is not for a state of feeling, but for a certain state of *being* and of *knowing*—for light rather than heat.

19. Clement of Alexandria, "Exhortation to the Greeks" (*Protreptikon pros Hellenas*, usually referred to as *Protreptikon*), Chap. II. Another translation is by G. W. Butterworth in the Loeb Classical Library. Although he condemns the Mysteries as "mere custom and

vain opinion" and "a deceit of the Serpent," he promises to describe them "in accordance with the spirit of truth, without burlesquing them as Alcibiades is said to have done."

## 9. Expressive Statement and Truth

1. I. A. Richards, *Science and Poetry* (Norton, 1926), especially Chapter VI, "Poetry and Belief." Cf. my earlier discussion of Richards' critical views, in Chapter Four above. His corrective definition of "pseudo-statement" is published in *Speculative Instruments* (University of Chicago Press, 1955).

2. From Carolyn Wells, *A Nonsense Anthology* (Scribner, 1902, 1930). It is possible that some of the component statements may originally have had satirical meanings: cf. *Oxford Dictionary of Nursery Rhymes*, edited by Iona and Peter Opie (Oxford University Press, 1951). That possibility does not affect the point I am making, however, which concerns the meanings of the various statements, component and total, for the modern reader.

3. L. C. Harmer and F. R. Norton, *A Manual of Modern Spanish* (London: University Tutorial Press, 1935), p. 6.

4. Margaret Schlauch, *The Gift of Tongues* (Modern Age Books, 1942; paperback, Dover Press).

5. The illustrations from Old French and Ronsard are on the authority of Ferdinand Brunot, *La pensée et la langue: methode, principes, et plan d'une théorie nouvelle du langage appliqué au français* (Paris, 1922; rev. ed., 1936), pp. 8-9.

6. *Mundaka Upanishad,* II. i. 1. Perhaps the most accessible version is that in Volume I of Swami Nikhilananda, *The Upanishads* (Harper, 1949). It might be interesting to try the same kind of sentential analysis on the pair of sentences that follows (II. i. 2): "Self-luminous and formless is the Supreme Person (*Purusha*), uncreated and existing without body or mind. He is devoid of vital breath (*prana*), devoid of mind, pure, and higher than the surpeme Imperishable." Does not the paradoxical notion of "higher than the supreme" suggest that the declarative element is not here the most dominant?

10.   *Thematic Imagery in the* ORESTEIA

1. Suggestive material for this chapter has been found in Jean Dumortier, *Les images dans la poésie d'Eschyle* (Paris, 1935); also, but less pointedly, in Gilbert Murray, *Aeschylus, the Creator of Tragedy* (Oxford University Press, 1940); George Méautis, *Eschyle et la trilogie* (Paris, 1936); E. T. Owen, *The Harmony of Aeschylus* (Toronto: Clark, Irwin & Co., 1952); and Chapter III of H. D. F. Kitto, *Greek Tragedy* (London: Methuen, 3rd ed., 1961). Since the present chapter remains the same, except in its opening pages, as in the orignial 1954 edition, it is unaffected by later publications. Four of these should be mentioned, however, as throwing light on interpretative problems of the *Oresteia:* H. D. F. Kitto, *Form and Meaning in Drama* (Methuen, 1956), Chapters I-III; Richard Kuhns, *The House, the City, and the Judge* (Bobbs-Merrill, 1962); Anthony J. Podjecki, *The Political Background of Aeschylean Tragedy* (University of Michigan Press, 1966), Chapter V; Leon Golden, *In Praise of Prometheus: Humanism and Rationalism in Aeschylean Thought* (University of North Carolina Press, 1962), Chapter IV. Often very useful, though somewhat limited by its special political viewpoint, is George D. Thomson, *Aeschylus and Athens* (2nd ed., Progress Books, 1946).

2. E. T. Owen, "The *Oresteia* of Aeschylus," in *The Toronto Quarterly,* Vol. VIII (July, 1939).

3. References by line number are to the edition of the *Oresteia* (text and translation) by Herbert Weir Smith in the Loeb Classical Library, Vol. II of Aeschylus.

4. Cf. Jean Dumortier: "Aeschylus has made of this metaphor of the hunt a sort of diptych. The first panel shows Paris and Troy being hunted like wild beasts by the sons of Atreus and enveloped in a fatal snare. On the second panel we see depicted Agamemnon caught, in his turn, in the meshes woven by Aegisthus and Clytemnestra. The city of Priam and its conqueror suffer the same fate: the law of retaliation applies rigorously: eye for eye, tooth for tooth." *Les images dans la poésie d'Eschyle*, p. 76.

5. *Aeschylus, Translated into English Prose*, by F. A. Paley (2nd ed., Cambridge and London, 1871). Based on the Greek text as

given in *The Tragedies of Aeschylus,* edited with an English commentary, by F. A. Paley (London, 1855).

## 11. *Pilgrim in the Wasteland*

1. "The Music of Poetry" (1942), in T. S. Eliot, *On Poetry and Poets* (Farrar, Straus, 1957), p. 32.

2. T. S. Eliot, "Tradition and the Individual Talent," in his *Selected Essays* (Harcourt, 1932, 1950).

3. "The Music of Poetry," loc. cit. Eliot's qualification should not be overlooked, however: "But I believe that the properties in which music concerns the poet most nearly, are the sense of rhythm and the sense of structure. I think that it might be possible for a poet to work too closely to musical analogies; the result might be an effect of artificiality."

4. Lloyd Frankenberg, *Pleasure Dome* (Houghton, 1949).

5. S. Marshall Cohen, "Music and Structure in Eliot's Quartets," in *The Dartmouth Quarterly,* Vol. V (1950).

6. St. Peter is the speaker in this passage (Acts 5:30). He uses the same description in Acts 10:39: "And we are witnesses of all things which he did both in the land of the Jews, and in Jerusalem; whom they slew and hanged on a tree." The King James Version is used in both Biblical quotations, as being closer to the still older version that Kyd must have used.

7. *The Divine Comedy of Dante Alighieri,* translation and comment by John D. Sinclair: Part I, *Inferno* (Oxford University Press, 1948). Max Picard, *Flight from God* (Regnery, 1951).

8. Washington Matthews, "The Night Chant, a Navaho Ceremony," in *Memoirs of the American Museum of Natural History,* Vol. VI (1902). The prayer to the Owl God is less directly connected with anything in Eliot, but invites quotation. According to Dr. Matthews the Navahos were wont to recite it during the ceremony of cigarette rolling, while the chanter "applies pollen to the essential parts of the patient, making a motion as if bringing it from the sun, and takes pollen on his own tongue and head." The cigarettes are

then transferred to the patient's hand while the following prayer is chanted responsively:

> Owl!
> I have made your sacrifice.
> I have prepared a smoke for you.
> My feet restore for me.
> [*Repeated for afflicted parts of the body*]
> Today take out your spell for me.
> Today your spell for me is removed.
> Far away you have taken it.
> Today I shall recover.
> Today my interior shall become cool.
> My interior feeling cool I will go forth.
> No longer afflicted I will go forth.
> Feeling light within I will go forth.
> Happily I may walk.
> Happily abundant dark clouds I desire.
> Happily abundant showers I desire.
> Happily abundant vegetation I desire.
> May it be happy before me.
> May it be happy behind me.
> May it be happy below me.
> May it be happy above me.
> With it happy all around me may I walk.
> It is finished in beauty.
> It is finished in beauty.

While abridging and modifying Dr. Matthew's version for clarity and economy's sake, I have nevertheless quoted at such length in order to preserve the rhythmic character of the hymn, as well as the relating of personal therapy to prayer for the restoration of health in nature.

9. Ian Dishart Suttie, *The Origins of Love and Hate* (London: Kegan Paul, 1935; New York, Julian Press, 1952).

10. Helen L. Gardner, *The Art of T. S. Eliot* (Dutton, 1950).

11. Jessie L. Weston, *From Ritual to Romance* (London, 1920; Anchor Books paperback).

12. My two main sources of information on the Fish symbol have been: Franz Josef Dölger, Ἰχθύς *Das Fischsymbol in frühchristlicher Zeit,* 5 vols. (Rome, 1910); and C. R. Morey, "The Origins of the Fish-Symbol," *Princeton Theological Review,* Vol. VIII (1910). That

the symbol may also have possessed magical properties is shown by Miss Weston (op. cit., p. 127): "That the Fish was considered a potent factor in ensuring fruitfulness is proved by certain prehistoric tablets described by Scheftelowitz, where Fish, Horse, and Swastika, or in another instance Fish and Reindeer, are found in a combination which unmistakeably denotes that the object of the votive tablet was to ensure the fruitfulness of flocks and herds." Such may indeed have been the case, but I would have said "probably" instead of "unmistakeably," and would think that the magical might have been one motive among others. It is unlikely that primitive man separated his utilitarian, his speculative, and his devotional interests with clear bounding-lines.

13. The Abercius-epitaph occurs in the "Life of Abercius," *Patrologia Graeca*, CXV, col. 1211 ff. Evidently the pious Christian compilers of that monumental collection had no doubts of the epitaph's Christian character. The translation is by Professor C. R. Morey, op. cit., Part IV.

14. Epitaph found near Atun, 1839, now in the museum of that city, as reported by Morey, op. cit.

15. "Sed nos pisciculi secundum ἰχθύν nostrum Iesum Christum in aqua nascimur, nec aliter quam in aqua permanendo salvi sumus."—Tertullian, *De Baptismo* I. iii; written about A.D. 205, in answer to a certain Quintilla, who had published a polemic against the Christian sacrament of baptism. The quotation from the second-century Alexandrian hymn is given in German by Dölger, op. cit.

16. Roger S. Loomis, *Celtic Myth and Arthurian Romance* (Columbia University Press, 1927), pp. 182 ff. Loomis quotes the thirteenth-century romance of *Sone de Nansai*, on the wounding of Joseph of Arimathaea, who becomes one of the resurrected embodiments of the Fisher King: "Neither peas nor wheat were sown, no child was born to man, nor maiden had husband, nor tree bore leaf, nor meadow turned green; neither bird nor beast had young, so sore was the king maimed." Op. cit., p. 185.

17. Sir John Davies, *Orchestra; or, A Poem of Dancing* (1596). Edited with introduction and notes by E. M. W. Tillyard (London: Chatto and Windus, 1945).

18. *Bhagavad-Gita*, Canto II, Vs. 69. Among the nearly fifty English translations of this Hindu classic, the one by S. Radhakrishnan (Allen & Unwin, 1948), offers the triple advantage of quality of translation, juxtaposition verse by verse of the transliterated Sanskrit text, and good notes.

19. Eliot's echoings of Heraclitus are not limited to the two fragments which stand as prefatory mottos to *Four Quartets*. Referring to the fragments as numbered in my volume *Heraclitus* (Princeton University Press, 1959; Atheneum paperback, 1964) I would invite attention in particular to the following: besides 2 and 108 (Eliot's two mottos), 15, 16, 18, 21, 46, 47, 109, 116, 121, 124. The inner, arcane meaning of Heraclitus' "way up and way down" is intensely moral as well as cosmological. It applies not only to transformations of matter (from rock to earth to mud to water to cloud to air to aether to fire, and the reverse) but also to the aspirations and degradations of men's souls.

# Index

Words followed by "(S)" are employed mainly in a symbolical sense.